My Friend You

Donald Clark

ISBN 978-1-64191-974-6 (paperback)
ISBN 978-1-64191-975-3 (digital)

Christian Faith Publishing, Inc.
832 Park Avenue
Meadville, PA 16335
www.christianfaithpublishing.com

Printed in the United States of America

Contents

Introduction...7

Marine Corps Recruit Depot, San Diego, California 12

Nearly Getting Busted at Boot Camp 22

Aviation Technical Training 29

Presidential Helicopter Squadron 35

Aboard Ship, the USNS Gaffey 47

Brief Tour of Okinawa...56

Arrival—South Vietnam...70

MCAS—Marble Mountain 79

Mail Call at Marble Mountain 100

Brave Navy Corpsmen...109

Medevac—Rescue of Children 116

Little Kim—a.k.a. My Friend You 127

Purchasing Guitar Strings...144

Lanh's Survival...166

Lanh's Best Friends 191

Finding the Care Home 215

First Care Home Visit 220

Care Home Donations 225

Fifth Care Home Visit...233

Last Care Home Visit..237

Attack Preparation..249

VC Attack on MAG-16 at Marble Mountain 261

Post-Attack Assessment 285

Search for the Children 296

Finding the Children..302

Thien's Concluded Statements...............................320

New Base Assignment 326

This book is dedicated to all my fellow U.S. servicemen and women who fought to liberate South Vietnam. Also the brave Vietnamese people... particularly the children. And, to my beautiful wife Marjorie, our lovely daughters Carla and Pamela, and my fine grandchildren. As well as my hometown family and friends of Lawrence, Kansas consisting of my brother Kenneth and Burrieta White, Willy Mumford, Duane Vann and Marine Corps buddies: Billy Shepard and William Tellis (aka Tee).

Introduction

*M*Y *FRIEND* *YOU* IS A true story chronicling a young man's four-year tour of duty in the United States Marine Corps. It begins by discussing his senior year in high school, then describes his boot camp training in San Diego and how he nearly became the first marine to get "busted" while graduating boot camp.

The story describes his MOS training of an aeronautical engineering clerk received at the famed Naval Aviation Technical Training Center, in Memphis, Tennessee. Graduating tops in his class earned him a transfer to HMX-1, the prestigious Presidential Helicopter Squadron, located in Quantico, Virginia.

After serving sixteen months at Quantico, he was informed he had failed to obtain the top-level security clearance that was necessary to remain there. Out of frustration, he put in a request to join the war effort in South Vietnam; his request was quickly granted.

So off he went, traveling by sea to Okinawa, then finally by air to Da Nang, South Vietnam. He was then trucked to a newly constructed Marine Corps Air Station named Marble Mountain and assigned to MAG-16's Aircraft Engineering Office.

He enjoyed his MOS duties and totally understood the importance of accurately recording aircraft component and flight data. Yet he and his closest friend (Tee), who held the same MOS, would jump at the opportunity to fly as a volunteer crew member aboard UH34D/ UH1E helicopters. They mainly flew on medevac "rescue" missions but, on occasion, flew on what was termed "combat missions."

On the fourth of July 1965, the young marine was flying as a volunteer crewman when his aircraft was dispatched to rescue a party of seventeen children. During the rescue, the marine was awkwardly introduced to a pretty ten-year-old girl (Kim) and her older teenaged brother (Lanh). As time passed, their interaction inexplicably triggered the marine's paternal senses to befriend them both—thus, changing his life forever.

Lanh and the young marine quickly bonded. And Lanh told him in vivid detail about the medevac'd children's courageous escape, led by his aunt Thien, from a nearby village that had been overran by VC.

Lanh explained how the rescued children had all been placed in the same care home (orphanage) inside Da Nang, and that it was owned and operated by a lady named Tuyen and her older policeman brother, Trang.

Ultimately, the young marine and ten of his marine buddies at Marble Mountain monetarily provided support to the care home. They also periodically visited the rescued children at the care home and became closely attached with many of the kids.

Donald Clark is my name, and I'm the young marine in this story, which has taken some fifty-two years to complete. I made a promise to two beautiful children in South Vietnam that I would tell the world about their incredible life journey, and, God willing, I plan to do . . . just that!

The reason the story is entitled *My Friend You* is when our helicopter landed with the rescued children, they were taken to Marble Mountain's newly constructed hospital for a medical exam. While waiting for her exam, a frightened little girl was crying and yelling at the top of her lungs while tightly holding onto her older brother.

I had volunteered to assist with the children during their exams and was called upon to quiet down the little girl. I managed to stop her from crying by simply offering her some sugar mints I was carrying in my shirt pocket.

Shortly afterward, the little girl's brother walked up to me and, in perfect English, told me his sister's name was Kim and that his name was Lanh. He then said his sister wanted to "thank me" for providing her sugar mints and that she wanted to know my name. I told Lanh to tell his sister my name was *My Friend You*.

To this day, I'm not sure why I said those three words, but I did, and his sister sincerely enjoyed the name, and she quickly learned how to pronounce it. And each time we subsequently greeted one another, I would say, "Kim, what's your name?" She would take a deep breath, close her pretty little eyes, then shout out, "My Friend You."

Then I would say, "What is the name of that big bad marine that will always protect Kim?" Kim would close her pretty eyes, take a deep breath, and yell out, "My Friend You." Calling each other in this manner became our fun-loving ritual, so each time we saw each other, we would say it. And we really enjoyed it; we enjoyed it—a lot.

On the night of 27 October 1965, an estimated ninety-five VC soldiers attacked our base (Marble Mountain). Their objective was to destroy our parked helicopters, which was why many of them were only armed with satchel charges and hand grenades.

During the thirty-minute attack, they had managed to destroy nineteen helicopters and heavily damaged thirty-five others. Forty-one VC were killed, and many or more wounded. Our side lost two marines and one navy corpsman, and four were wounded.

I awkwardly got caught up in the middle of the fighting during this attack by disobeying a direct order to cease working late and sleeping over in my work station. Obviously, I survived the attack and only ended up with a slight wound on my backside, and *a lesson about fear and war that I'll carry to my grave.*

Soon after the attack, I and my nine buddies began to check on the status of the children and shockingly learned from Trang (Tuyen's older brother) that Tuyen had gathered up the children and left the area. Trang told us Tuyen had been witnessing heavy VC movement in close proximity to her care home and, fearing for her children's safety, had them driven overnight to her favorite uncle Tho's estate, who lived in a small hamlet called Quang Ham.

Unknown to Tuyen, the hamlet of Quang Ham was where the VC had been recruiting many of the fighters they used to attack Marble Mountain. Trang further said he had been contacted by reliable sources living in Quang Ham, saying that there had been several killings there by a ban of VC and, due to some of the people believed killed, that it was imperative for him to go there to identify some of the bodies.

I managed to accompany Trang to Quang Ham, and soon after our arrival, Trang went about his business of identifying the dead bodies of his beloved sister (Tuyen), his favorite uncle (Tho), and six care home children. Among the dead children lay the body of Lanh. We quickly noticed that Lanh's body wasn't being prepared for burial like the others. Instead, many of the villagers were lined up to view his body.

They were praising Lanh like he was some kind of god. The witnessing villagers told of his bravery and how Lanh had overheard the VC leader instruct his men to harm Kim in order to stop her from yelling out the three words *My Friend You*. The VC leader arrived at the conclusion the three words were a secret code.

The villagers told us of how Lanh broke loose from his captives, grabbed their rifle, and killed five of them prior to being mortally shot in the back.

I spent the entire night at Lanh's makeshift memorial. Reflecting over the wonderful and eventful times we had shared together . . . like that time we beat the shit out of Dung's pimp. The many talks we had at the hamburger cafe. To this day, I've never ran across a person that can eat a burger as fast as Lanh. Trang had to literally drag me away from his body, but it was now morning, and Trang and I needed to turn our focus toward locating Little Kim, a.k.a. My Friend You.

One of Trang's childhood friends told him that Kim's aunt Thien was the last person to see Kim, and he even told us where Aunt Thien was currently staying which was a nearby hospital, only a few blocks from where we stood.

We arrived at Aunt Thien's hospital early in the morning and were informed she had been shot in the arm and nearly beaten to death by VC soldiers. When we walked into her hospital room, she was so thrilled to see us that she collapsed and didn't come out of it until two hours later. When we finally got a chance to talk to her, she was in severe pain but did manage to tell us the whereabouts of Little Kim.

Speaking the best she could, her jaw had been broken in two places. Aunt Thien told us a girl named Mai was truly the last known person to see Kim alive. And Trang found out that, yesterday evening, Mai had given birth to a baby girl, and, luckily, she was located in this same hospital of Aunt Thien.

Mai was very cooperative and attempted to answer all our questions. She said she witnessed four VC soldiers dragging this cute little girl through the jungle and that the little girl had both of her hands tied behind her back. Mai said the little girl was being hit in her head and face with fists and rifle butts, and it looked as if the soldiers were hitting her to stop her from shouting three English words.

Trang asked Mai, "Did the English word she was shouting sound like *My Friend You?*" And, without hesitation, Mai said, "Yes, oh yes, that was exactly what the pretty little girl was shouting." We both thanked Mai, and Trang provided the hospital staff a check that would cover both Mai and Aunt Thein's medical expenses.

While packing up and getting ready to make our return drive back, I began to sincerely contemplate whether Trang and I had done enough these past two days. As I was recollecting my experiences in Quang Nam, up walked two of my closest friends, Corporal Tee and Cpl. Chris Fabris. They had been flying as volunteer crew members on UH1Es, on what was termed "cleanup missions" these past few days.

Tee said he had a chance to visit with Thien most of last night. And that they had just left visiting Lanh's makeshift memorial. And they were deeply moved with what they saw; then we began to discuss Little Kim. And I broke down, crying uncontrollably. Then the three of us engaged in a long embrace, and Tee led us in a nice prayer. Then, after a long period of silence, I spoke up and said that I didn't understand why Little Kim continued shouting out, "My Friend You," when she was ordered to stop.

Chris stood up, embraced me, then softly said, "Don, my brother, Little Kim was calling out for that big bad marine that had promised to always love and protect her."

"So Little Kim was calling out for me to save her, and I failed to show up. Guys, I get it! I truly do, and it hurts. It hurts real bad." Then I began to cry again and have been crying ever since.

—*Donald J. Clark Sergeant E-5 USMC, July 31, 1962–November 12, 1966*

Marine Corps Recruit Depot, San Diego, California

ALL KINDS OF THINGS BEGIN running through your head when you become a senior in high school. Some of my buddies were planning on getting married after graduation. I hadn't yet met that special person, so marriage was not on my agenda. Several of my graduating buddies were talking about working at various jobs in town upon graduation. This didn't interest me, because the starting pay wasn't enough to live comfortably on, and I wanted something larger.

A few of my friends talked about joining the military service upon graduation, and I kind of liked that idea because it sounded exciting. In a few days, I would be graduating from Lawrence High School, along with three hundred other youngsters, and there was plenty of excitement in the air on our campus.

LHS was located in Lawrence, Kansas, and our school campus was only a mile from nearby Kansas University. Several friends had parents who were professors there, so it stood to reason that many of my school classmates were set on attending Kansas University upon graduation.

Going to college on a football or basketball scholarship was my plan, but during our first football game of the season, I suffered a severe knee injury. I was devastated because I was destined for stardom, and this injury halted my hopes of obtaining an athletic scholarship for playing football. The doctors removed torn cartilage from my right knee and told me I couldn't play football again.

This injury also halted my hopes of obtaining an athletic scholarship for basketball. As a result of the blown knee, I could no longer jump or run fast.

Lacking an athletic scholarship to finance my college education equates to my college aspirations appearing slim and dim. My mother and father were hardworking people but not making enough money to send me to college.

Thinking my college hopes went by the wayside, I hobbled around on crutches, feeling sorry for myself for several weeks. Then I was informed by my basketball coach that if I joined the military and served honorably, upon completion of service, I could graduate from college on what he termed the GI Bill.

Immediately, I began checking on the qualifications needed and discussed the requirements with several friends who were in the military and was informed that all I had to do was enlist in the one of the four military branches for a period of four years and receive an honorable discharge. This seemed simple enough, so I figured I had a second chance.

Soon afterward, I began discussing joining the military with one of my closest friends, Billy Shepard. He was pro navy, and it took several weeks to talk Billy into joining the marines. He had been set on enlisting in the navy because he had this notion that sailors saw the world.

We had some good discussions concerning which branch to join, and finally I said to Billy that if we're going to join the military, why not join up with the best?

His older brother, Donald, had been in the marines, and he told Billy the marine corps had a great tradition and, in his opinion, was the superior branch.

Soon afterward, Billy and I visited a marine corps recruiter and were informed that we return upon high school graduation and he would assist in joining us up.

He further informed Billy and I that, after our swearing-in ceremony, we would be flown out to San Diego, California, to undergo thirteen weeks of boot camp training and four weeks of infantry training.

It all sounded exciting. Billy and I were all pumped up and ready to embark on our career as a United States marine. Our careers began on July 31, 1962. Two marine recruiting sergeants arrived at my house with Billy already in their car to drive Billy and me to Kansas City, Missouri, to board a TWA jet airliner to San Diego to begin our boot camp training at MCRD (Marine Corps Recruit Depot).

This was my first plane ride and Billy's second, so he wasn't afraid, but I was scared shitless, particularly when the Boeing 707 lifted off. Each time the plane hit an air pocket, I would damn near faint. It was frightening, and I kept saying to myself, "I have to be cool and not appear to let this bother me because, after all, I'm beginning my life as a United States marine."

While flying, I tried to appear strong and kept saying to myself, "What would my film idol John Wayne do if he's sitting in this seat? Would he sit tall and proud in his seat or constantly be reaching for a barf bag, like a little bitch?" I tried to be cool and sat tall in my seat while the plane hit air pockets, but any observer could easily tell I was scared out of my mind simply by eyeballing my shirt and noticing the large amount of perspiration coming from my armpits. It was embarrassing, and Billy didn't help things by laughing at me each time I reached for the barf bag.

The plane finally landed, and I was totally relieved and thankful to God for the safe ride. As we walked down the unloading ramp, a tall suntanned marine sergeant was saying that all marine recruits aboard the plane should fall in formation at the end of the loading ramp, where the two marine corporals were standing. The majority of the passengers aboard the aircraft were marine recruits, and we quickly fell into formation and were herded into several marine buses, called cattle cars, that transported us to MCRD.

MCRD in San Diego, California, had been training young marines since the early 1920s, and it was within a stone's throw from the city's airport, so the trip in the marine cattle cars was a short one.

MCRD was situated on 388 acres; and it contained personnel barracks, warehouses, messing facilities, an exchange, medical and dental facilities, an auditorium, a large swimming pool, and ramps for beach craft landing training.

As we drove onto the base, there wasn't a cigarette butt on the ground. This place was literally spotless and perfectly manicured.

Our buses came to a sudden stop, and we were instructed to fall out on the grinder in formation. I soon found out the grinder was this gigantic asphalt area situated adjacent to several large administrative buildings. The grinder was where we would soon be marching on, and for hours at a time.

We were hurried off our bus and fell in line. Soon two more buses of marine recruits pulled up, and they were hurried off their buses and fell in line adjacent to where we were standing.

The lined-up recruits totaled about seventy in number, and we all stood there in the hot sun for a good twenty minutes, chatting and getting to know one another; and then, all of a sudden, we heard a person say, "Attention!" It was a neatly dressed marine staff sergeant, and he announced he would be our head drill instructor during the thirteen weeks we would be at MCRD.

Drill instructors were normally a spit and polish marine, and his mission was to shape new recruits into becoming marines. He began by getting his new recruits to listen and adhere to each one of his commands because discipline would be the foundation for his new recruits turning into marines.

Adherence to marching signals instills discipline, and every marine recruit marches hundreds of miles before graduating from boot camp. And that's a fact.

We were trained not only physically and mentally but morally as well. This formed the bedrock of our character and our core values of honor, courage, and commitment.

From conventional warfare to counterinsurgency and disaster relief, marines are known to be the first to deploy on a wide array of missions. If we endure the strict training and earn the title of marine, we will be prepared to handle each mission successfully.

At MCRD, we learned martial arts and how to overcome a larger opponent in hand-to-hand combat. We were taught marksmanship and how to measure and adjust for the effect of the wind on a rounds (bullet) trajectory. We were made familiar with the world's ever-evolving spectrum of threats and how to quickly improvise and adapt to overcome them.

Week 1

A recruit trains to earn the title of marine for twelve weeks at MCRD. The first week of attempting to become a member of the world's finest fighting force is for the drill instructor to explain the Uniform Code of Military Justice. Then we're issued "gear" and undergo a ton of medical evaluations, as well as perform an "initial strength test." Word to the wise, don't be the weakest member in the platoon because it's very difficult to live it down. Marines are known to be tough, and strength goes hand in hand with toughness.

Week 2

The second week is basically one of the drill instructors enforcing a daily routine of discipline. There are normally three DIs to each platoon. There is the head DI or the platoon sergeant who is in charge of the platoon, and he normally is a staff sergeant. He has a buck sergeant and a corporal assisting him, and they all are noncommissioned officers who use every moment of the daily routine to teach and enforce discipline and teamwork. In the barracks where the recruits sleep and call home are a number of Marine Corps Regulations concerning hygiene and protocol that must be followed. Drill instructors teach us recruits how to follow these regulations and care for our equipment by inspecting every detail. We learn to move as a unit while quickly completing tasks to instill order.

Week 3

Week 3 consist of "finding the warrior within." In essence, drill instructors work relentlessly to bring out the warrior in every recruit. For example, on the Bayonet Assault Course recruits learn to channel their intensity toward a target. Drill instructors teach recruits how to properly use a bayonet to kill an opponent. After bayonet training, recruits will be able to attach a bayonet quickly before charging toward an aggressor.

Week 4

During week 4, recruits undergo more close combat training, this time against an adult opponent. Using a device called a pugil stick which is simply a padded pole used to simulate rifle combat. Two recruits at a time must fight on wooden bridges and in simulated trenches. For many recruits, pugil stick training is the most intense physical combat they have ever experienced. They have to learn to act despite fear in order to outmaneuver and overpower their fellow marine opponent. The fighting is intense, and that damn pugil stick hurts when hit by it.

Week 5

One learns very quickly that the motto of the Marine Corps Martial Arts program is "One mind, any weapon." We were taught how to combine unarmed techniques from various martial arts with armed techniques designed for hand-to-hand combat. More than merely self-defense training, this training fuses together mental and character building with combat disciplines. We also study martial arts culture and the history of marine corps values. There are five colored belt levels during this training. In order, they are tan, gray, green, brown, and black. To earn the title United States marine, every one of us recruits were required to qualify for at least a tan belt.

Week 6

You learn very quickly after joining the marine corps that quitting is not an option either in combat or in life. You're made to overcome fear, and you're trained in rappelling which is a controlled slide down a rope that helps to prepare recruits for deployment from troop-carrying helicopters, navigating difficult terrain and gaining access to buildings during raids. Recruits must learn to overcome their fears and prove they can rope down, brake, and land safely. DIs employ proven training methods to instill confidence and courage in recruits.

Week 7

During week 7, you literally live with your rifle. Every marine is a rifleman, but there is a difference between pulling a trigger and being a rifleman. A good rifleman has complete control over their rifle and their body at all times. Recruits learn safety and marksmanship principles as they practice firing their M14 without ammunition. They learn how to shoot from every firing position: sitting, kneeling, standing, and in the prone position. I remembered as a young boy growing up in Lawrence, Kansas, when my dad bought me my first rifle; it was a Remington .22, and Dad would tell me, "Son, you and your rifle must become good friends in order to be successful in hunting rabbits and small game. In the marines, your rifle becomes your good friend, your lover, and your wife.

Week 8

After we have learned the basics, recruits start training with live rounds (real bullets). Drill instructors make sure recruits are concentrating on taking well-aimed shot from all positions with their M14. Building accuracy, recruits begin with fifty rounds of slow fire, one shot at a time, and move up to rapid fire, ten shots in a row. At the end of week 8, recruits undergo qualifications and strive for their highest score out of 250 points. We either earn the Rifle Marksman badge, the Rifle Sharpshooter badge, or the coveted Rifle Expert badge. My scores earned me the Marksman badge, and during this period of my training is when my poor eyesight surfaced. I needed and received eyeglasses in order to see the target. If I had worn eyeglasses during the first day of rifle training, I would have achieved the Expert badge, no doubt. Oh well, life goes on, but a marine recruit cherishes the thought of achieving expert status.

Week 9

When we reached week 9, we were taught that marines must be ready to move toward the sounds of chaos without hesitation. The success of their mission demands complete focus and confidence. Drill instructors focus on building confidence in recruits by motivating them to overcome the eleven unique challenges of the Confidence Course (commonly referred to as the Obstacle Course). During the first phase of the course, recruits complete the Obstacle Course individually. During the second phase, taller obstacles are added, and recruits must complete the obstacles in four-man fireteams. DIs push each team of recruits to work together and, above all, to "leave no man behind."

Week 10

This phase of training is commonly referred to as Day Movement exercises, and here recruits learn to stay together in simulated tactical scenarios and ensure the safety of the marines to their left and their right. To avoid shouting over the deafening noise of simulated weapons fire, marine recruits communicate with hand signals as they navigate their way over walls and under heavy barbed wire. Combat-experienced drill instructors show recruits how to respond to evolving situations on the battlefield and complete the mission together.

Week 11

The Crucible is the final phase of Marine Corps Recruit Training which tests every skill learned and every value instilled. Recruits will be challenged for fifty-four continuous hours with little food and sleep. To complete this final test, recruits must have the heart and the intestinal fortitude, the body, and the mind . . . the desire, and the ability. The recruit must pull together or fall apart. Win as one, or all will fail. Succeed, and you will carry a sense of accomplishment that will last forever. I've attempted to explain this sense of accomplishment to my two lovely daughters, but I found it impossible to verbalize. One has to go through it, and only then can this sense of accomplishment be explained.

Week 12

At the end of the Crucible, recruits march to the Emblem Ceremony where drill instructors present their platoons with the Marine Corps Emblem—the Eagle, Globe, and Anchor—and address recruits as "Marine" for the very first time. Over the past twelve weeks, the recruits have been transformed from individual civilians into a tight-knit group of marines. Every struggle and challenge has prepared them for this moment when they will stand beside their instructors at graduation as "marines." This was one of the proudest moments of my life, and I will never forget the feeling when my DI addressed me as a marine for the first time.

I was a platoon squad leader during the twelve-week boot camp training period and was awarded the rank of private first class (PFC) upon graduation. The four other platoon squad leaders also received their PFC stripe, along with our platoon guide, who received his PFC stripe, and a brand-new dress blue uniform.

My platoon #356 graduated late in October of 1962, along with three other platoons in our company. Platoon #356 achieved the title of Regimental Honor Platoon. Each one of us gave all we had in order to compete with the other three platoons, and we became brothers. Graduating from boot camp was no small feat; it took a "man" to complete this training, and we all made it. *We were a proud bunch of guys who earned the title of United States Marine.*

"DON CLARK IS MARCHING DIRECTLY BEHIND THE MARINE IN DRESS BLUES"

Nearly Getting Busted
at Boot Camp

WHEN MY CLOSE FRIEND BILL Shepard and I enlisted, we were told by our recruiters that we could spend our marine corps career working in the field of aviation if a score of 70 percent or above was achieved on a series of tests we took shortly after enlistment. Due to the superb academic training we received at Lawrence High School, we both scored well above 90 percent.

After completing boot camp, we both were on our way to the world of Marine Corps Aviation. Prior to traveling to our assigned aviation school, Bill and I went home directly from boot camp and enjoyed a much-deserved vacation for a period of thirty days. We spent quality time with our families and friends, said our goodbyes, and boarded the train from our hometown of Lawrence, Kansas, en route to Memphis, Tennessee.

Our train ride from Lawrence to Memphis took nine hours, and once we arrived in Memphis, we were to take a bus and travel twenty-four additional miles to the small town of Middleton, Tennessee. Middleton was where the Naval Aviation Technical Training Center (NATTC) was located, and was where we would undergo aviation MOS training.

While traveling on a Greyhound bus to Middleton, Bill and I were met up with Alex, one of our friends while attending boot camp. Alex sat beside us during our bus trip to Middleton, and he began telling jokes that weren't funny.

He could sense the joke telling wasn't going so well, so he reminded us of how he and I were the only two marines in all the history of the marine corps who came an inch of getting busted from PFC (private first class E-2) back to PVT (private E-1) while still assigned to a platoon undergoing boot camp training.

Each boot camp platoon consisted of about sixty marines, and the platoon was divided into four squads. Each squad had a squad leader, and upon boot camp graduation day, the four squad leaders and the platoon guide would normally be awarded a promotion from private to private first class. The promotion signified they were superior in most tasks undertaken at MCRD and performed as an outstanding leader during the thirteen-week training period.

Alex, Bill, and I were three of the five marines who were awarded our PFC stripe the day of graduating from boot camp because we were three of the four platoon squad leaders. Our platoon guide was the fifth marine to be awarded PFC. He also was awarded a dress blue uniform which signified he was the most outstanding marine in our boot camp platoon.

We were extremely proud of our achievement and worked and marched our asses off in order to obtain our PFC promotion. The episode that caused Alex and me to almost lose our PFC status happened on the night prior to boot camp graduation. Bill followed instructions and, to his credit, wasn't involved in this episode.

The night prior to our graduation day, our platoon sergeant ordered the platoon to hit the rack and to get a good night's rest in preparation of the graduation ceremony that was to take place precisely at 1100 hours the following day.

I'm not sure who came up with the idea, but Alex and I decided to disobey orders and slipped out of our Quonset hut (small barracks) when lights went out and tiptoed to the "head" (restroom) to celebrate the fact that we were about to graduate from boot camp in the morning as a marine and promoted to private first class.

I can't overemphasize the fact that we disobeyed a direct order and should have been like all the other marines in our platoon in our racks sleeping or attempting to sleep. Again, I don't remember who came up with the idea, but as that particular evening unfolded, I can assure you, we wished it would have never happened.

It just so happened that during our so-called private celebration, the officer of the day which was a first lieutenant walked in the head to relieve himself and stumbled upon the two of us laughing, telling jokes, and most of all disobeying our platoon sergeants direct order. The first lieutenant was furious and yelled at the top of his voice for us two to fall out on the road in front of the head.

We were scared to death and practically shit in our skivvies (underwear). We panicked and ran out the head and down the path to our platoon's Quonset huts as fast as we could. We quickly jumped in our racks and pretended to be sleep like all our other fellow platoon members.

It was about one hundred yards to our Quonset hut from the head, and both of us must have set a one-hundred-yard dash record. We never discovered the marine that squealed on us, but within ten minutes, our platoon sergeant was yelling our names to fall out on the road. As commanded, Alex and I fell out on the road and stood at attention in the cool night air for over twenty minutes.

The three drill instructors (DIs) were all very upset at us, and the junior drill instructor ordered us to perform three hundred step-ups. We felt as if our legs were going to fall off. He then ordered us to do push-ups until we couldn't do anymore. Then our platoon sergeant stepped in front of us and, at the top of his voice, ordered us to hit the rack.

Neither Alex nor I got an ounce of sleep that night. We realized we had seriously screwed up and laid there in our bunks wide awake, imagining how severe our punishment would be the following day. It seemed the next day came quicker than usual, and sharply at 0600 hours, we were ordered out in front of our Quonset huts and lined up into formation and marched to morning chow.

We began marching to morning chow, and for some crazy reason, we, Alex and I, felt that maybe all had been forgotten because we were ordered to assume our positions of squad leader. After marching about ten steps toward the mess hall, our platoon sergeant suddenly halted the platoon.

He then slowly walked to the head of the platoon and came to Alex and me, and quietly ordered us to fall out and report to the Officer of the Day's office with all our gear. We were stunned at this action and didn't know what to think.

Without saying a word to each other, we managed to pack our gear in our duffle bags. Then we nervously walked to the Officer of the Day's office, all the time thinking we possibly were going to receive brig time or was going to be disgracefully booted out of the marine corps. Words can't describe how frightened we felt walking to the Officer of the Day's office.

We finally reached our destination, and the Officer of the Day, a seasoned decorated Captain, was impatiently waiting for us while standing on the front steps of his Quonset hut office.

The captain said we were late; he then angrily ordered us inside his office. He ordered us to stand at attention in front of his desk for nearly ten minutes. Then, in a controlled voice, he commenced to explain how we had disgraced the marine corps. He then looked straight at us and sternly said that he had never heard of boot camp squad leaders about to be promoted to PFC perform such a dumb and stupid act. He said he was disgusted at us and should throw the book at us.

The captain then stood up from behind his desk and firmly asked us if we understood our platoon sergeant last night when he said to turn out the lights and hit the sack. We answered that we understood and stated we didn't have an excuse for our actions. He continued by stating that if we failed to follow a direct order in combat, we could cause fellow marines severe harm, or even death. He ended his lecture by instructing us to wait in the small room adjacent to this office.

The small room was no larger than a broom closet, and it didn't have lights. The captain ordered us, most emphatically, not to sit down on the floor or speak a single word to each other. While entering the small room, the captain stated we were to remain in the room until our platoon's commanding officer makes the decision about our fate.

The captain then left us in the small room and left the door cracked open. We pointed to the cracked door and, in sign language, said to one another not to talk. It seemed we were in that room for eternity, but we didn't say one mumbling word or attempt to rest our legs by sitting. We followed the direct order just as the captain instructed.

We reasoned, by the captain leaving the door cracked open, that possibly someone was listening and checking to see if we would follow his order to keep our mouths shut and stand on our feet. We followed the direct order. We were too frightened to talk or sit down anyway. After standing in that broom closet for a solid two hours, we were finally ordered back in the captain's office and informed the decision concerning our fate had been passed down.

We remained at attention as the captain informed us that we would graduate as scheduled. The captain said no word concerning getting our planned PFC promotion we had worked so hard for during boot camp. We were too scared and ashamed to ask the captain about our planned promotion.

When we were dismissed, we commenced to hump our gear back to our assigned Quonset hut. When it came time for our platoon to march to our graduation ceremony, we were ordered to fall in, and we didn't know if we were to fall in as squad leaders, so we held back. Our platoon sergeant came over to where we were standing and, with a half smile on his face, said, "Fall in, marines, as squad leaders." He went on to say that we had deserved our promotions today to private first class.

As we took up our position as the leader of our respective squads, we looked over at each other and smiled with pride. We were elated and learned our lesson, and we would be better off as marines because of the experience. Alex and I were the happiest marines on the parade deck that day, and probably the face of the earth. We figured our so-called PFC-celebrated act of stupidity in the head last night was a first and most likely will never be topped. We were so thankful that day to God and the marine corps for showering us with mercy.

After boot camp graduation, we were bused about thirty miles up the Pacific Coast to Camp Pendleton, California. As the buses rode north, on Highway 1, the two of us sat in our seats, so proud. We had learned a valuable lesson, a lesson that we would never forget.

While in boot camp we trained as a platoon, in infantry training (ITR) we would be trained as a company (four platoons). We were about to undergo four laborious weeks of infantry training. The training consisted of hard noise and basic marine infantry training, and the instructors were drop-dead serious about their training lessons.

We were housed in Quonset huts just like at boot camp, but in boot camp, our Quonset huts were surrounded by flat land. At ITR, our Quonset huts were surrounded by hills, lots of hills. All three of us had assumed that during ITR training, we would be humping those hills in full combat dress. Our assumptions were dead-on, because hump we did until we were completely exhausted.

Teamwork was the theme at ITR whether it was your assigned fire team, your squad, your platoon, or your assigned company. We were taught the common skills needed in combat. We were also taught the basics of combat marksmanship, counter-improvised explosive device technique, how to conduct the defense of a position, convoy operations, combat formations, fire team assaults, patrolling, and the use of correspondence devices.

We were trained in basic military intelligence; land navigation; and the use of hand grenades, grenade launchers, rocket launchers, and automatic weapons (BAR, M60 machine gun). We engaged in combat conditioning by navigating various obstacle courses. We went on several hikes in full combat dress. We also underwent various physical training techniques and received advanced training in the Marine Corps Martial Arts Program.

Upon graduating from ITR, the marine was to have gained skilled combat knowledge, an ability to operate in a real combat environment as a basic rifleman and to perform his called-upon duties under enemy fire.

Once ITR was completed, we were granted a thirty-day leave (vacation), and this was more than well deserved. The vast majority of us that completed ITR went home for the leave period. Home for me was Lawrence, Kansas, where my parents and younger brother would be happy to see me. I didn't have a hometown sweetheart, but I knew my three-year-old German shepherd would be there and happy to greet me.

"If you walk with the Lord, you'll never be out of step."

"RECEIVING MY LAST RIFLE INSPECTION IN BOOT CAMP"

Aviation Technical Training

THE FIVE-MONTH TRAINING I RECEIVED at NATTC (Naval Aviation Technical Training Center) in Middle, Tennessee, was professional and challenging. The instructors taught with a no-nonsense attitude and made sure you earned your credential.

There were some fifty MOS training schools on campus at NATTC, and it wasn't easy to pass the requirements needed to obtain a desired MOS certification. So when the necessary requirements were achieved for graduation, celebrating the achievement was warranted.

While stationed at NATTC, I visited the city of Memphis practically each time I was awarded a liberty pass. Normally, I would end up on Beale Street which was famous for its many bars and nightclubs. Some of the best blues and soul singing acts in the world would perform in these places.

On one particular Sunday, I attended a large Negro church in downtown Memphis, and the Lord blessed me with the opportunity to see the famous James Brown perform. He was called the "Godfather of Soul," and on this particular Sunday, he lived up to his billing. He sung his heart out, and while being accompanied by the church choir, this living legend had everyone in the church standing up, stomping their feet and joyously singing along. Everyone attending church that particular day (including yours truly) witnessed the Holy Ghost.

April 26, 1963, was my MOS Training School "graduation day." My MOS was that of an aircraft engineering clerk, and I was thrilled to learn I had graduated number one in my class. Several of the other aviation training schools on base were graduating young sailors and marines that week, and it seemed as though most everyone I made contact with were in a serious partying mood.

Most of us who were graduating headed to Memphis to celebrate. We planned to dance and party the night away with one of the many pretty girls who frequented the many nightclubs located up and down Beale Street.

While leaving the base, headed to Memphis, we were seriously warned by our senior NCOs to avoid getting intoxicated and ending up in the slammer. They told us that civilian cops loved arresting young marines. This warning was a little difficult to comprehend, because many Memphis policemen were retired marines.

My hometown enlistment buddy, Bill Shepard, was scheduled to graduate on the same day, and we decided to hook up with a couple of our friends and roll into Memphis.

The group of marines Bill and I traveled with were nondrinkers, like we were, and while driving into Memphis, we couldn't help but to notice a large number of cops out in force and on the lookout for intoxicated celebrating servicemen.

Our carload of celebrators consisted of five marines. We were pretty close and stuck together. We also looked out after one another. One of the marines in our group had just graduated from my MOS school, and the remaining two guys graduated from Bill's MOS school.

As stated earlier, we were all nondrinkers, but there were a couple of hotheads in the group who would fight at the drop of a hat. Prior to exiting the vehicle, we all pledged we wouldn't engage in any bar brawls. We also pledged that we would remain together and not drift off after some hot skirt. We reasoned the worst thing that could happen to ruin our celebration was to do something stupid, like fighting, and end up behind bars.

After exiting our vehicle, we immediately walked to a popular nightclub that staged some great soul singing acts and had a ball. None of us got into any trouble that night, but a good many celebrating jarheads we heard did in fact find their way to a cold Memphis jail cell. I felt bad for the guys who ended up in jail, because I sincerely knew they were only trying to have a little fun.

That following morning, many of the guys who had celebrated the night before received their orders for their new base assignment. *I received orders to report to HMX-1, the Presidential Helicopter Squadron, located in Quantico, Virginia.*

A staff sergeant, who was one of my class instructors, found out about my assignment destination and told me that HMX-1 only accepts top graduates from the various schools at NATTC and that I should feel proud and honored to be awarded the opportunity to serve in the prestigious Presidential Helicopter Squadron.

I told the staff sergeant that I appreciated him providing me with the "heads-up" concerning *HMX-1*. He ended our little talk by saying they would be expecting great things from me, and he knew I wouldn't disappoint them. I assured him I would do my best and sincerely thanked him for everything.

The first chance I got, I ran to our base library to read up on HMX-1 because, until the staff sergeant discussed it with me, I was totally unaware of this squadron but was aware of Quantico, Virginia. I was knowledgeable that Quantico was the place where the majority of our key officers in the marine corps were trained. Secondly, that Quantico was where senior officers from the other four branches of our military received advanced training. I was also aware that it was the place where members of the FBI and the CIA received much of their training. In essence, it was a special place where advanced training was performed.

That afternoon, I ran into Bill, and he said that he received orders to go to Lakehurst, New Jersey. Bill graduated tops in his class from Parachute Rigging School. He had worked hard, and I was proud of his achievement. By Bill receiving orders to New Jersey, this would be the first time that we would separate since enlisting in the corps. We had figured it was going to happen eventually.

We were excited about our orders, and I informed him I was riding into town again this evening with some of my classmates to boogey once again. He said since we were granted another liberty pass that he was going to take advantage of it and that he also was riding into Memphis to party a second straight night with a couple of guys he graduated with and that he would look for me on Beale Street.

Bill and I managed to join up at a nightclub on Beale Street that we frequented and began partying the night away. Early in the evening, we hooked up with PFC Barr, a mutual friend at base, and decided to go to another club about a half mile down Beale Street. During our walk toward this nightclub, a most unusual thing happened to us three young celebrating marines.

We three stopped at a popular clothing store on Beale Street and were checking out the threads. And, all of a sudden, three fine-looking sisters walked up and began staring at us up and down. Then a strange thing happened. The leader of the three stepped up and asked each of her two buddies, "Which one of these handsome young marines do you want?"

Like a scene straight from the movies, each one of the three fine ladies walked toward us and put their arm around their chosen marine for that evening. Barr, Bill, and I were in total disbelief until the young ladies said in unison, "Do you want to party, Marines, or just stand here inside this storefront?"

Off we went, and party we did. We partied with these three fine-looking ladies until the early morning hour. This sounds like fiction, but it actually happened. Bill and I, to this day, laugh about this particular episode. The girls were young, pretty, and ready to party; and I'm going to simply leave it at that and conclude by saying we had a ball for the remainder of the evening.

After all of these many years, I must fess up . . . Billy, I know I told you and Doug that I nailed my little sweetie pie to the cross . . . but, in actuality, I was unable to get it up . . . Don't laugh. It happens to the best of men.

We said goodbye to our three beautiful sweeties; and Billy, Doug, and I began our short bus ride back to base. Also, on our bus were eight white navy sailors who apparently had been drinking earlier that evening because they were trying very hard to start trouble with us, and we at first paid them little or no attention. Then they began repeatedly saying the "N" word, and saying it often and louder.

We remained calm concerning the situation until the taller sailor walked over to us and asked us where we were headed. Doug told the guy we were headed to Middleton; then he laughed and said that "he thought we were headed to Africa to be with our monkey brothers and sisters."

As the tall sailor talked, the closer his seven buddies walked toward us. Then, to our surprise, one of the sailors came over to our side and said he wasn't a part of the name-calling and insulting behavior.

As the friendly sailor walked toward us, I could clearly see that he wasn't totally white and mixed with something. When he reached us, we asked him why he was coming over to our side, and that's when he proclaimed to be Rican.

As soon as he said he was a Puerto Rican, the other seven sailors began calling him "sand nigger," and worse. When one of the sailors attempted to hit him, then that's when it was on. The Rican quickly did away with his opponent (we later learned the Puerto Rican was a black belt karate expert). Doug loved to fight and began kicking the shit out of two of our opponents. Bill and I were pretty good with our hands, and we took on the remaining four.

Billy and I was having a little trouble with our four sailors until the Rican stepped in and, in a matter of seconds, disposed of all four of them. Our fight aboard that bus traveling to base lasted about ten minutes . . . thanks to the help of the Rican. His name was Eugenio Perez, and we remained friends the entire time I was in the corps.

That following morning, I was one of four graduating marines from NATTC that boarded a Boeing 707 and flew into Dulles Airport. After arriving in Washington, DC, we boarded a marine military bus and set out on a three-hour ride to my new base inside Quantico, Virginia.

"Begin each morning with a talk with God."

"DON CLARK STANDING ON THE TOP ROW. SEVENTH FROM THE RIGHT."

Presidential Helicopter Squadron

AFTER ARRIVING IN QUANTICO, THE bus I was riding on spent an hour driving through the base, dropping off marines at their assigned barracks. During the ride to my assigned barracks, I couldn't help but to notice how well manicured the lawns were, and there wasn't a piece of trash on the ground anywhere. Not even a cigarette butt on the ground. Quantico was a beautiful base. Red brick three-story buildings served as personnel housing and administration buildings. I was totally impressed by what I was seeing.

As our bus meandered its way around the base, I observed field officers and staff officers walking to and from buildings from all five branches of our armed forces. I also observed staff officers from foreign countries walking about the grounds and was informed they were receiving advanced training at Quantico. The smartly dressed civilians walking about the grounds were personnel from the various FBI and CIA schools.

Finally, the bus stopped in front of my assigned barracks and, while departing, noticed a sign across the street that read Marine Corps Air Station—Quantico, Virginia.

After checking into my barracks, I walked back outside to observe the four large aircraft hangars that were lined up directly across the street. The four hangars housed the helicopter's belonging to HMX-1. I attempted to take a peek at the choppers inside but, due to tight security measures, was unable to get close enough. My fatigues didn't have the proper tags hanging from the lapels of my shirt—thus, not allowing me to enter the hangars.

As my first day on base came to an end, I quickly became indoctrinated to being assigned to the most prestigious helicopter squadron in the marine corps. This was a spit and polish outfit, with a no non-sense attitude. I went to sleep that night impatiently waiting on the next morning to arrive so I could report to my duty station and meet my coworkers and superiors.

Morning finally arrived; I quickly ate morning chow and reported to my work station. It was the Aircraft Engineering Office located in the north wing of hangar number 2. There, I was officially introduced to my fellow workers and my direct report. My direct report was a muscular built staff sergeant. He was short in height but extremely well-groomed. He was of Greek heritage and a career NCO.

The staff sergeant and I appeared to get along from day one. I was a fast learner, extremely accurate, and performed my job duties with a no-nonsense attitude. In a short time on the job, the staff sergeant was pleased with my output and several times told me he admired my positive attitude.

Several members of our Aircraft Engineering Office staff privately informed me the staff sergeant was impressed with my work ethic. And that he had told some of them that he had not witnessed a marine fresh out of NATTC performed his aircraft logging duties as fast or as accurate as I had proved to be the short time on base.

The staff sergeant had stressed the importance while working in the capacity of my MOS to be accurate while logging flight data against our helicopters and their main components. He was personally checking my work and, after three weeks, ceased this activity because he felt I could perform my work accurately.

It was my third week on base, and it only takes one a short time to realize marines assigned to HMX-1 take their jobs drop-dead seriously. They personify a proud bunch of men, who strut around with an air of cockiness about themselves.

As the days passed on, I also felt a great sense of pride being a member of HMX-1's staff. Additionally, it was a thrill to be able to tell family and friends that my military duty afforded me the opportunity to be associated with our commander in chief, the president of the United States.

Many Washington, DC, civilians I talked to about my association with HMX-1 asked me if I flew in those big green-and-white helicopters they would see on television taking off from the White House lawn. The green-and-white helicopters they were referring to were named "Marine One," and they were the aircraft used to fly the president, his family, and key staff members around on short trips.

When asked the question, did I fly in Marine One? I would answer by saying all marines attached to HMX-1 play an important role in the president boarding Marine One, flying off and returning safely. I would further say that many of my friends at HMX-1 flew with the president, his staff, and family. I would say they were extremely proud of their duty. Then I would abruptly change the subject.

Due to exceptional job skills, I was promoted from PFC to lance corporal ahead of schedule. There was another young black marine who held the same MOS at HMX-1 and worked as efficient as yours truly. William Tellis was his name, and he was promoted to lance corporal during the same time.

We both were nondrinkers and simply celebrated our promotions by listening to Motown record albums in our barracks. As time would passed, William Tellis and I would grow into very close friends. I called him Tee, and he called me DC.

Tee, I, and a corporal aircraft mechanic were the only three black marines assigned to HMX-1 at the time.

Tee and I became acquainted, and, in some cases, friends with our squadron's pilots, copilots, and helicopter flight crewmen. And the reason was when a helicopter would complete a flight mission, the flight logbooks were subsequently dropped off at the squadron's Aircraft Engineering Office where both Tee and I worked. Either one of the pilots or one of the flight crew performed this task, thus, enabling the acquaintance.

By Tee and I being in contact with the aforementioned personnel, we were able to strike up conversation that would lead to Tee and I having the opportunity to fly in their helicopters when they flew up and down the eastern Atlantic seaboard.

Both Tee and I had a likable personality, and this made it easy for crew members to enjoy taking us with them on certain flights. Getting flight crew members to like me was not by accident. My dad taught me my personality skills. He preached to me while growing up that the key to getting ahead in this world is to have people open doors for you, and this occurred most likely if people liked you.

These trips were normally training exercises or courier missions. Tee and I could care less about the type of flight mission; we were just thrilled that they allowed us to fly along at times as voluntary crew members.

On occasion, I requested to fly with them when they flew to Cherry Point, North Carolina, or Pensacola, Florida. There were a couple of marines stationed at these sites whom I had become friends with during my training at NATTC. I made at least three flights to these two places and got a chance to see my friends each time. And the good thing about these trips is we returned to Quantico on the same day.

Although I was the rookie in our Aviation Engineering Office, I was working longer hours than my MOS counterparts. The main reason for working the long hours was I had been attempting to learn the helicopters nomenclature.

I reasoned that logging time against key mechanical components of a helicopter could be performed in a more efficient manner if I were mentally familiar with the aircraft's nomenclature . . .

the logging process would take less time, thus, making my job more efficient.

I had been stationed at Quantico and assigned to HMX-1 a little over four months and, as yet, hadn't logged any time against the helicopters the president, his family, or his staff flew in. A promotion to NCO (Corporal) was required in order to perform this function. In addition, I needed to obtain a high-level security clearance.

I was informed on the first day stationed at HMX-1 that, in order to remain in this most prestigious helicopter squadron, it was mandatory that I be granted a top-level security clearance, referred to as a "White House Clearance." To secure this top-level security clearance, a marine had to have his shit supertight. He had to provide the correct answers to tons of questions.

This process of providing personal information went on for several months until, one fall day in 1963, I was called into the squadron's Administration Office and informed a decision was pending concerning my top-level security clearance.

A friend of mine who worked in the admin office told me in confidence that he heard from valid sources it was likely I would have to leave HMX-1 because of my lack of knowledge concerning my biological father.

Upon hearing this negative information about my sperm father and all, even though it was unofficial, it made me feel real mad inside. I saw red and reasoned it wasn't my fault my biological father swept my mother off her feet, laid his seed, and broke her little heart with the news he was already married.

I couldn't help but think what difference would it make if I knew his whereabouts anyway. I felt as though I had proven myself and that I made the grade. I reasoned I should be able to receive this so-called high-level clearance because I had nothing but good marks throughout my short marine corps career.

I would lie awake nights sweating this one out and would have many bad dreams over this clearance thing. In my dreams, I would get so mad at the whole situation I would want to hurt somebody. The main problem I had was I didn't know fact from bullshit while listening to people telling me I would pass or wouldn't pass. I reasoned I had to pass because I felt I was a sharp candidate and possessed the right stuff.

On some sleepless nights, I would dream on the negative side and see me not being granted the clearance. During these nights, I would dream that when the clearance was not granted, I would play out the rejection by envisioning me running to the squadron's Administration Office and demanding they provide orders to ship my ass out as soon as possible. Then I would awaken, take a cold shower, and start the new day.

I seriously wanted to remain in HMX-1 so bad that this entire clearance thing was driving me crazy and often moody. I guess about three weeks or so of this uncertainty passed by, and finally I was ordered to the Administration Office and was officially informed I failed to qualify for the high-level security clearance required to remain at HMX-1.

They further told me I had several choices of Marine Air Base destinations requiring the duties of my MOS. Upon hearing the official rejecting news, I became fighting mad and, for a few minutes, completely lost it and demanded I receive orders to be shipped to a squadron engaged in combat operations in South Vietnam.

At the time, I wanted to take my frustrations out on the enemy our nation was currently fighting. I figured if I would put the hurt on somebody, why not this enemy they kept referring to as the Viet Cong? They informed me they couldn't promise me duty in South Vietnam but that they would try very hard to satisfy my request.

The day prior to Thanksgiving in 1963, I was informed by a friend who worked in HMX-1's personnel office the true reason I didn't qualify for the high-level security clearance was the "fact" that when I was sixteen years of age, seven other high school students and I were caught and charged with stealing pizza pies from a Pizza Hut delivery truck.

All seven of us were popular school athletes and well liked in our community. The county judge that was to hand down our sentence was aware of our reputation as good athletes and was an avid high school sports fan. He gave us a strong lecture about being a good law-abiding citizen, and by the strike of his gavel, he dropped all of our criminal charges. The pizza bandits (as we were referred to in the town's newspaper) did, in fact, have to spend one night in jail. We were told the one night behind bars was the judge's way of teaching us a lesson.

That night we spent behind bars was not what taught us a lesson. We did our one night of jail time standing on our head. As a matter of fact, we had a fun pillow fight and were playing around in our jail cells that night. What taught us our lesson was the serious ass whooping each of us received from our parents. They tore our ass up when we got home the next day, and that experience was what really taught us not to get in trouble stealing in this life, or the next, ever again.

My marine buddy who worked in the personnel office further informed me there were a large number of marines who also failed to receive the top-level security clearance. He seriously stated it wasn't a racial thing or anything of that nature. He simply said I should not have taken the pizza pies.

I bought him a few round of beers at the enlisted men's club for providing this information, and we both got a little tipsy. I really did appreciate him telling me the true reason. I felt relieved with his info, and the anger I had about the whole situation suddenly vanished.

Because of my failure to obtain the high-level security clearance, I only remained at HMX-1 a total of seventeen months. I loved every minute of duty there. And, by this time, I had begun to strut around base with a noticeable swagger like the other proud marines stationed at HMX-1, because this truly was a proud and special place to serve our country.

While waiting on orders to be shipped out of HMX-1, I spent some time reflecting on my time spent there. During most of my stay at HMX-1, I didn't go on weekend liberty much and mainly hung around the barracks and read books. This wasn't the case for most of the other marines in my squadron. They would catch a ride into Washington, DC, party and have a great time.

A few weekends, I would get bored hanging around base and would take my weekend liberty pass and catch a ride into Washington, DC. While in the city, I would either see a show at the famed Howard

Theater or simply visit with my father's sister and her husband. They always made me feel real comfortable and were great conversationalists. I enjoyed the dozen or so times I visited with them.

Continuing with my reflections of duty at HMX-1, there were two spectacular events that occurred. The first being the famous march on Washington that took place August 28, 1963. The second was the assassination of President John F. Kennedy that occurred on November 22 that same year.

The March on Washington was one of the largest political rallies for human rights ever staged in the United States. Its primary purpose was to call for civil and economic rights for African Americans. It was estimated some three hundred thousand people participated; and the March was organized by a group of civil rights, labor, and religious organizations.

During the March, Dr. Marin Luther King Jr. delivered his historic "I Have a Dream" speech in which he called for an end to racism in the US. It was estimated 80 percent of the marchers were black, and the March is credited with helping to pass the Civil Rights Act of 1964 and the Voting Rights Act of 1965.

Many of the military bases in and around Washington, DC, were on high alert during the March. Several military bases, including Quantico, had trained "riot control squads." Their purpose was to prevent participants of the March from rioting and getting out of control.

Eighteen riot control squad members were chosen from the Marine Corps Air Station in Quantico, and yours truly was one of those chosen. Prior to the date, we would practice several times weekly on methods to control and contain a rioting mod. I truly hated being a part of these squads but, like a good marine, followed orders.

I wanted so badly to travel to DC and participate in the March because, as a black person, I viewed the March as a means to end racial discrimination and achieve racial equality in America. It was humiliating to be assigned to a riot control unit, and to harm if necessary marchers who got out of line. I felt like a "racial turncoat" and was praying the marchers didn't riot or anything, because the last thing I wanted during that time was to inflict bodily harm on people who were sacrificing their time and energy for "my equality."

The second most remembered event that took place during my tour of duty at HMX-1 was shocking news around the world. John Fitzgerald Kennedy, the thirty-fifth president of the United States, was assassinated on November 22, 1963, in Dallas, Texas.

It's very difficult to express into words the depressed feeling each member of our helicopter squadron felt that awful day. Marine One, the helicopter the president flew in, was, of course, on site in Dallas, as well as two other of our squadron's aircrafts.

Our entire base was in deep mourning after Kennedy's assassination and couldn't believe a former marine (Lee Harvey Oswald) had, in fact, fired the fatal shot.

I clearly remember how tight security around HMX-1 got directly after the incident, how all marines at Quantico were placed on high alert because it wasn't known at the time that Oswald acted alone. During that time, the majority of the American public suspected JFK was killed as a result of a conspiracy.

JFK was extremely well-liked by all marines in HMX-1 who had come in contact with him. And many people in our squadron had close ties with him, especially the pilot and crewmen of Marine One. During this period, I heard several stories from members of Marine One's flight crew expressing how nice JFK and his entire family members were and each time a tear would fall when they talked about him. It was a sad time in and around our base during these troubled times in US history.

There were several other significant events that took place while stationed at HMX-1, like the time my mother came to visit me in May of 1964. With a borrowed car from a marine buddy, I picked Mom up at Dulles Airport on the day of my birthday in 1964. I drove Mom around the city, showing her many of the historical sights. I showed her the Capitol Building, the White House, and the Lincoln Memorial. She was very happy to have seen these places, and I was extremely happy she came to visit me on my twentieth birthday.

Mother only stayed that one day; and during that time, we had a ball, went sightseeing, and talked about old times. It was one of the best days in my life, and I'll never forget the joy on her face when I showed her where the March on Washington had taken place.

While we were viewing the Washington Monument, Mom tearfully and sincerely thanked me for showing her around. Then suddenly because of joy in her heart, she tightly embraced me for a good five minutes. Then we held hands as she said a prayer that I'll never forget because she ended her prayer with these words: "God, please protect the safety of Dr. King, and don't let the demons out there cowardly assassinate him because we as a people need his leadership in order to achieve equality."

There were so many significant events that occurred while stationed at Quantico that I could write a book about. I'm going to close this topic of discussion, but before I do, I have to spend some time telling about the time a marine buddy and I visited his grandmother in a small town located on the outskirts of Fredericksburg, Virginia.

We were driving to his grandmother's home on Labor Day 1964 and, because we were getting low on fuel, had to stop at a gas station. My friend was driving, and I told him to stay in the car and I would fill his car up with gasoline. The station attendant was sitting on a stool talking to four of his buddies, and I kindly walked up to him and asked him to unlock the gas pump so I could fill our car up with gasoline.

It was difficult getting the attention of the station attendant because he was busy telling fish-catching stories to his buddies that were sitting alongside him in broken-down chairs. When I finally got his attention, he said without even looking at me, "This filling station doesn't do business with niggas." Naturally, I was stunned and didn't know what to say. So like an idiot, I asked him to repeat his statement. He stood up, along with his four buddies, and repeated his statement. Then he spit on my shoes and said I better hightail it down the road.

Each of these guys weighed in over two hundred pounds and stood over six feet.

I'll never forget the hatred in their eyes as they began to surround me. My marine friend was Italian and grew up in South Side,

Chicago. He ran around with black marines and simply loved to fight. He was six feet four and weighed 220 pounds of solid muscle. He saw and heard what was happening and immediately jumped out of the car and ran over to where the confrontation between me and the five rednecks were taking place.

Realizing we were totally outnumbered, I attempted to defuse the situation by saying to my friend that this gas station is not for us, and we should drive further down the road to seek another. I even asked the station attendant if he could provide direction to the nearest one. His reply was, "I don't provide directions to niggas, and you best move your ass on down the road."

Soon after the station attendant finished his remark, my marine friend hauled off and hit him in the nose so hard that his entire nose shattered. Then my friend hit the biggest of the attendant's four buddies in the mouth so hard that teeth went flying everywhere. I figured the brawl was on, so I hauled off and hit one of the bigots in the temple, and the guy immediately fell to the ground, knocked out.

By this time, the remaining three rednecks had retreated and began to run away from the scene. Meanwhile, blood was still pouring from the nose of the station attendant, and it was an ugly sight. So, as a good gesture, my marine buddy gave the station attendant a shop rag to catch some of the blood pouring from his face.

It was so ironic, my friend giving this asshole a rag for his nose, but he did, and we reasoned it was best we depart this place before the law arrives on the scene. As we walked to our car, it was hard to believe the remaining three bigots ran like little bitches and didn't engage in the fight. They outnumbered us, but I guess after my friend damn near knocked their buddies nose off, they reasoned they didn't want that to happen to them and figured marines were kick-ass crazy and opted to run instead of joining the fight.

It wasn't that all marines were kick-ass crazy; it was my Italian friend who was fighting crazy. He was well-known around Quantico for kicking ass, and he would demonstrate his skills at the drop of a hat. I bet those gas station bigots will think twice the next time a couple of marines drive up seeking petro.

The date for my departure to leave HMX-1 had finally arrived and, on October 7, 1964, I must have shook hands with and/or hugged nearly every marine in the squadron. It truly was an emotional departure; and while riding in the military bus headed for Dulles Airport, in Washington, DC, I remember being overwhelmed with joy.

I had experienced a fantastic seventeen-month tour of duty at HMX-1, and although I didn't qualify for the high security clearance, I did have the grand opportunity to be a part of the most prestigious helicopter squadron in the world.

I'm so very grateful for my friends. I take this time to give thanks for their many blessings of friendships.

"YOURS TRULY IS THE HANDSOME MARINE DIRECTLY BEHIND THE PLATOON GUIDE – FAR LEFT."

Aboard Ship, the USNS Gaffey

P ERSONALLY, I KNEW VERY LITTLE about Southeast Asia and knew absolutely nothing about the country of South Vietnam. However, I was aware the country of France, had troops fighting in Vietnam for the past twenty years, but didn't have a clue as to why they were fighting.

By the time my tour of duty at HMX-1 came to an end, the news media was reporting Vietnam's civil unrest had escalated into a full-blown civil war. The news media further reported that people living in North Vietnam were fighting the people of South Vietnam. And people in South Vietnam were fighting each other. And they referred to the communist fighting forces as Viet Cong.

Practically all major newspapers, television networks, and radio stations were constantly providing daily news updates of Vietnam's civil war. They also were reporting that American GIs were being shipped to South Vietnam by the thousands, with the marines and army forces leading in the buildup.

Three weeks had passed since I received my security clearance rejection, and on October 1, 1964, I was requested to report to our squadron's Administration Office to fill out some beneficiary forms. While waiting to turn the forms in, a strange urge came over me. I approached the desk clerk and asked, "Is there duty in Vietnam that requires the services of my MOS? If so, I want a duty assignment in Vietnam ASAP."

Several marines in the office overheard my request and looked at me like I was crazy. A staff sergeant walked over to me and quietly stated there were several openings for my MOS and that I could go to South Vietnam, assigned to a Helicopter Squadron, as early as next week.

About a week after my request, I had signed orders to board a naval troop carrier named USNS *Gaffey*. The USNS *Gaffey* was scheduled to ship out the following week, and she was to leave from the naval docks in San Diego, California.

Mainly marines were to board the ship, and it was to transport us to the island of Okinawa. While in Okinawa, we were to undergo several weeks of jungle survival training. From Okinawa, we were to fly to Da Nang, South Vietnam, aboard C-130s.

Prior to embarking upon my journey to Vietnam, I was granted a ten-day leave pass and flew into Kansas City International Airport where my parents met me and drove me the remaining distance to my hometown of Lawrence, Kansas.

During the forty-five-minute ride from the airport to home, they brought me up-to-date concerning the hometown news. During the ride, my dad asked me how I ended up with orders to Vietnam. I told him I volunteered to be sent to Vietnam.

He commended me for stepping up to defend human rights and told me he was proud of me. His words made me feel good inside.

The following ten days I spent at home was most enjoyable but went by quickly. The next thing I knew, I was saying goodbyes to my family and boarding a Boeing 707 in Kansas City that was scheduled to fly into San Diego, California. The plane ride was not enjoyable, and it must have hit every air pocket in the sky.

Each time the 707 hit an air pocket, the plane seemed to fall five thousand feet and would scare the ever-living shit out of me. Each time the aircraft hit an air pocket, I ordered from the stewardess a rum and coke. The plane hit a lot of air pockets, and I was damn near drunk when we landed four hours later in San Diego.

After landing in San Diego, we were sent to Camp Pendleton to await our ship to dock and be prepared for our long sea voyage to Okinawa. We couldn't go on liberty during our eight-day stay at

Camp Pendleton, and about all we did was write our loved ones back home.

Finally, the time came for my group to take the fifty-mile ride from Pendleton to the San Diego shipyard. It was nearing the time to ship out, and on one hand I was thrilled, but on the other I dreaded the ship ride. I had never been out to sea aboard a large vessel and had heard many stories about seasickness.

My group was next to board ship, so with my barf bag in hand, I promptly slung my overpacked duffle bag over my shoulder and began my walk up the long plank to board our ship, the USNS *Gaffey*, along with my fellow marines.

Once aboard, I quickly noticed how clean and orderly the ship appeared to be. I reasoned the sailors assigned to this vessel had nothing to do but to keep it clean. The entire ship was spotless, and it seemed everything had been freshly painted.

The chow was good, damn good actually. Most of the cooks aboard our ship were "brothers," so I figured that was the reason the food was so tasty. Eating aboard ship was no doubt the best chow I had eaten since joining the corps.

As soon as our ship pulled anchor and launched out to sea, several other marines and I were stricken with seasickness. My stomach was extremely upset, and at times it felt like gas was trying to escape but couldn't. I began getting severe stomach cramps. It was embarrassing, but I wasn't alone. Other marines suffered, and the sailors aboard the ship got their kicks out of watching us seasick victims suffer and throw up all over the place.

At times, I attempted to be cool with my seasickness, but it's hard to uphold your dignity when barfing all over the deck. It was a miserable feeling. And I must have looked like a little bitch running around on deck with my neck hung over the railing attempting to barf. It was a miserable feeling, but there was nothing we could do to stop it.

The mission of the USNS *Gaffey* was to transport 1,100 marines and 400 army soldiers to the island of Okinawa. The infantry marines and army soldiers would undergo jungle survivor training while on the island. And aviation marines on board would be temporarily assigned to units and soon be flown out to Da Nang, South Vietnam.

About 70 percent of the marines and army personnel on board ship were infantrymen. While the remaining held an MOS in aviation, communications, or transportation. Both branches of the armed services aboard our ship for the most part seemed to get along fine with each other and appeared to enjoy each other's company during the long ship ride.

There were three marine recon squads and two army special forces units on board ship. The recon marines and army special forces units would compete with each other every morning at 0500 hours by performing various physical exercises. They would pair off and compete with one another by performing push-ups, step-ups, sit-ups, chin-ups, and several other physical endurance tests.

When they competed, noncompeting marines and army personnel awake and on deck that early in the morning would place side bets of quarters and half-dollars on who would win the various endurance competitions.

There was also a small unit of Navy SEALS on board ship, and they also took part in the endurance competition. The SEALS won the majority of these physical endurance exercises. And they were the ship's crew's odds-on favorite, and they would bet accordingly. Some days the betting pot would reach well over two hundred dollars.

Each team member of the Navy SEALs, the Marine Force Recon, and the Army Special Forces would completely exhaust themselves in attempting to win the endurance exercise competitions. One of the Navy SEAL members damn near died from getting totally exhausted during the sit-up competition. And the ship's commander put a stop to the competition for the remainder of the voyage.

The three teams normally would end their physical endurance sessions by running a one-hundred-yard sprint on the ship's deck. The Army Special Force's team had the only brother competing, and this guy was a world-class sprinter. He won so often that nobody would bet against him, so eventually they dropped the sprint running contest. I was a little upset at this decision because this was the only event that I won money betting on.

Betting and cheering for either of the three sides to win was about the only excitement we experience doing our sea journey, and several guys picked up a few dollars along the way. I made friends with a few of the navy and army GIs aboard the ship, and we would have fun singing songs and playing cards together.

We also engaged in some exciting and intense conversations concerning the war. It was split right down the middle between those who felt positive toward our nation being involved in the conflict versus those who felt otherwise.

Normally, after our heated discussions concerning our views toward the war, we would end those conversations with some serious prayer sessions. And these sessions would last well over an hour.

Some evenings aboard the ship, the brothers would get together and sing R&B "doo-wop" songs that many of them grew up singing on street corners back in the world. There was one brother who sounded just like Wilson Pickett and another who crooned like Nat King Cole. Listening to these guys sing their hearts out became a pleasant way to pass time.

After several days out to sea, we received word that we would be docking in Yokohama, Japan, for an eight-hour liberty call. We were all thrilled with the knowledge we would to be getting off the ship for a few hours of fun on dry land.

Several of the navy crew members had docked at this port before and knew their way around town. I had become friends with a couple of the sailors aboard the ship and overheard them talking about the best places to go in town. I told my marine buddies we should try to stay close to these sailors because they knew the hot spots and we wouldn't have to spend most of the day trying to learn their whereabouts.

Finally, we reached port and dropped anchor. About an hour later, the ship's commander sounded "liberty call." As we began to walk down the plank to exit the ship, all we could see were little compact taxicabs lined up waiting to take us to the town hot spots.

I climbed into one of the taxicabs, along with a marine and two sailor friends I'd met on ship. The sailors had been in this port city before and instructed the cab driver to drive directly to the Red Cock

Club. The sailors told me and my marine buddy this particular club had the prettiest women. We were also told this club played the kind of R&B music we all liked.

Upon entering the Red Cock Club, I noticed there were hardly any GIs present. It was early in the evening, but I figured this nice-looking club would be crowded with GIs by now. Then one of my sailor friends informed me GIs would be arriving soon.

He could sense I didn't understand the reason for their delay. So he explained that most of the local cab drivers had driven the liberty departing marines and sailor to nearby "red-light districts." He said the cab driver would wait while the horny GIs received their two-dollar quickie, then drive them to the Red Cock or one of the many other clubs that were in close proximity to where our ship was docked.

My sailor buddy also told us that since we were the first GIs in the club, we would most likely have our preference to dance and party with the prettiest girls present in the club. And that, as long as we bought drinks, they would party with us the entire evening.

What my sailor friend failed to tell me was the dancing girls got paid at the club by the quantity of drinks brought to their table and also the quality of the drink. For example, beer cost twenty cents, while a shot of cognac was a dollar.

As soon as we were seated, just like the sailor had predicted, the prettiest Japanese girls I had ever seen approached our table. After brief introductions, we all began to dance and party. The girls seemed to enjoy partying with us, and they're drinks consisted of cognac, and they seemed to be very thirsty.

My marine friend and I only bought thirty dollars with us, so our drink-buying time with the pretty girls was limited. As a matter of fact, we were broke by 1800 hours, and the two pretty girls we were dancing and having fun with quickly vanished from our table when our funds dried up.

The two sailors we rode into town with were monetarily prepared for the evening. They both had docked in Yokohama twice before and knew that, in order to have a grand time at the Red Cock Club, a serviceman had to spend handsomely. My marine friend and I borrowed twenty dollars from our sailor friends, and soon the two girls we were dancing with returned to our table. In order to preserve our limited funds, we slowly and carefully bought drinks for the ladies the remainder of the evening.

While showing off my many dance moves with the ladies, I suddenly got the urge to urinate. I was capable of drinking beer for an hour before I would begin to urinate a lot. At first, I thought I had a medical problem but found out a lot of marines experienced the same problem, which was once we began to urinate, it became difficult to turn off the faucet.

The more beer I drank, the more I partied—thus, the more I urinated. It was embarrassing, running back and forth to the restroom, but I was having a great time and soon didn't care about the amount of urination I was donating to the club's restroom.

As the evening wore on, I continued to run to the restroom located down a narrow hallway inside the club and relieved myself. About the tenth time I raced to the restroom, I bumped into a marine that was also racing to the restroom to relieve himself. I leaped in stall number one, and he hit stall number two. After we both relieved ourselves, *I heard a familiar voice say, "Donnie, is that you?"*

I quickly turned around, and it was *the voice of Bill Shepard*. Wow, I think the probability was something like a billion to one of a person bumping into one of his closest friends in a restroom some six thousand miles out to sea. We were so excited to see each other that we accidently pissed on each other's shoes.

What an incredible feeling to be halfway around the world and bump into the person you grew up with . . . trying to take a leak. Bill and I joined the marine corps together directly after graduating from high school. We kept saying to each other there is truth in the statement "What a small world." Would anyone believe us back home when we tell them of this incredible moment?

After introducing Bill to the group I traveled to the club with, we found a table in the back of the club and spent the last hour of our liberty time discussing hometown news. The two of us recently had been promoted to corporal and discussed how proud we felt about our achievement of reaching NCO (Noncommissioned officer) status at such a young age.

It was getting late, so I located my marine and sailor buddies I had traveled to the club with and informed them I was leaving and that I was catching a cab and riding back to our ship docks with Bill. They said they would see me back at ship and continued getting their party on.

Bill's troop-carrying ship had docked next to the USNS *Gaffey*. During the short taxi ride back to our ships, we spent quality time together discussing our families and hometown gossip. We finally reached our destination, hugged, said our goodbyes, and departed up our respective ramps to board our troop carrier.

Due to the excitement experienced while on liberty, it became difficult for me to sleep that night. I tossed and turned while thinking about the odds of running into Bill like I did. I also must have awakened from sleep during the night a dozen times to relieve myself of the gallons of beer consumed at the club. What a special evening—an evening I will never forget.

Bill ended up pulling two tours of duty in the Nam. Upon returning to the States, he spent two years as a drill instructor. After putting in twenty years of duty, Bill eventually retired from the marine corps. He retired as an officer, a captain. He is currently living happily with his wife and family in a new home he built on his father's land in Lawrence, Kansas. To this day, we remain close friends.

Evidently, the news media was correct by stating thousands of GIs were being sent into South Vietnam to assist in the fight against communism. Because in talking to Bill, I learned that, along with our troop-carrying ships, there were two others docked in Yokohama that were also transporting troops.

The following day, our ship left port, and it seemed as though the USNS *Gaffey* took forever to reach Okinawa. When it finally landed, many of us aboard were thrilled to death. We were looking forward to once again, eating and being able to hold our food down.

While most navy men enjoyed a long sea journey and liked riding the ocean waves. I reasoned this kind of enjoyment is not suited for the kid. I'm a land person myself and damn proud of it. Give me land, or give me death, that's what I'll always say. Hello, Okinawa!

"A smile is a crooked line that sets a lot of things straight."

"DON'S FIRST DAY AT HMX-1"

Brief Tour of Okinawa

THANK GOODNESS WE STOPPED OVER in Yokohama to dance with the ladies, drink an ocean of beer, and have a down-home great time. Damn near every marine I talked to concerning our eight-hour liberty call in Yokohama said they had one of the best times during their entire time in the military.

The poor guys who caught the clap and no telling what other type of VD didn't see it that way. These guys were laid up in the ship's sick bay with needles in their ass, resulting from their visit to the infamous red-light district, and getting a two-dollar quickie from the local hookers.

Some unexpected excitement occurred on ship when one of the marines who visited the red-light district walked into the ship's sick bay with a red pecker. That's right. His sex organ appeared bright red, and the doctors on duty that night said they had never seen anything quite like that, and all they could do was give him shots of penicillin in the buttocks.

The following morning, the marine woke up, and the head of his pecker had swelled up as large as a cue ball. And if that wasn't bad enough, the head had even turned to a different color. This time the color of his pecker had turned from red to a bright purple.

That poor marine was ordered to stay in his sleeping quarters and not to mix with other servicemen on ship. No one wanted to catch this poor jarhead's disease, and they stayed clear of his presence. The medical staff worked on the guy for several days and kept pumping penicillin in his ass, and for some crazy reason instead of curing his problem, the head of his pecker kept swelling. Corpsmen who administered aid to him said the guy's pecker head grew even larger in size and, eventually, ended up the size of a major league baseball.

We were never officially informed of the outcome of the marine's pecker head problem, except that we all reasoned he would think twice and twice again before his ship docks at a port town, and he goes on liberty and engages in sexual rodeo.

We all sincerely hoped he learned his lesson and hoped next time he'll use his five fingers and call it a night. Shortly after his situation, people in the marine corps began calling each other "pecker head." Maybe this is where that phrase originated.

Other than the pecker incident, our voyage to the island of Okinawa was brief and uneventful. Our ship, the USNS *Gaffey*, dropped anchor; and once on land again, it was a calm feeling, and most passengers were extremely grateful their sea-sickened ship ride had ended.

It seemed like mass confusion when over a thousand marines and army troops began falling into formations on the loading dock. Platoon sergeants were barking off orders at the top of their lungs.

I was ordered to fall into formation with the small group of aviation marines. After a brief waiting period on the loading docks, we commenced to march to awaiting buses that were to take us to a base named Futenma.

Futenma was a Marine Corps Air Station several miles inland. Shortly after arriving at Futenma, I was ordered to report to HMS-36, the helicopter maintenance squadron, attached to MAG-36.

Marines assigned to HMS-36 checked into single-story barracks that would be their housing for the next few months. During this checking in process was where I ran into my Quantico friend William Tellis. I call him Tee and was extremely excited to see him.

He calls me DC and informed me his troop-carrying ship had docked one day ahead of the *Gaffey*.

We both carried the same MOS (aviation engineering clerk) and soon realized our MOS was critically important. Accurate recording of flight data in aircraft's logbooks was life-saving important. If inaccurate logging of flight data occurred, serious consequences could result.

It was crucial that, during our logging process, we accurately flagged an aircraft or its components "not flyable." If by chance Tee or I recorded inaccurate flight data against an aircraft or its main components, there was a possibility a component malfunction would occur due to the component not receiving proper scheduled maintenance. This activity could result in a pilot flying an aircraft that became unmanageable to the extent of crashing.

Knowing totally well the importance of performing our jobs accurately constituted pressure we both daily dealt with and successfully managed. We were proud of our work, and we reasoned that was why the both of us were due to get promoted to the rank of corporal E-4, next month, many months ahead of the normal scheduled time.

Tee and I had become close friends and running buddies during the seventeen months stationed together at Quantico. We hit it off the very first day we met and remained friends throughout our tour in the corps.

Tee was from Clearwater, Florida, and I from Lawrence, Kansas. Maybe that had something to do with our solid friendship. We were both raised in small towns, and our parents had taught us good old-fashioned down-home hospitality.

It was so great to run into Tee again, and I can't tell you how gratifying it is to have a close buddy like Tee around when you're ten thousand miles away from home on an island like Okinawa where the island locals hate your very existence. As days passed, we would spend most of our free time socializing together and listening to music.

In addition, Tee and I would practically always go on liberty together. There was a popular area that most marines visited while on liberty, and it was called the "Ville." The Ville was famous for its many bars and "red-light district." It was located in the town of Ginowan about five miles from Futenma.

Tee told me that he also was assigned to HMS-36 and, as I was unpacking my gear, informed me he had learned a few things about Futenma and began sharing them with me. Tee started out by saying Futenma was located about six miles from Okinawa's capital city of Naha. He then said Futenma was a beautiful base, with newly built barracks and home to 1,500 marines who were assigned to MAG-36, which was attached to the First Marine Aircraft Wing.

He said Futenma had been a US military airbase since the island was occupied following its famous WWII battle in 1945, and that marine corps pilots and air crewmen were primarily assigned to the base for flight training and air support to other land-based GIs on the island. The best thing he said about the base was the food was superb at the dining hall.

After Tee helped me fully unpack, he stated it was chow time and that our chow hall was only two blocks from our barracks. We walked to the dining hall, and, while eating, Tee started back up again and explained Futenma occupied roughly 1,200 acres of the island and was strategically situated in the center of a city named Ginowan which had a population of around sixty-five thousand people.

He further said our base took up about one-fourth of the city, and many of the locals were not fond of that. He was emphatic in stating be very careful while on liberty because the townsfolk didn't want US servicemen in their country, and many of them would openly display their disproval.

As we were finishing chow, Tee stated that within the boundaries of the Ville, there was a hooker in residence named "Hammerhead" and that she was beautiful, built like a thoroughbred, and famous for rocking a GI's world.

Tee further stated that any GI who had pulled duty in Okinawa within the past ten years had experienced the charms of Hammerhead . . . She was that good. He finished by stating Hammerhead was one of the wealthiest ladies on the island.

While strolling back to our barracks, I asked Tee if he had nailed Hammerhead to the cross and experienced her inner charms. He just smiled and changed the subject. All while we were in Okinawa Tee never confessed, but he did slip up and say one day that Hammerhead never allowed a GI to ride bareback. Now I wonder how he knew that. I think he revealed the truth.

While preparing to hit the sack, Tee informed me that we would undergo some jungle orientation training. He was told it wasn't that difficult and was informed that air wing marines underwent about a quarter of the jungle training compared to the marines in the infantry.

Later in the week, I talked to some infantry marines who had just completed a tour of duty in the Nam and were on their way back to the States, and according to their statements, the jungle training they received in Okinawa was big-time necessary and, in isolated cases, wasn't thorough enough.

My direct report was a gunnery sergeant who was well-liked by almost everyone in our squadron. He was a career marine who took his job and everything that surrounded it very seriously. We got along real well, and he quickly noticed how fast and accurate I was in my logging duties. Tee was my equal in fast and accurate logging, and he also reported to the gunnery sergeant.

When it came time for providing names for a meritorious promotion, our gunnery sergeant submitted our names without hesitation, and after being on the "rock" (Okinawa) less than forty days, Tee and I were promoted to corporal E-4.

After our NCO promotion ceremony, Tee and I entered our barracks that evening, and a couple of our close friends had a ceremony planned of their own. As soon as we entered the barracks, we were hit with about thirty water balloons and completely soaked. What a bunch of great friends we had during our time on the rock.

It seemed as though from the very first day on the rock, Tee and I were having fun with these guys. We became a tight group and took good care of each other. We got drunk together and roamed the red-light district together. We fought local gang members and known GI enemies together. Seemed as though everything we did together was fun and enjoyable.

The following is a list of guys I would later pull duty with in the Nam, and because of our many experiences together, I'll never forget them as long as I live.

Corporal Tee, Aviation Engineering Clerk:

Born and raised in Clearwater, Florida. My closest friend for most of the time I was in the marine corps. He was always there when I needed him and the best friend one could ever have.

Corporal MacDonald, Administration:

Born and raised in New York City and the only group member who was married. Mac is what we called him, and he was the oldest of the group. He kept us in line while on liberty and truly tried to keep us from getting into trouble. He was successful, because not one member of our group spent any time in the brig while stationed on the rock. Mac had a likeable personality, and we all admired his loyalty to his wife.

Corporal White, Aviation Mechanic:

Born in Atlanta and raised in Dallas, Texas. He was muscular built and strong as a bull. White continually wanted to prove his strength, and it seemed every night in the barracks he was arm wrestling one of us in order to demonstrate his strength superiority. Upon completing the contest that he always won, he would brag about his win, take a smoke brake, and brag about his win some more. He was the only member in our group that I personally got into a fight with. Guess I got sick and tired of his bragging and decided to test him. We fought hard. I got the best of him, and he ceased bragging afterward.

Lance Corporal Tony, Aviation Ground Transportation:

Tony was born and raised in Philadelphia, Pennsylvania. According to Tony, he had belonged to one of the infamous street gangs in Philly. He was thinly built, and to listen to him talk, he had whooped everybody's ass in Philly, and then some. He constantly stated he only joined the marines to put the hurt on people. He was well-liked, and the consensus among our clan was Tony truly had our backs. Consensus among our group is we would fight in a foxhole with Tony on any day of the week.

Lance Corporal Chris, Aviation Door Gunner:

Born and raised in Chicago, Illinois, Chris Fabris was the only blue-eyed soul brother in our group. He carried himself like a brother, and the only thing white about Chris was his skin color. While growing up, he had always run with brothers, and it showed. Chris was a fun guy to hang with, and he would stand with you when everyone else had abandoned you. Chris also stated that kicking ass was the reason he joined the corps. Like Tony, we would fight in a foxhole with him on any given day.

Lance Corporal Bernie, Aviation Maintenance:

Bernie was also from Chicago, and he was a tiny fellow in statue, but a giant of a man when it came to his gift of gab. He was smooth in everything he did, and while on liberty the girls simply adored him. He would cheat his ass off when we played cards, and seemed to also win the jackpots. He kept all the guys laughing with his witty bullshit, and everyone that came in contact with him seemed to like old Bernie. The jury was out as to whether or not we would want Bernie as a foxhole partner.

PFC Carlton, Aircraft Security:

Carlton was the quiet one of the clan. He grew up in Atlanta and was genuinely a nice guy. Without any hesitation, Carlton would give one of us his last dime. He was always attempting to stop Chris and Tony from fighting a fellow marine. We nicknamed Carlton the "peacekeeper," which is why it's so ironic that he was the centerpiece of one of the largest brawls ever to take place in the Ville.

In summary, Carlton was severely beaten up by a couple of army soldiers while on liberty in the Ville. He managed to catch a taxi and ride back to his barracks in Futenma. He stumbled into his barracks all bloodied up and managed to tell us what had happened. Immediately, Chris, Tony, and the rest of us caught cabs headed for the Ville. We were joined by other marines in our barracks, so we must have reached a total of twenty marines. Not a single one of us knew the true identity of the army guys who had kicked Carlton's ass, but that didn't matter.

As soon as we reached the Ville and exited our taxi, we began fighting with anyone that was army. It turned out to be a giant brawl right in the heart of the Ville, and it ended with a couple of army soldiers getting beat up pretty bad. Once we felt we had kicked enough army butt, we calmly loaded back into cabs and headed back to Futenma.

Subsequently, there was an investigation on base by our MPs, but they failed to discover the responsible parties. When Carlton found out about the fighting on his behalf, he was upset at us and said he felt sorry for the army guys that we beat up. He was alone in his assessment, because we all enjoyed the festivities.

For the most part, the time spent with our clan was enjoyable. Normally, when we were granted liberty, we all went to the Ville. We would attempt to avoid riding in the cab that hauled Corporal White. Reason was each time White crammed his wide ass into one of these small cabs, it appeared he had to let out one of his gigantic Texas farts. When he would bust a good one, his farts were so loud they hurt our ears, and the smell of his breaking wind was enormous and would knock an elephant to its knees.

Our clan normally rode in two separate taxicabs, and as soon as our cabs entered the Ville, we would pour out and begin to enjoy our liberty. We all reasoned it was safe and wise for us to travel around the Ville in pairs.

Tee and I paired up the majority of the time, and we would go to a guitar shop we had stumbled on to during our very first liberty on the rock. We would rent guitars for a couple of hours and paid a small sum for guitar lessons provided by the shop owner.

The people of Okinawa were called Ryunkans, and most of them didn't speak English. Most of the time, Tee or I didn't understand the guitar shop owner's remarks, but Tee and I somehow managed to communicate well enough to get through the lessons. We were both beginners, so the lessons were not difficult.

We had both purchased inexpensive guitars soon after arriving in Okinawa. We practiced playing our instruments in the evenings in our barracks. We thought we were getting pretty good at picking the thing until some white Marine would grab our guitar and "really" play it. This action only made us want to learn how to pick that much more. We practiced at every opportunity and received a lot of assistance from our fellow white marines who actually knew how to pick.

The two Chi Town boys, Chris and Bernie, normally paired off and roamed the Ville together. Tony and White were an odd pair, but they hung together in the Ville. Mac and Carlton both enjoyed oriental cooking, and they would often pair off and walk to a nearby eatery.

The first thing that was on Chris, Bernie, White, and Tony's agenda while entering the Ville was to go directly to the "red-light district." Like so many fellow horny GIs, they would soon end up in some dark dingy room, shelling out two dollars and seriously praying the hooker they were with didn't have VD. After enjoying the hooker's delights, the guys would reappear on the streets of the Ville with a big shit-eating grin on their faces.

It seemed as though each time we all returned to base and began telling about our past liberty adventure. Tony would always begin by telling on White. He would tell how White would steer him down an alley and to his favorite "red-light district" cathouse. Tony would tell how White's cathouse of choice was where elderly hookers worked. He further explained that White associated with the old folks' home because he could receive their sexual charms for half the normal price.

We would all crack up when Tony talked about White's money-saving tactics. Then we would ask old Tony what was he doing while White was visiting the elderly. White would then tell on Tony, and he stated Tony would sprint through the Ville to his favorite hooker with his private parts in his hand, standing tall at the "ready."

White reported that Tony's favorite hooker was none other than Hammerhead herself. Furthermore, it was reported that old Tony was one of only a handful of GIs who had ever completely satisfied Hammerhead.

During the end of my tour of duty on the rock, Tony was hospitalized, and one of the medical personnel who cared for him leaked the word that the reason for his hospitalization was Hammerhead screwed him so hard one evening that she literally pulled his private parts from its socket. This was probably true, because she was known to have the capability to activate vacuum-like sensations with her moneymaker. We felt sorry for Tony.

Meanwhile, Bernie and Chris were known to frequent a cathouse that was famous for giving head jobs. This "dynamic duo" thought no one knew that they were sneaking off and frequenting the elderly ladies who specialized in greasing knobs. These old chicks charged one dollar, and in most cases, they were gumming the GIs' joint. Most of them had lost their teeth due to many years of poor teeth hygiene.

I sincerely apologize for the distastefulness of much of the aforementioned, but I'm writing about reality here, and if a veteran of Okinawa reads this work, they know what they're reading is truthful. At least it was true back in the mi-1960s. I'm assuming Hammerhead has retired or passed on by now. Any GI who spent any time on the island during this period was aware of Hammerhead.

Mac, Tee, nor I spent our money on working girls. We also didn't frequent the many bars lined up in the Ville. Mac was a devoted husband and married to a lovely Jamaican girl who lived in Harlem and cared for their two-year-old daughter. He was admired by the guys for being true to his mate.

When the group exited our cabs, Tee and I normally went to our guitar lessons or simply sightseeing. We never visited the cathouses or paid for hookers. We didn't participate simply because we were taught during our upbringing not to engage in this activity. I know this sounds corny, but it's the truth. Our parents taught us it was a sin to participate in sex prior to marriage, and we adhered to their teachings.

The clan thought Tee and I was full of bullshit and, even a few times, spied on us to see if we were really, in fact, attending music lessons. They found we were, and consequently, we were ridiculed and made fun of. They said things like Tee and I walked the base with a giant monkey crawling all over our back. This didn't bother us, and we reasoned it's better to be ridiculed than to end up with a giant dose of VD.

Our tour on the island was coming to an end. I remember vividly the excitement Tee and I displayed when we received knowledge that the both of us received orders to fly out of Okinawa on the same plane and to the same destination, Da Nang, South Vietnam.

Bernie, Chris, and Tony also received orders to fly out with our group of three hundred marines this coming Friday, the sixth of March 1965. Mac, White, and Carlton were to fly out to Da Nang three days later. After five months of residency, we all were ready to leave the "rock."

The eight of us immediately began planning our "leaving the rock" party. It only took a few minutes of planning to arrive at the decision as to how we would celebrate. The eight of us agreed to go to the Ville and get wasted as a group—and not engage in any two-dollar quickie.

As soon as our planned liberty call sounded the mighty eight boarded two cabs and directed them to drive straight to the Ville. We drove to our favorite beer bar, exited our cabs, and commenced to drink the evening away. It was fun; and for the first time, the eight of us stayed together, drank plenty of beer, and totally enjoyed the evening.

Our celebratory conversations went from positive remarks about Okinawa to negative remarks pertaining to the country. Positive remarks were directed to how friendly many of the island people appeared to be and how clean the inside of their small homes seemed to appear. Also discussed on the positive side was how great the weather was and how the temperature seemed to remain mild.

On the negative side, we all stated "boredom" as number one. Tee and I went on several island bus tours and enjoyed taking pictures, but we were beginning to see the same old places, and both felt it was time to move on.

We were having a supergood time, and everything seemed to be going great during our departure celebration. Then, all of a sudden, about a dozen or so army soldiers began calling us names and giving us the finger just to piss us off. It only took a couple of their foul remarks to get us into a fight, and fought we did. Luckily, no one drew knives or other like weapons, and the fight consisted of only using our hands.

The army guys we were fighting were big guys who could really take a punch and hurt you when throwing one. Their blows were softened a bit by us marines being intoxicated; thus, not one of us really got seriously hurt that evening.

I had a severe headache for at least a week after the fight resulting from a powerful blow to the right side of my head, but survived. Tony thought he received a broken nose but later was told by a navy corpsmen his nose was only badly bruised. Tee sustained a bloody lip, and Chris damn near broke his hand by hitting the jawbone of one of the army soldiers.

In addition, one of the army guys received a mighty blow to the chops by Corporal White, and the guy's teeth flew everywhere. White was as strong as a bull, and loved to fight. So, when the name-calling began, he jumped on the guy who was shouting the loudest and damn near knocked all of his front teeth out.

The army soldiers' number grew to a dozen guys, compared to only eight of us.

The brawl didn't last long, because most of us were drunk and didn't have our novelties together. In many cases, both parties were swinging in the wind and only hitting air. The locals must have enjoyed seeing twenty American GIs beating up on one another.

Okinawan policemen were called in to put a stop to our action and to separate us from the army guys. The soldiers continued to shout obscenities, and my group reciprocated. Brawling with the army guys was dumb as hell, because we could have been placed in jail and not able to catch our scheduled flight to Vietnam.

The fight should have never happened. There is simply no excuse for a US serviceman beating the shit out of one of his own.

The Okinawan police held us captive for thirty minutes, and after writing out their report, they released us with a warning that if this happens again, we would go to jail. We all reasoned that it was time to leave the Ville and boogey back to base.

We put up a courageous fight but eventually ended up getting our butts whipped. While riding in our taxicab back to base, we boasted that we kicked ass, knowing all along the army guys kicked the ever-living shit out of us. We were too ashamed to admit that we got beat down.

We arrived at base well ahead of our curfew time, and every single one of us stumbled to our bedding and went fast asleep. When morning came, we were hung over from our celebration—from the huge consumption of alcohol while in the Ville. We were also terribly bruised up from the fight.

There was a brief inquiry into the fight by our base security. They somehow had found out marines on their base were involved in the brawl. I was even called into a room to testify, but like the other members of the group, I said absolutely nothing and was shortly released back to duty.

As 1200 hours approached, we all somehow managed to pack our gear and pick up and stage our gear at the selected station in front of our barracks. We then fell into formation and awaited loading into military buses for our scheduled twenty-minute bus ride to Kadena Air Force Base.

At Kadena, we were scheduled to begin loading onto C-130 aircraft at 1400 hours for our flight into Da Nang, South Vietnam. "Goodbye, Okinawa, it was good while it lasted." And so long to the Hammerhead!

*"The beauty of life is to be found in thoughts
that rise above the needs of self."*

"STAYING CLEAN ABOARD SHIP – CHECK OUT DON'S MUSCLES."

Arrival—South Vietnam

THE DAY HAD FINALLY COME for many of us aviation jarheads to leave Okinawa. Some of us were very happy, and some were sad. Personally, I was extremely happy. The time had finally come, and my exodus from the "rock" officially began on March 7, 1965.

Large buses transported 150 marines to Kadena Air Force Base from Camp Hansen, and another 120 aviation marines were bused into Kadena from the Marine Corps Air Station at Futenma. And, as soon as the large buses pulled to a stop, marines from Hanson and Futenma quickly unloaded and fell into formation at specified areas on the large runway.

Kadena was busy on this day because, minutes later, buses began arriving from Fort Buckner with one hundred army soldiers aboard. The soldier boys unloaded and fell into formation alongside our group. While waiting and standing at ease in formation, I looked down the line at the many marine and army faces and couldn't help but to think how many of them would end up as KIAs.

My thoughts and daydreaming soon came to an end as our senior NCOs began to shout out loading instructions. Our group from Futenma was marched to two waiting C-130s that sat on the runway with their engines roaring. We quickly loaded up into the two large aircrafts, buckled up, and impatiently waited.

Our wait time was short, and soon afterward the large entrance door of the aircraft was shut and secured. A marine first sergeant led us in saying the Lord's Prayer. Then suddenly we were in flight and on our way to Vietnam. The flight was bumpy, and our plane seemed to hit every air pocket in the sky. And, only a few on board cared, because the majority was excited at the thought of soon landing in the country known as South Vietnam.

While airborne, we could have been mistaken as being in church, because some serious praying took place high in the sky. I said a few prayers as we climbed aboard, and I continued to pray during the entire flight. I prayed that the Lord protect me while in-country and that I have a safe return home. I said this simple prayer over and over, and over again. I fell asleep praying.

As the plane ride continued its journey, a good feeling suddenly came over me. I felt good inside about being from America and part of a fighting force that was helping to liberate the South Vietnamese people who were fighting for their freedom.

Just as quick as the good feeling came over me, a sad feeling took its place. The sadness came from the thought that good young men, some I probably got to know back in Okinawa, were going to lose their lives in a war that many of them didn't clearly understand, I included.

The flight lasted a short time, and as we neared the landing, the air force pilot spoke over the plane's intercom system. He warned that it was possible our aircraft would be the recipient of small arms fire as it would begin its descent to land. The pilot said for us to remain seated and keep our seat belts buckled until told otherwise.

Our many prayers must have helped, because our C-130 safely landed without an incident. As our aircraft taxied to its docking destination, the majority of marines aboard were cheering with excitement. They had actually landed in the country they had heard so much about, and they felt deep down that their presence would make a big difference in the war's outcome.

I clearly remember not only that I was elated to be in South Vietnam, but how I had visions of kicking the enemy's ass, and returning home a war time hero, just like I had seen in the movies.

Speaking of the movies, there was this one particular movie actor that was my favorite, and when he starred in a war time film, I'd manage somehow to view it at least twice. And, while viewing his heroic feats as a marine in a couple of WWII films, I knew that, someday, I, too, would stand tall in a marine corps uniform, just as he had. As a matter of fact, my enlistment in the marines was a direct result of wanting to emulate this actor's many feats of heroism in those epic WWII movies.

Two, and sometimes three, times I would watch his war movie. I admired the manner in which he was portrayed as a brave soldier, without fear, and that he kicked the enemy's butt, and was awarded high-level medals for his heroic acts of bravery.

He also was seen as a man of courage, and I wanted to be just like him when I grew up. The actor was a white man, with the first name of John, but that didn't make any difference to me back then. He was truly my hero during this period of my life.

As we were about to exit the C-130, I was reflecting on the fact that during the time I was growing up in the late 1950s and early 1960s, young Negroes, like myself, failed to have any screen actors of color that wore a US military uniform to idolize or want to emulate. The screen actors of color in uniform during those days seemed to portray either a comic or a servant character type.

While further reflecting as our aircraft was unloading, I remembered how the colored screen actor was always viewed as serving military officers, by shinning their shoes, pressing their uniforms, or serving them meals. The colored actors in uniform were never shown as fighting men or anything close to resembling.

While everyone else on the plane was gathering up their gear and preparing to exit the aircraft, I was deep into thought as to "why colored actors weren't portrayed as military fighting men. I remember having a rough time with this, because, at that time, about every boxing weight class had as its champion, a colored man. So the world knew colored men could fight, so why weren't they shown fighting in military films? It just didn't make any sense to me.

By this time, I was knee-deep into my colored movie actor reflections until, suddenly, I heard Corporal Tee shout, "Snap out of it, Corporal Clark." My daydreaming abruptly came to a halt, and my old buddy Tee caused me to return to reality. But, even after Tee's shouting, the colored movie actor thought lingered a bit longer.

As we began pouring out from our aircraft, we couldn't help but to notice marines, army soldiers, and naval corpsmen already standing on the tar mat. They had flown in on other C-130s. Our C-130 was packed full of marines, and we fell into formation at a specified location on the tar mat at parade rest and waited in that position for further instructions.

It seemed as though further instructions never came, because we must have stood at parade rest for a good half an hour. Our legs began cramping, and because of the 105-degree temperature this warm spring day, a couple of marines grew dizzy and had to be carried off the runway lying on a stretcher.

Lance Corporal Chris Fabris had apparently experienced dizziness and was being carried past Tee and I on a stretcher. As the two corpsmen who were carrying Chris walked next to us, we witnessed Chris give us the thumbs-up. He was faking it, and we later learned he hadn't experienced dizziness at all. He was like that, if he didn't like something, he would fix it to his liking some kind of way, and, evidently, he didn't like standing in the heat on this sun-soaked runway.

Chris was carried to an air-conditioned van, and from there, he was transported to a makeshift sick bay station that was set up close to the runway. While Chris was being carried off the runway, I couldn't help but notice the sad look on the faces of the marines and army soldiers whom we were replacing.

Four hundred American fighting men were returning stateside, and they were standing in formation, waiting for us to unload so they could load up and fly back home where their families and loved ones were waiting for their arrival.

As I observed the many GIs waiting to load our aircraft, it was written all over their faces the many tales of horror they had experienced while in-country. In addition, as they moved about, they appeared totally drained of emotion. Many of them simply stared at the ground, as if they were happy to be just standing there, healthy, and alive. A few had tears dripping from their eyelids. They were a sight to see, and it wasn't pretty.

As soon as we completely unloaded our aircraft, the sick and wounded returning GIs began loading. It must have been at least ninety wounded GIs, and as they began loading and getting assistance in loading, an unhappy feeling came over me as I stood there witnessing seriously wounded fine-looking Americans.

Each of them had a pale gazed stare on their face. The stare told one hell of a story, and it was not pleasant. These men had experienced purgatory while in the Nam, and it was extremely obvious they wanted to get the hell out of Vietnam as soon as possible.

One of the marines loading into our C-130 was a black corporal being rolled in a wheelchair. I caught his eye and gave him a thumbs-up. He tried hard to reciprocate but was unable to; then he tried to muster up a smile and was unsuccessful as well. The only response he could give me was to stare at me with tears filling in both his eyes.

That stare in that wounded marine's face stayed with me for a long time, and after a few short months in-country, I began to figure it out, and I, too, began to stare in the same manner. It's a stare that is difficult to emulate or explain. But after a tour in-country, we all seem to adopt it. *Only those of us who have experienced the horror(s) of fighting in South Vietnam understand that stare's true meaning.*

Meanwhile, our standing at parade rest on the hot runway had come to a climax, because suddenly several large military buses began rolling onto the runway and began loading us up and driving us to our newly assigned base.

While we were loading into the buses, there was a small party of South Vietnam civilians standing alongside the bus paths. Due to the bullshit I had read in the news media, I had this vision that when United States marines arrived on foreign soil like South Vietnam, they were warmly greeted, cheered on by the crowds, and received as heroes by a large welcoming committee of townsfolk.

When we landed at Da Nang's Airport, there was no welcoming party warmly greeting us, and the runway was completely absent of the town locals. As a matter of fact, the entire airport was absent of anything that even slightly resembled crowd "fanfare."

It was a sad occasion because many of the 370 marines and army soldiers arriving that warm afternoon in March 1965 thought they would be welcomed by important members of the South Vietnamese community and possibly provided "keys" to the city. Instead, only about fifty people were present, and they were unruly and appeared not to like us one bit.

In pure marine corps fashion, we marched from the giant planes, not by the beat of some citizen hometown band but by the cadence of a marine gunnery sergeant; and the fanfare we all expected turned out to be the Da Nang townspeople spitting in our direction, shouting obscenities, and giving us the finger. It was difficult to believe they were giving us the finger. Hell . . . we thought the finger "thing" was American born and originated. And wondered how in the world they were privy to this American tradition.

Giving us the finger pissed many of us off. We simply couldn't believe this shit was happening, because we were certain the people of South Vietnam would be laying out the red carpet for us so-called "freedom liberators."

Not a single marine who walked off the plane was ready for this sour-ass treatment. We were in this country prepared to lay down our lives to liberate these people from oppression; and here we were, being treated like shit, taunted, and being called nasty names—and for no apparent reason. It just didn't make any sense, and, personally, I felt hurt and real bad inside.

Due to the deviant and improper behavior on the part of the locals, there was an investigation into this incident, and it was determined this particular crowd of locals that were performing the taunting and giving us the finger was assembled by factions of the Viet Cong, who were reportedly working very hard recruiting locals in and around the Da Nang area to join their forces.

They even had members of the foreign press present, taking pictures and taping the incident. Our officers and senior NCOs reported that the incident was staged to make the United States involvement in the war look bad and to make it look as though the South Vietnamese people didn't want us there to assist in their war effort.

In essence, this was one big propaganda ploy, and as far as many of us were concerned, it worked. Most people viewing our arrival on this tape, which was distributed around the world by the VC, would have thought our rejection by the townspeople was, indeed, legitimate.

Additionally, we were informed Victor Charlie didn't allow the people to view the film of our arrival revealing a large segment of townspeople who were "happy" to see marines and army personnel arriving on their soil.

This crowd was smaller in number than the VC-staged body count, but you could certainly tell by the joy on their faces, and even some tears coming down their cheeks, that they were sincerely thrilled Americans were arriving in their country to assist in fighting for their democratic cause.

American GIs arriving that afternoon felt this small group of locals displaying friendliness totally alleviated most of the hurt caused by the VC orchestrated anti-American staged protest that the GIs had experienced earlier in the day.

Finally, our C-130 was fully unloaded of all its GI passengers, and we were standing tall on the huge runway. We loaded some of our gear into trucks to be driven to our various base destinations. Then we commenced to pile into military buses that were arriving and transporting GIs to their assigned bases.

Corporal Tee and I managed to ride in the same bus that was packed full of jarheads. Our bus exited the Da Nang Air Station and began traveling through the city. Its destination was the Marine Corps Air Station located in East Da Nang—referred to as Marble Mountain.

While our bus traveled the six miles to our base, a cute little Vietnamese boy about nine years of age began running after it. Then the boy picked up and threw a large rock at our bus that broke out a back window. The bus driver didn't stop and kept right on driving. We learned later on that this was common practice for some of the locals who were anti-American.

Soon after the first rock-throwing incident, another young lad about the same age broke from a small crowd and began running after our bus. Several marines riding in the lead witnessed the boy throw an object that appeared to be another large rock of some kind.

His throw was not as accurate as the first kid, because his object hit a telephone pole.

Some of us were voicing our thoughts about the bastards who put these kids up to do this, and our truck driver, who was a Vietnamese marine corporal, overheard our concern and told us the rocks were probably given to the boys by factions of anti-American locals, or maybe even the VC—and that they had instructed the boys to throw them at US servicemen riding in buses leaving the airstrip. One of us said how he couldn't believe it, and the truck driver shot back with emphasis, "Marine, you best believe it. This sort of thing happens all the time."

The bus driver further said the boys probably were carrying out these rock-throwing missions because some anti-American faction most likely had captured some member(s) of their family and told them they would harm them if they disobeyed.

Our bus driver slowed down a little in order to provide us a good look at an elderly woman working road construction. He said, "Boys, I bet you don't find this back home."

One of us asked the driver, "What's the point?" And the he said, "The point is this nearly seventy-year-old woman is performing a function that normally her husband or her son would be doing, but they are most likely are dead or currently engaged in their country's bloody civil war."

As our bus driver sped up a little, he further said that this type of situation is prevalent throughout this country, and it's so sad, so sad, indeed. I think most of us riding that old shaky bus didn't comprehend the driver's full meaning by pointing out that old woman performing men's chores, but after a few weeks in country, we all understood.

While steering his bus onto Marble Mountain, the bus driver ended his comments by saying, "Fellow, Marines, don't be surprised at anything while in Vietnam."

"And good luck to each of you."

"Cast all your anxieties on Him, for He cares about you."

—*1 Peter 5:7*

"BILLY WAS MY CLOSE BUDDY THAT JOINED THE MARINE CORPS WITH ME….along with Karen his girlfriend."

MCAS—Marble Mountain

URING THE SIX-MILE TRIP FROM Da Nang's airport to the Marine Corps Air Station, known as Marble Mountain, I must say I was not impressed with the view of the terrain. I had envisioned a tropical setting, but as we traveled, the view was anything but scenic. I couldn't figure out why they were calling this place Marble Mountain and finally asked the bus driver.

He informed me Marble Mountain consisted of five separate mountains, and each one represented one of the five elements of the universe (water, wood, fire, metal, and earth). He told me I should take a tour of the area after getting settled in, and then maybe I would enjoy the surroundings a little better.

We finally arrived at Marble Mountain, and soon after unloading from the large buses, we began searching for our personal gear that had arrived earlier in military trucks. While retrieving my gear, I couldn't help but to notice all the construction activity being conducted on base.

After inquiring, I was informed the Seabees were putting the finishing touches on a new Naval Field Hospital and finalizing the construction of helicopter landing pads.

A staff sergeant stood in front of our transporting buses and began directing us to our new tent homes. When I entered the entrance of my assigned tent, I quickly noticed at the far end of the tent my friend Tee unpacking his duffle bag.

Tee and I had somehow managed to be assigned the same tent, and we were overjoyed; not only were we good friends, but we could practice plucking our guitars together, that we purchased in Okinawa.

Tee and I soon learned that construction of the Marine Corps Air Station at Marble Mountain (MMAF) was 80 percent completed when we arrived in March 1965 and, eventually completed in late summer of 1965. The base would first be occupied by Marine Aircraft Group 16. MAG-16 was made up of primarily helicopter squadrons.

The following day, Tee and I were assigned to work in the Aircraft Engineering Office of Helicopter Squadron HMS-16. We were happy with this assignment and couldn't believe our good fortune of not only getting the opportunity of sharing the same tent but also being assigned to the same squadron and working right next to each other.

HMS-16 was a helicopter maintenance squadron, and its primary mission was to perform aircraft maintenance on the entire fleet of helicopters contained in Marine Air Group 16. HMS-16 was made up of UH34D, and UH1E Helicopters assigned to it, and its helicopters mainly were used as backup aircraft during combat missions alongside the other helicopter squadrons contained in MAG-16.

The majority of HMS-1s helicopter deployments were medevac rescue missions. During some of these medevac flights, Tee or I was awarded the opportunity to join the flight crew as a voluntary support crew member. We would jump at this opportunity because logging flight data against our squadron's aircraft at times was a bit boring.

The Marine Air Base at Marble Mountain (MMAF) was also referred to as East Da Nang and was located about five miles southeast of Da Nang Air Base on a strip of beach between China Beach and the Marble Mountains. MMAF was located about six miles from the city of Da Nang, where most American GIs enjoyed liberty.

As prior stated, it was nothing less than a miracle that Tee and I were both assigned to the same squadron and sleeping tent. During our first several weeks together on base, we spent most of our off-duty time lounging around inside our tent and attempting to play our guitars.

Our two buddies from Okinawa, Lance Corporals Chris and Bernie were also assigned to HMS-1, and although they were housed in an adjacent tent, we all managed to get together most nights for our evening bullshit session, prior to "lights out." Bernie was a pint-size marine. But to hear him discuss his many episodes of kicking ass, you would think old Bernie was a giant of a man.

Chris told more ass-kicking stories than old Bernie, and trust me, this was hard to do. These two guys kept Tee and I rolling in laughter. Their bullshit storytelling helped considerably in alleviating the stress of being new to the war zone.

Tee and I were granted liberty in our third week at Marble Mountain. We joined a small group of marines and went on a tour of one of the main mountains in Marble Mountain that represented "water." We were bused to a certain point and had to hike the remainder of the way. We climbed to the highest part of the mountain, and the view of the city of Da Nang and its surrounding landscape was beautiful.

We began to hike down the mountain, and during our hike, we came upon an ancient shrine. It was very old but well-preserved. As we walked along, we came across deep caves that made pockmarks in the sides of the mountain. We didn't venture inside the caves, because Tee and I were informed by our guide these caves were haunted by spirits of ancient enemies.

The guide spoke good English and told us we should tour China Beach on our next liberty. We called him when our next liberty arrived, and off to China Beach we went, along with seven marines. It was about a six-mile ride from MMAF, and when we arrived, we were surprised by how dark the sand appeared on the beach.

This was nothing like the white sand beaches I had envisioned. We also thought we would see beautiful tall palm trees like in San Diego. We didn't see anything that came close to resembling a palm tree, and, instead, we saw many young kids running up to us with their hand out, begging for money. We gave them all the money we could spare. And we promptly told our guide we wanted to vacate this area.

We were telling the guide about how enjoyable the tour had been, and, all of a sudden, we were attacked by tiny sand crabs. The beach area we were at was full of these hungry sand crabs that would eat anything you threw their way. These tiny little guys would eat you if you stood in the sand long enough.

This was the last tour Tee and I joined for a very long time. We mainly hung around the base during our free time. Like most of our marine friends, we tried many different things to keep occupied during our free time. We even joined a group of jarheads that pumped weights in order to build up our bodies, so when we returned to the world, we would be admired.

Some of the jarhead brothers would group up and sing various R&B songs in the evenings to pass the time. Some of these guys were pretty damn good. One corporal in particular could flat-out sing his ass off. He sounded like Curtis Mayfield, and would sing for hours.

Singing to pass the time away or simply engaging in fun-type activities wasn't the case for most marines assigned to Marine Aircraft Group-16 at Marble Mountain. And the reason was most marines assigned to MAG-16 were helicopter pilots, helicopter crewmen, or aircraft support personnel. And they were busy working around the clock, engaging in deadly combat missions or conducting grueling medevac rescues.

Volunteering for Medevac Rescue Missions

The primary purpose of the helicopter squadron Tee and I were attached was to assist other aircraft squadrons in MAG-16 by providing an aircraft maintenance function.

Our helicopter squadron would also provide backup aircraft to its sister squadrons when applicable and perform medevac rescue flights when called upon. As stated earlier, Tee and I would volunteer to fly as a crewman on these missions every chance we got.

I didn't enjoy flying on the medevac missions as much as Tee, and as a consequence, he must have flown at least three times as many. The reason I didn't enjoy flying on these missions as much as

Tee was I wasn't big on seeing my fellow marine infantrymen being lifted into our choppers all shot to shit and barely hanging on to life.

I know these horrific sights bothered my friend Tee as well, but he handled it better, and I had serious trouble getting to sleep at nights. To this day, I still see some of the faces of shot-up marines, and it still bothers me.

During my first four months stationed at Marble Mountain, I volunteered in joining the medevac crew well over a dozen times and, during this period of time, must have witnessed about a half-dozen GIs transported in body bags and over a dozen GIs or South Vietnamese soldiers badly shot up and clinging onto life as we flew them to Marble Mountain's newly constructed base hospital.

While discussing our medevac flight history one afternoon, Tee said his most memorable was when he had volunteered to fly as a crew member on his third medevac mission, and the mission was to lift twelve army soldiers out of the bush after they had been attacked and wounded about twenty miles north of Da Nang.

Tee explained how four of them were placed in his UH34D medevac helicopter and that two of the four were seriously wounded. He said they were all white guys and must have all been raised in the deep south because they voiced their concerns about riding in the same chopper with a colored person, such as Tee.

The gunnery sergeant crew chief told the wounded army soldiers that Corporal Tee couldn't help the fact that he was colored and that he was there to help them. Tee said they still insisted on being racist, and even uttered the "N" word his direction a few times. He went on to explain how two of the four had eventually died while in flight and how he had attempted to assist the naval corpsman in placing them into body bags.

His attempt was resisted by the two bigots that apparently would survive their wounds because they demanded that Tee not place a finger on their fallen buddies. Tee said that, suddenly, he impulsively stood up and began leading the five crew members in the belly of that medevac aircraft in prayer. And, to his surprise, the two bigots joined in, and by the time they finished, all seven men in the belly of that helicopter were crying like newborn babies. Tee ended by telling me as he was assisting in unloading one of the two bigots from the chopper that he grabbed his arm, smiled up at him, and whispered, "Thank you."

When Tee asked me for my most memorable medevac mission, I quickly began telling him about my fourth medevac mission. I thought I had told him about it already, but he wanted to hear it again.

It just so happened I was selected to join this medevac crew as a volunteer on my twenty-first birthday, and we were informed our assignment was to airlift some wounded men back to base hospital. We flew about thirty miles north of Marble Mountain; and as our UH34D helicopter hovered over the landing zone and dropped to the ground, I figured we would most likely be picking up wounded marines, army soldiers, or South Vietnamese Rangers.

To my surprise on that late spring evening, our medevac mission was to pick up and fly back to base hospital four wounded Viet Cong fighters. Three of the four had suffered multiple gunshot wounds, while the youngest one in the group was uninjured. The VC that suffered the worst wound was identified as the leader. He had been shot twice in the midsection.

All four of the Viet Cong fighters were extremely young in appearance and didn't appear to be combat warriors by any means whatsoever. These little guys actually looked like a bunch of dirty little junior high school boys.

They were brave little warriors because not a single one who was shot cried out in pain during the medevac corpsman's in-flight examination. Actually, they didn't show hardly any sign they had been shot at all. They all had their eyes on me as if they hadn't seen a colored marine before.

Every one of them wore black pajama-like clothing. And they smelled very badly. As a matter of fact, they smelled like shit. It was hard to see where they were shot because their bodies were so muddy and filthy. The corpsman spent a lot of time wiping away mud and dirt from these little fellows prior to his medical examination.

The navy corpsman assigned to our chopper was a dedicated medic, and he made a serious effort to ensure the four captives were properly treated. He even attempted to administer morphine to the VC leader. The leader resisted the morphine several times while lying on the floor with two 7.62 mm rounds in his gut.

Finally, I asked the corpsman if he needed assistance in holding down the VC leader while he administered the morphine shot. He promptly replied yes, and I began restraining the VC leader. Holding him down was not a problem, but I'll never forget the wounded leader's concentrated stare. Although he was in obvious pain, not once did he take his eyes off me.

His constant stare was making me a little nervous, and I attempted to stand in a position where he couldn't stare me down, but his cold black eyes easily found my location. He never said a word or did anything inappropriate.

And if eye contact could kill, I would have been one dead GI.

To sum up this episode, the VC leader failed to make it to the hospital and died while in flight, staring directly in my direction. The corpsmen attempted to close his eyes after he had passed on, but his eyelids wouldn't remain in the closed position and kept opening. I said to myself this little guy is even staring me down while he's traveling to his maker. I guess one can call it "enemy respect," but at that moment, I bowed my head and said a silent prayer for this brave young warrior.

My first six months stationed at Marble Mountain flew by, and I was performing brilliantly in my MOS field and, as a result, was receiving "Good Conduct Medals, and "Meritorious Mast Awards." During the same time frame, my close friend Corporal Tee was receiving the same type of recognition, and both of us sincerely appreciated the fact that the marine corps had recognized our hard work and dedicated service.

While Tee and I were stationed in HMX-1, at Quantico, Virginia, we learned the importance of accurately logging flight time against the aircraft and its components. We reasoned the same caution should apply in the Nam, as it did at Quantico. Because, whether at war or stateside, if flight time was inaccurately reported against an aircraft or its key components, it could result in placing the pilot and his crew in danger of an inflight malfunction or possibly cause a mission to abort, or even result in a fatal crash.

Practically, all the pilots, copilots, and crew chiefs in our squadron were cognizant of our desire to be the best damn aircraft engineering clerks in the corps and applauded our efforts. They also were aware of our desire to fly as volunteer crew members on medevac rescue missions. And granted our request most of the time an opportunity arose.

Tee flew on three times as many medevac missions as yours truly, and he had a ton of exciting stories to tell as a result of those flights. Our medevac flights were not always simply flying into a combat zone, picking up wounded marines and flying them to a field hospital. As Tee and I witnessed up close and personal, the medevac missions we took part in weren't always "safe and easy."

There were frightening moments during some of our flights, especially when our helicopter began taking hits from hostile small arms ground fire. This is a unique sound when the enemies round rips into the magnesium fuselage of your helicopter. It's a frightening sound, and a sound that lives with those who have experienced it for the remainder of their life. .

Navy Corpsmen's Acts of Courage and Bravery

The 1965 Independence Day Celebrations were taking place back stateside, and I'd volunteered and been chosen to fly as crew member on our sister squadron's medevac helicopter. (Due to our MOS and popularity with flight crews, Tee and I often flew as volunteer crewmen on one of our sister helicopter squadrons that was attached to MAG-16).

I remember it being a warm and beautiful holiday afternoon. By the way, Sundays, and national holidays was when a volunteering crew member was readily selected for medevac flight rescue mission.

By this time, I had been stationed at Marble Mountain going on five months and was beginning to feel like a seasoned jarhead around the base. I had made friends with a good many marines aviators and navy corpsmen, and was feeling right at home.

The naval corpsman assigned to our medevac crew that Independence Day was a person whom I had flown with at least two times before. He was a petty officer second class (PO2), and his name was Borrero. He was born in Puerto Rico and raised up on the hard streets of the Bronx in New York City.

Our pilot received the emergency call at 0300 hours, and our UH34D helicopter was airborne at 0315 hours. The medical rescue mission was only fifteen miles from Marble Mountain, so our chopper was hovering over the landing zone in just a few minutes after takeoff.

Due to the dense vegetation growth on and around the LZ, the pilot had a difficult time negotiating the landing where the orange flare had been tossed by the ground forces to signal the LZ. Finally, the pilot managed to land, and it was a hard landing. The jolt of his landing was so severe that it caused the two mounted M60 machine guns to become unsecured from their brackets.

The two lance corporal marine door gunners immediately began repairing the M60 mounting situation because it just so happened we had landed only a thousand meters from where a small firefight was in progress. A squad of recon marines who had been wounded was our chopper's assigned medevac mission.

There were four marine helicopters dispatched on this particular medevac, and our chopper was the last one to land. The other three helicopters on the medevac consisted of two UH34Ds and one UH1E gunship.

The UH34D's medevac mission was to airlift wounded marines and South Vietnam rangers from the combat area, while the UH1E's mission was to protect the three UH34Ds involved in the rescue mission.

The UH1E was doing all it could to protect the UH34Ds that were currently picking up their assigned ground personnel. The UH1E gunners were blasting away with M60 machine gun fire. On one occasion they got careless and accidently scraped one of the UH34Ds. Thank God no one was hit or injured because the UH34D was hit with about a dozen rounds.

Our helicopter door gunners were also firing their M60s, and the noise from the two M60s firing was deafening. Our mission was complete (so we thought) because we had successfully loaded the team of six recon marines into our aircraft and our corpsman, and other crew members began immediately administering aid to them.

Flight Corpsman Borrero was shouting orders so fast it was hard to understand him, and sometimes he would speak in Spanish. He was frantically hoping from one wounded marine to the other, because all but one of them had been badly wounded.

Just as we were about to lift off, the recon team leader shouted that not all of his team was aboard and that a lance corporal was still out there. The team leader was a sergeant E-5 and was badly wounded. He had been hit twice in his lower torso and kept spitting out blood. Although he was hurt real bad, he was adamant about not leaving behind one of his team members, the lance corporal.

Meanwhile, our pilot and copilot were conducting their countdown procedures to lift off and were seconds away from taking off when, all of a sudden, Corpsman Borrero leapt out of the helicopter and began running toward the direction the team leader had directed him in order to locate the missing lance corporal.

The pilot shouted out to the corpsman to get back into the chopper for liftoff. The corpsman ignored his command and kept running in the direction the team leader had directed him. Borrero was determined to locate the missing lance corporal and acted as if he didn't hear the pilot's instructions and disappeared into the tall monkey grass, out of our view.

The pilot was just about to lift off, and all of a sudden, Corpsman Borrero reappeared and shouted to the pilot that he heard a sound that sounded like someone moaning and that he was going to continue his search.

By this time, the two door gunners, the uninjured recon marine, and yours truly leapt from the helicopter to assist in the search of the missing lance corporal and to provide cover fire for Corpsman Borrero if needed.

Tall monkey grass was densely covering the terrain, and in order to recover a body in this stuff, a person would almost have to stumble upon it. Corpsman Borrero was running as fast as he could toward the area where he thought he had heard the moaning sounds.

Our marine pilot, a decorated captain shouted, with extreme emotion that he was giving all of us a direct order to reboard the chopper and that for the safety of the entire crew he must take off. As soon as these words left his mouth, Corpsman Borrero shouted, "Captain, I've located the missing lance corporal." Corpsman Borrero had, in fact, stumbled upon the shot-up body of the missing marine.

Out of pure excitement, those of us who had exited the chopper began firing in all directions, and this action continued for a short time until we saw the pilot motioning for us to cease firing.

By hearing the shouts of discovery by Corpsman Borrero, the marine pilot instantly aborted his planned takeoff and ordered all able-bodied marines to provide assistance in helping Corpsman Borrero lift the wounded lance corporal into his helicopter.

By this time, the enemy had us dialed in, and we were taking fire from all directions. In addition, our crew was beginning to run extremely low on ammo from firing our M60s and M14s so often.

Our crew chief informed our pilot that the lance corporal was aboard and instructed the marines on the ground providing cover fire to board the chopper. Once all were aboard, the pilot lifted our helicopter off the ground and quickly into the air to safety. God was with us that day, and we were all thanking him as our helicopter made its turn to base.

After we had flown out of danger and finally caught our breath, we also began thanking Corpsman Borrero for his heroic effort in saving the life of the lance corporal. There was positively no doubt in any of our minds that our fellow marine lance corporal would have died from gunshot wounds lying in tall monkey grass had not Corpsman Borrero went searching for him.

After receiving medical care from our base hospital, the lance corporal would survive his facial, leg, and chest wound. In addition, we were informed not a single one of the seven recon marines airlifted to the base hospital and out of harm's way died from their wounds.

We all figured that much of this success was attributed to Corpsman Borrero who was shouting out medical instructions to the crew in order to save the lives of the recon team like a crazed person during our flight back to the base hospital.

Our crew chief was also highly instrumental in providing instructions to his crew, which helped considerably in ensuring our recon marines were attended to adequately during the flight. I, personally, was extremely impressed with our crew chief's medical actions and felt he was equally responsible in saving the lives of all the recon marines.

While administering aid to the recon marine's team leader, Corpsman Borrero suddenly fell hard to the deck of our chopper and rolled over on his back and began to breathe very heavy. Our crew chief rushed to his aid and determined Corpsman Borrero had taken a small caliber round in his right buttocks area while running around in search of the lance corporal.

Our flight crew chief, a much-liked marine staff sergeant, took over for Corpsman Borrero and assumed the overall responsibility of administering the first-aid effort. His small staff of four crewmen followed his instructions as if he were a doctor, and even some of the wounded recon marines chipped in and helped. Meanwhile, Corpsman Borrero had passed out but soon awakened and began providing verbal assistance prior to passing out again. This time, Borrero remained passed out until we had returned to Marble Mountain and landed.

After safely landing, our crew assisted in carefully unloading the wounded and carried them inside our base hospital. Then we all rushed to the room where Corpsman Borrero was being treated by navy doctors and nurses.

We didn't leave that Borrero's bedside until he was moved into the operating room. Even then, we mulled around outside the operating room until the doctors completed removing the round from his backside.

Our crew remained at the hospital until the naval surgeon informed us Corpsman Borrero was going to live and expected to have a full recovery. We were all elated to hear this report, and only then did we finally begin to leave the hospital and report back to our assigned work units.

While walking to the Aircraft Engineering Office, I reasoned that Corpsman Borrero most likely would receive a Purple Heart for getting shot in his buttocks and that he would not receive a medal for his act of bravery. But for the six marine crew members and the seven recon marines who were aboard the medevac chopper, we all unquestionably feel Borrero should receive the highest medal of our land.

We had just witnessed this corpsman place his life in total danger in order to save the life of another. His heroic actions wasn't a movie, a play, or some novel. This was, in fact, a real person saving the life of another real person. This was for real.

Thus far, I had been stationed at Marble Mountain for seven months, and during the remaining four months of being stationed there, I must have volunteered to fly as a crew member on about a dozen missions. On nearly every one of those medevac missions, I witnessed courageous acts of bravery on the part of a navy corpsman. And not once did I recall hearing about a corpsman receiving his or her due recognition. In essence, these corpsmen damn well deserved high-ranking medals, and, in some cases, the Medal of Honor.

Speaking of medals given out during wartime, I was informed, or personally witnessed on a few occasions, where a marine had been slightly wounded during a firefight but didn't report it to his superiors. And the reason these marines failed to report their injuries was in some cases the fact they didn't want to be taken away from their combat unit and sent back to some faraway hospital.

In these instances, they failed to receive a Purple Heart or any appropriate medal. These individuals I'm referring to didn't care for that kind of recognition, but, on the other hand, I've witnessed where a marine cut his ear shaving and, after a firefight, reported his injury, and he was awarded a Purple Heart and, in fact, didn't deserve it.

So, in essence, for many a marine who fought in Vietnam, a medal didn't mean a whole lot. What was important in our minds was simply to "win" the war and return home with "favorable recognition" from our families, our friends, and our fellow Americans for the many sacrifices we had made.

In many cases, this failed to happen, and in fact, when we returned home, some of us were spit upon and called nasty names by fellow Americans. These people didn't approve of America's involvement in the Vietnam war and took their disproval out on returning servicemen.

We didn't like their actions then, and to this day, we still are pissed at what they put us through. The only reason some of us didn't strike back and we could have done some serious damage was we love our country. We love our country so much that we would not stoop that low and hurt our fellow Americans physically, like many of the war haters hurt us returning servicemen mentally.

We put our lives on the line to protect our country and its way of life. And will do it again in a heartbeat. We truly love America, and it damn well didn't matter if we were white, black, brown, or yellow. We all fought together as one. Many of us died or were badly hurt, but even if we stand with the aid of a cane, *"we stand proud."*

VD Avoidance while on Liberty in Da Nang

When marines properly performed their work and conducted themselves in a satisfactorily manner at Marble Mountain, they were rewarded and granted a liberty pass which occurred normally on Saturdays. This pass consisted of obtaining permission to leave the base and getting bused or taking a taxi and traveling five miles into the city of Da Nang.

Da Nang was the second largest city in South Vietnam, and GIs on liberty would normally visit one of Da Nang's many bars or taverns spread across town in search of recreation and/or physical enjoyment.

Upon arrival in Da Nang, a marine's liberty typically began with downing a couple of cold beers, socializing a bit with the town locals they were acquainted with, and, soon after, ending up negotiating a quickie with one of their favorite working girls.

After price negotiations, the working girl and the marine would quietly disappear into a small run-down house. After ten minutes or so, the marine would reappear after releasing the giant monkey from his back and walk to a nearby café and order up a fat juicy hamburger. He would down the hamburger, with a large mug of beer. He would socialize a little with the townsfolk, possibly return to the working girls' shack for a second round of sexual rodeo; then he would begin his return to base before the curfew hour.

While traveling back to base, the marine would be hoping and praying that he was returning to Marble Mountain, VD free. He wouldn't be alone with his fear of contracting a disease. Paying a working girl for a two-dollar quickie was normally the agenda for the majority of marines who enjoyed liberty in Da Nang.

Naturally, there were a handful of marines who refrained from buying sexual pleasure. Tee and I were included in this category. We were constantly subjected to harassment from our jarhead buddies, who felt we were trying to be better than them.

It wasn't that we were trying to be better than them or that we were even trying to be Christian like. The sole reason we didn't partake in the two-dollar quickies was we were scared to death of catching Vietnam VD. This was the honest-to-God truth. It was as simple as that. We witnessed what Vietnam VD had done to the private parts of a few of our marine buddies, and we didn't want any part of that horrific experience.

There were a few types of VD in Vietnam that would drop Sonny Liston dead on his ass with a single bout and in a matter of seconds. I was told some of the girls entertaining in the arena of the two-dollar quickie was as good as Hammerhead back in Okinawa, but was the risk of catching VD worth a Hammerhead thrill?

Catching VD in Vietnam was no joke. Tee and I witnessed young strong marines literally running to sick bay, crying like a little bitch, with their VD-stricken pecker in their hand. It was a sick sight to see. These guys would literally have tears in their eyes, crying out uncontrollably, and they would scamper about the base with their sex tool literally in their hand because the pain was so excruciating.

These VD-stricken marines normally ran to the base hospital, seeking help from the on-duty navy corpsmen with their pants pulled down and their peckers standing tall, at the ready. Their pants were down because normally the corpsman jammed a long needle in their ass to counteract the VD they had caught. I had actually seen the needle the corpsman would use, and it was every bit of four inches in length.

I was informed by a corpsman I knew that there were several types of Nam VD our medical professionals working in sick bay were not familiar with and nothing like the types of VD found stateside. This Nam VD was extremely painful and, if not readily treated, was even deadly. Naturally, Tee and I were much afraid of the consequences of catching Nam VD, and this contributed highly to the reason we didn't engage in sexual rodeo with the many working girls in Da Nang.

A couple of my marine buddies on base experienced Nam VD and in grand style. Bernie experienced catching Nam VD firsthand. Bernie arrived in Vietnam with a brown normal-colored pecker. He left Vietnam with a bright pink penis. Bernie's friends on base gave him a nickname of "Pinkie."

Bernie stopped taking showers with the rest of us in the squadron because he didn't want to expose his bright pink pecker. Bernie was a short fellow and rather thinly built, but Bernie was hung like a racehorse. And to have his bright pink pecker flashing all over the shower was most embarrassing and too much for little Bernie to take.

For the remaining time Bernie spent in the Nam and stationed at Marble Mountain, he stopped taking showers after catching Nam VD. His buddies began to stay clear of him because of the manner in which his ass stunk. Poor Bernie, what a price he paid for a two-dollar piece of ass.

You can rest assured that old Bernie was not the only marine who caught VD in the Nam and walked around our base smelling like a dead rat. There must have been many of Bernies walking around Marble Mountain at the time, dangling a bright pink one and smelling like skunk dump.

Tee and I both felt sorry for our friend Bernie, but he knew the consequences of buying a two-dollar quickie. He heard the same VD lectures we did and saw the same-sex educational movies. But I don't think in his wildest dreams he thought he was going to be the guy to catch this rare disease.

Bernie hit the jackpot, and most marines in our squadron made fun of his situation almost every time they laid eyes on him. This was another reason that Tee and I didn't yield to the temptation of the flesh. All we had to do was think about the humiliation Bernie was experiencing.

We were later informed that Bernie and marines like him caught a rare form of VD and the chances of contracting the pink pecker disease were one in a thousand. Every GI who had served in Vietnam was warned of the possibility of catching VD by their medical staff. Additionally, we were forced to listen to many lectures and was forced to watch sex-oriented movies detailing the fact that old Mr. VD was out there, and he was out there to stay, and was constantly searching for new victims.

The movies and lectures pointed out the venereal diseases we would most likely catch in the Nam. They were syphilis, trichomoniasis, genital warts, chlamydia, genital herpes, or gonorrhea.

The movies and lectures stressed there were side effects when catching each disease. For example, when you caught genital herpes, there was a good chance you would be stricken with shingles, cold sores, or even chicken pox. Many marines would be walking about the base sipping on lemon juice or some type of fruit juice because the lectures and movies pointed out that fruit juices were good combatants against venereal diseases. The service did a great job in teaching GIs the ABCs of VD. Tee and I were good students and seriously listened to the lectures. We wanted no part of Nam VD.

Another one of our friends was known to frequent the redlight district and keep the working girls employed. His name was Corporal Smith; we called him Smitty. He was known to run to his selected working girl with his two dollars dangling from his pockets. He would get his two-dollar quickie, his dose of VD, and run to his next selected working girl to repeat the process, all over again.

The navy corpsmen on our base had a special name for Smitty. They called him the "Double-Dose Kid." Most any corpsman at the hospital knew they would be getting a visit from Smitty every time he went into town on liberty, and they knew he would arrive back on the base with a sick pecker, and it was common knowledge that in many cases he would walk into sick bay with two kinds of VD.

Smitty had all the medical professionals scratching their heads one particular Saturday night when he came running into sick bay with a mystery case of VD.

The doctors and corpsmen attending to his sick pecker couldn't figure out what type of disease he had picked up, because he came into sick bay holding his sick pecker in his hands, and it was the size of a small football. The swelling of his penis was so enormous he couldn't zip and/or fasten his pants.

Just so happened I was on guard duty that night and was guarding an area close to the hospital and naturally was caught up in the commotion. When I saw Smitty crying and his swollen pecker, I briefly left post and tried very hard to console him, but he was in excruciating pain. It was a sight to see him sitting there, holding his enlarged pecker in both hands and crying like a little bitch.

After about three minutes attempting to console Smitty, I left him and assumed my post. I felt terribly sorry for him, but there was nothing I could do except laugh my ass off behind his back, like so many others were doing. It took seventy-two hours for the swelling of his pecker to subside and reach its normal size. We heard that the doctors at sick bay were baffled about the cause of Smitty's problem.

As predicted, when liberty call went out the very next weekend, the first marines on board the bus headed to Da Nang with his two dollars dangling from his pants pocket. Old Smitty was at it again. This time the lectures and movies were "not" ignored. Old Smitty had several packages of protection on him, and he planned to use them. We think.

Mixing It Up with the People of Da Nang

During our day liberty passes, Tee and I spent a lot of time enjoying the privilege of mixing it up with the local townspeople of Da Nang. We sincerely liked most of the locals we met, and most of them were nice, as well as friendly. I didn't know if they were friendly to us because we were soldiers or because of that big ass smile Tee would constantly have flashing on his face.

Tee had the biggest and friendliest smile I had ever witnessed in my entire life, and I think the native people of South Vietnam responded to it. In essence, Tee would smile, and the townsfolk would reciprocate and smile back.

The town locals we knew would talk to us, but we didn't understand a damn thing they were saying most of the time, but for some reason, we pretended to always understand. I think what we enjoyed most was their hospitality.

I even pretended most of the time to enjoy their home cooking. The seasoning they would use when cooking was not in line with my taste buds, and sometimes when I ate the locals' cooking, it served as a good laxative.

I tried hard to stay away from their home-cooked dishes as much as I could, and when invited to eat their meals, I would pretend I had stomachaches to avoid eating their cuisines.

On the other hand, Tee loved their cooking, and he thought they seasoned their food very good. He was from Florida and was used to eating food prepared Cuban style, and maybe that was the reason he could stomach their dishes. He would eat up and smile his ass off, and the locals loved it.

I liked the Vietnamese children and felt they were the cutest and prettiest young kids I had ever seen. Many of them were mixed with French blood which could explain their unique facial features. The children living in Da Nang were so much fun to be around that Tee and I spent much of our liberty time trying to communicate with them and taking pictures of them.

Their parents had a funny sense of humor, and they would laugh at almost anything Tee or I did. They would laugh at shit that we thought was totally the opposite of funny. As I would reflect on my visits with them back at the base, I would think that maybe they were laughing at Tee and me all the time. I don't mean laughing with us, I mean laughing at us. They always had a certain gleam in their eyes as they were laughing that I didn't clearly understand. Maybe they were Viet Cong, and that gleam in their eye was saying,

"Marine, beware, because when nightfall rolls around, we will be using your ass as target practice."

After about a dozen or so times of getting day liberty passes and mixing with the people of Da Nang, I started to realize marines were nothing special to many of the locals that appeared to be prodemocratic. For the most part, they only put up with us because we were fighting their war for them. In reality, they wanted marines and other US servicemen to leave their country as soon as the war ended.

Many of the Vietnamese people wanted us to simply disappear the day the war ended. I discussed this topic with other marines on base, and it was clear that many of them felt the same way I did. They also noticed how the locals communicated this message by the look in their eyes. The look in their eyes would say, "Marines, please leave our country when the war ends as soon as possible, and never come back." And, of course, they would smile and laugh.

Many marines were saddened that many locals felt this way and didn't let it get next to us in a big way, and, honestly, we felt we were there fighting in their country for a mission, and the mission we thought was to ensure that South Vietnam remains a democratic free country.

After being in country for a while, you also soon came to realize that there were many locals who wanted us in their country and were much thankful that we were their upholding peace and providing safety for them and their families.

*"The beauty of life is to be found in thoughts
that rise above the needs of self."*

"MY BEST FRIEND – {TEE} STANDING BESIDE A HEAD (RESTROOM)."

Mail Call at Marble Mountain

THERE WERE ALSO SOME UNDESIRABLE locals who were "extremely" happy we were in their country. These were the pimps and their workingwomen. These locals were making more money than they had ever dreamed about. They may even had been the VCs shooting at us at night, but during the day, they were smiling their ass off and gladly taking our money.

Marble Mountain was under heavy construction when our unit arrived. And I was placed in charge of erecting my squadron's Aircraft Engineering Tent, the place of which I would soon put in some very long hours . . . updating and maintaining our aircrafts flight logs. Erecting our tent on the newly laid matting was fairly easy work. The hard part was setting it up with all of its necessary components . . . *as shown sprawled out directly behind me in the below picture.*

Evening chow call, at the newly built mess hall, at Marble Mountain began at 1630 hours. Most marines on base would eat chow and rush back to their tent locations on both Tuesdays and Friday evenings with hope they would hear their names shouted out during the evening mail call services.

The mail delivery team consisted normally of two NCOs that practically everyone on base loved to see drive their jeep full of mail cargo to a certain location close to their tent area.

Goodies contained on the mail jeep was the link between marines and their loved ones back in the world. So mail call was serious business, and GIs came scampering to the mail delivery drop area in hopes of receiving a letter from a loved one.

When one's name was called, that individual would rush to the mail carrier, retrieve his mail, and find a quiet place to absorb the letter's contents. These letters were from their wives, girlfriends, mothers, fathers, or anybody back home in the world who cared to take the time to drop them a line.

Some marines or navy personnel stationed at Marble Mountain received mail regularly and would brag about it, while some only received a letter or package every so often, and when they hadn't received mail for a while, they were not happy troopers to be around.

Not all mail recipients were cheerful after reading their mail's contents. Some guys who received mail would throw the letters down and begin kicking them around and eventually tearing the letter in half prior to discarding it into a nearby trash container.

In the majority of cases, this activity resulted from a jarhead receiving a Dear John letter.

This type of letter was sent to GIs in the Nam quite often, and the reaction on the part of the recipient was normally the same, which was noticeable outrage at first, then ultimately a calm of quiet sadness; so it was easy to spot those who had recently received such a letter. It was known knowledge to provide a marine his space during this time in his life. I would say to myself after detecting a Dear John recipient, "I feel sorry for Charlie's ass, if he ever came in contact with this brokenhearted marine in the bush."

A Dear John letter was never written to yours truly. I didn't have a sweetheart back in the States whom I was dating prior to be shipped to the Nam. The only female person writing me regularly was my dear mother.

In some occasions, I would lie and tell my fellow marines I received mail from a sweetheart back in the world, but if they were able to actually read the letters contents, they would quickly realize the letter was from my dear mother.

Guess I lied about receiving mail from a sweetheart back in the States because I was jealous of the guys who actually received letters from one and wanted my fellow marines to think I had a love life back in the world as sweet as theirs. The only person who knew I was bullshitting about a love life was my dear friend Tee.

I even cut out a picture of a beautiful swimsuit model from *Jet Magazine* and pasted it on my bunk in my tent directly over my pillow area and told the guys this was the sweet thing who was writing me back in the States. Now that I look back . . . so much wasted time and energy.

Most marines bunking in my tent didn't just receive letters. Many of them would routinely receive "goodie packages." These packages consisted of all sorts of goodies. Sometimes, they consisted of home-baked cookies or home-baked bread, or even store-bought candy treats. Many of the guys would share the contents of these goodie packages with other jarheads in their tent, and 99 percent of the time the contents in these packages were absolutely delicious.

One marine in my tent of Italian descent would religiously receive a package from his mother almost weekly. He shared its contents with all marines in our tent, and we all damn near got fat off his mom's home-baked goodies.

Items distributed from the two NCOs during mail call wasn't just letters or goodie packages; also delivered to our tents were the latest edition of the *Stars and Stripes*. Marines and sailors who didn't receive love letters would practically fight over who would first get the chance to read this military newspaper.

There were only a couple of *Stars and Stripes* newspapers contained in the mail carrier's bag. Tee and I witnessed some damn good fistfights over who won the opportunity to be the first to read this military newspaper. I used to tell Tee that if we fought "Charlie" like we fought over who was first to read this crazy newspaper, this war would be over in a week.

In many instances, arguments and debates would result in almost every tent after marines had read and absorbed the newspapers main articles. In some cases, the arguments would get out of control and ultimately result in a fistfight. For those of us who have had the opportunity to serve in the marine corps, we are most cognizant of the fact a marine is willing to fight at the drop of a hat, and it didn't take much argument over the contents in the paper to get a fistfight started.

Some of the articles contained in the *Stars and Stripes* were primarily written, it seemed, to upset the average combat serviceman. I say this because the newspaper would contain articles detailing the many "war protestors" assembling back in the world and strongly protesting our role in South Vietnam.

The paper would graphically show college students marching in protest and denouncing the war effort. It would even show students and protestors burning their draft cards and harassing returning war veterans.

Obviously, the protesting activities on the part of these college students didn't sit well with marines at Marble Mountain and pissed us off to no end. Here, we were over in this hot-ass mosquito-infested place, getting shot at and spilling blood, and we read in the *Stars and Stripes* that, back home, rich college students were marching around, protesting that this war, that which our marine buddies were spilling blood in, was wrong and immoral. This was extremely hard to take.

These college kids were saying on TV news cameras the US military in South Vietnam was sticking its nose into a civil war that is the business of only the Vietnamese people and that we should just pack up and get the hell out of their country.

According to the *Stars and Stripes* articles we were reading, some of these college students would even go so far as to burn our national flag. I'll never be able to find words to explain how "hurt" this knowledge made us all feel—especially after we had just sent back home three popular brave marines in gray-colored caskets. It's impossible to find the proper words to adequately explain the hurt feeling we had then, and still have.

Many of these spirited discussions would go into the late hours of the night, and most marines in our tent felt these spirited war demonstrators who were against the war were also against fighting for democracy.

Our tents housed twenty-six marines, and each tent, it seemed, had one or two tent house scholars who agreed or semiagreed with the war protestors back home. So during the nightly bullshit sessions and particularly when tanked up on hot Budweiser, these minority thinking marines would reason that we didn't have a clue as to who the enemy was in South Vietnam. They would echo what the student protestors would say, and that is that this war we're engaged in is a civil war between North and South Vietnam, and that America has no right being involved.

The majority thinking marines would counter the minority scholarly marines by saying they were in Vietnam to stop communist aggression. If South Vietnam is overthrown, there will be a snowball reaction with more countries in Southeast Asia soon to be challenged. They reasoned they were locating the enemy daily and blasting them to hell and will continue to do so until South Vietnam is free from communist aggression.

This debate sometimes would go on until morning chow call. There were a many of mornings marines would go to work, skipping morning chow, and without hardly any sleep due to debating this subject throughout the night.

The *Stars and Stripes* also contained news articles about Negroes fighting for their civil rights back in the States. It would detail how they were infiltrating and integrating many popular eating establishments and practically everything else that didn't allow their patronage . . . such as movie theaters, retail stores, and even some public schools located in the southern states. The American Negro the *Stars and Stripes* stated wanted total freedom and, according to some of their leaders, was going to obtain it by "any means necessary."

In essence, there was a freedom war going on back in the States, and this was extremely troublesome to the servicemen of color who were risking their lives on a daily basis helping Vietnamese people whom they didn't even know obtain their freedom. Meanwhile, back in their own state, a Negro GI's own brother or sister couldn't sit down and eat a lousy burger at a lunch counter of a "five-and-ten-cent store." To many, including white marines, this simply didn't make sense.

The "civil rights" news when read in the military newspaper by GIs of color was more than depressing, and it's impossible to explain in words the humiliation and anger these fighting men of color felt when reading these articles in the *Stars and Stripes*.

Personally, I cried many nights after reading an article in the *Stars and Stripes* about this injustice that was happening back in my own neighborhood. I would awaken mad as hell and would ask myself in the mirror while shaving, "Why am I over here in this hot-ass jungle fighting these brown people of color, anyway?" Many of nights, I tried hard to answer that question but failed at finding any meaningful resolve.

On most nights, only anger would set in, and I didn't even know what or whom I was mad at. It sure as hell wasn't the white marine who was over here fighting alongside me, because I had witnessed him risking his life daily in an attempt to save the lives of my fellow Negro marines.

I'd reach the conclusion that I was mad at only the white people back home who didn't allow my brother to eat at their "white-only" lunch counter, and that I wasn't mad at the sixty-year-old white man who recently hand carried a nine-year-old black girl who had been involved in a hit-and-run accident to our community hospital and demanded they provide medical services that eventually saved her life. Finally, I came to the conclusion it is totally stupid to be mad at an entire race of people for some bad things a few had done.

Black GIs were receiving magazines and newspapers from the States that were published by groups like the NAACP and Black Muslims. Some of the news articles found in this media would graphically describe in great detail how the black GI had no business fighting in South Vietnam and that his or her fight was back home in the United States. The enemy they stated was not Vietnamese but bigoted white people living all around the United States.

It was in late spring of 1965, and the black and white racial situation in America was getting out of control. Positive civil rights legislation aiding Negroes had recently been passed in Congress, and some white people, particularly in parts of the South, had a difficult time accepting the fact they were required by law to eat in the same café beside a Negro and educate their children in the same public school classroom alongside a Negro.

History in our nation was being made on the civil rights front almost daily, and in some cases, these historical occasions were not made without the spillage of human blood. And far too many times, the blood was that of a fallen black brother, sister, or child back in the world.

In regards to mail call, black marines were constantly being bombarded with letters from friends and family members detailing the historic civil rights updates. My family and friends would send newsprint of how black citizens, sometimes children, were beaten by bigoted policemen, or how high-pressurized water hoses were utilized to turn back Negroes who were simply trying to integrate a community park facility.

Bernie's mother sent him an article from a black newspaper explaining how people of color in certain parts of the South weren't allowed to vote during open elections. This article was passed around among the brothers and infuriated those who read it or heard of its existence.

Black marines would say, "Can you believe this shit? There are places back home in America where I can't vote, and I'm over here putting my ass on the line for these people's right to vote. What kind of crazy shit is this?" This news article even pissed off many white marines who read it.

Chris, my friend and blue-eyed soul brother, would come to me time and time again and ask me after he had read one of these news articles and say, "Corporal Clark, how in the hell can you wrap your head around this type of shit?"

My answer to Chris was always, "It's hard, man. It's real hard." Chris would further state that he had a hard time understanding white marines and black marines fighting as a close-knit unit, but as soon as the firefight ceased, the white guys went their way, and the black guys went theirs.

In a most serious tone, I told Chris that during my time in the Nam, I had witnessed about a half a dozen bloody firefights while flying as a volunteer crew member on medevac flights. What I plainly saw was when the firefights broke out and the shooting began, all marines on the scene were fighting as one, and they put their racial hatreds aside during the battle. These men fought as a team and had each other's back.

But, sadly speaking, when the fighting was over, these same marines reverted to racially hating each other again. I did, in fact, witness that, in most cases, they hated one another a little less due to experiences encountered during the firefight. I told Chris that it was no doubt hard to hate a person with the same intensity when that same person of a different race had just saved your ass in battle.

Chris agreed and said he will never understand why people hate each other simply because of their skin color. My reply was, "God understands, and he will look after us while in this foreign land."

"DON'S FIRST DAY AT MARBLE MT."

Brave Navy Corpsmen

WHEN I RETURNED FROM VIETNAM in October 1966, the one thing that I kept saying during the many conversations held with friends and family was the numerous acts of bravery, I personally witnessed, on the part of our navy corpsmen. As soon as I would say this . . . I found myself always defining what a corpsman was or what he did.

And I would always walk away from our discussion, saying to myself, "Not only is Joe Public unaware of perhaps the bravest man alive during these celebrated war campaigns, but for the most part, Joe Public has never known this corpsman guy has ever existed."

I only flew on about four dozen or so medevac missions, and during my short amount of time airborne, I have witnessed bravery by corpsmen on the part of that I had never seen before, and as far as I'm concerned, this PO2 should have been granted the congressional Medal of Honor.

I don't recall the naval corpsman's name; all I remember was his rank and that he was of Hispanic racial origin. He spoke with a Spanish or Mexican accent, and he was rather tall for a person of his race. I think he was about six feet, two inches tall, because I'm six feet, two inches tall, and when he stood beside me, we were eye level.

As earlier stated, this activity on his part took place during my third or fourth medevac flight, and it happened a short distance (approximately ten miles) from our base of Marble Mountain. I remember the pilot had a pretty hard time landing our UH34D helicopter because the terrain was so dense with vegetation overgrowth. It was difficult to land our chopper where the orange flare had been ignited to spot our LZ, due to the aforementioned. The pilot finally, somehow, managed to land; and, believe me, his landing of the chopper scared the hell out of me because the plane dropped unusually hard on the ground when it landed that the six marines who were in the belly of the aircraft all fell from our seats to the deck when it landed. The jolt was so severe that it tore the two mounted M60s right from their secured brackets.

There were four helicopters dispatched on this medevac, and our chopper was the last to land in a formation of two UH34Ds and one UH1E. Our mission was to pick up the dead and/or the wounded. Again, our aircraft was the last to land in the formation and also the last to take off with wounded or dead marines primarily due to the action of a navy corpsman (PO2) who was assigned to our aircraft.

It just happened we landed about a klick (one thousand meters) from where a firefight was still in progress by a shot-up squad of recon marines, along with about ten infantry marines, accompanied by three South Vietnam soldiers. Our helicopter was last to take off because after we had successfully loaded four wounded marines and one severely wounded South Vietnamese soldier, the navy corpsman refused to jump in our chopper which was about to take off. He thought he heard a sound that sounded like a moan from a fallen serviceman who wasn't visible due to the abundance of tall monkey grass that surrounded our aircraft and the entire area. Our copilot even gave the corpsman a direct order to board the chopper for take-off, and still the corpsman refused. He was running and ducking from enemy fire around our aircraft in hopes of hearing that moan again and pinpoint its whereabouts. This time, the pilot shouted out to the corpsman to board the aircraft for takeoff, and yet the corps-man still didn't obey his instructions. Meanwhile, the two M60 gunners aboard our chopper began to fire their weapons in frontal fire spurts due to the increased fire we were experiencing. The fuselage of our chopper must have taken four to five rounds, and all of us aboard the aircraft were scared shitless, and we even began to shout to the corpsman to get his ass into the chopper. By this time, the navy corpsman was not in sight and actually had disappeared in the tall monkey grass surrounding our plane.

The chopper's marine corps pilot, a decorated captain, shouted out instructions to "Prepare to take off," because he focused on the safety of his crew and the wounded who had been put aboard his craft. A good five minutes or so had passed without sight of the corpsman, and just when the chopper began to lift off did one of the M60 door gunners sight the navy corpsman struggling to get to the chopper while rescuing a wounded United States marine. The corpsman was actually carrying the wounded marine on his shoulders when two marine crewmen jumped down out of the chopper that was lifting off to assist in the navy corpsman's rescue effort. The pilot witnessed this activity and aborted his takeoff and dropped the aircraft to the ground and ordered all crew members aboard the aircraft to provide cover fire in order for the corpsman and the two marine crewmen to successfully carry and lift the wounded marine into the helicopter.

As we all began firing our weapons, the noise was deafening, and we all began firing in all directions and praying that our aircraft take off without any of us getting shot. Finally, all was aboard, and the pilot lifted our chopper into the air as our M60 gunners kept firing away. We never saw the VC or the enemy we were firing at, but by the amount of incoming fire we were experiencing, the enemy was alive and well and in close proximity to our helicopter. God was with us that particular afternoon, and everyone inside the belly of that helicopter was congratulating the corpsman for his heroic effort in saving the life of that moaning marine. There was no doubt in anyone's mind that if the navy corpsman had adhered to the copilot and pilot's instructions, that wounded marine corporal would have died right there in that tall monkey grass.

The corpsman didn't hear any of our congratulating remarks because he was focused and busy attending to the wounded marine corporal he heard moaning in the jungle. Blood was literally pouring from the large gaping wound the marine corporal had experienced. Immediately, the corpsman, along with one of our crew, began administering aid to the corporal just as soon as he was aboard.

I was ordered by our crew chief to assist in helping the other wounded fighters aboard our aircraft and had to take my attention away from the brave, heroic navy corpsman who had just saved an American life. As far as I was concerned, I had just witnessed a scene directly from one of the John Wayne's war movies.

While attempting to assist with the administering of aid to the other wounded aboard our chopper, I and the other members of the flight crew were sliding all around the belly of the aircraft due to the slippery floor. As we began examining the chopper's deck, we quickly saw the reason the deck was so slippery. The deck of the chopper was covered with bright red puddles of blood. This was due to the vast amount of blood pouring from the wounds of all the wounded personnel aboard our chopper.

It was chaotic aboard our chopper, but due to the correct instructions provided by the brave corpsman and the crew chief, we all were doing our part to keep our fallen alive. All of a sudden, the brave navy corpsman fell to the deck of the chopper and rolled over on his back and began breathing very heavy. At that moment, all aboard the aircraft noticed that a large portion of the blood hitting the deck was coming from the navy corpsman.

The crew chief took charge of administering our first aid effort, and he personally worked on the navy corpsman. As he tried to keep the corpsman alive, all aboard that chopper were praying for the corpsman's life, as we witnessed, firsthand, that this navy corpsman placed his life in complete danger by searching for the wounded corporal, and that he was shot—and shot badly and didn't ask for any assistance to his wounds until he couldn't stand up and attend care to the wounded inside our aircraft.

After we had landed and had assisted in carrying all wounded inside Marble Mountains hospital, all of the crew aboard that chopper, including the pilot and copilot, stood guard around the bed where the wounded navy corpsman was being cared for by the navy doctors and nurses inside the hospital. We didn't leave that corpsman's side until he was moved into the operating room. Even then, we mulled around outside the operating room until the doctors completed operating on his wounds.

We didn't leave our heroic corpsman's side until the head doctor in charge that particular day said the corpsman was going to make it and that he would recover from his injuries. I don't have to tell you how happy and elated we all were. This guy was, and still is, a hero in my book and the book of so many others. He most likely only received a Purple Heart for getting wounded, but we who were there to witness firsthand his acts of bravery were certain that his heroic act of placing his life on the line and in serious danger to save a fellow marine was deserving of the Medal of Honor.

Afterward, I personally witnessed several acts of bravery during medevac missions that involved navy corpsmen. Maybe it's because many of them didn't carry a weapon, or maybe their bravery and life-saving gallantry were simply taken for granted. But, to this day, I don't understand why more of corpsman or similar caregivers shouldn't be granted high levels of recognition, because for what I witnessed in my short wartime experience, they damn well deserved "a ton" of high-ranking medals, and even the Medal of Honor.

Speaking of medals, I witnessed on several occasions where a marine or navy corpsman had been slightly wounded or sustained an injury and didn't report it, and the reason they failed to report their injury was they didn't want to be taken away from their combat unit and sent back to some faraway hospital. Therefore, they failed to receive a Purple Heart or, for that matter, any medal. These individuals I'm referring to didn't care for that kind of recognition, but on the other hand, I've witnessed where a marine cut his ear shaving and, after a firefight, reported his injury, and he was awarded a Purple Heart and, in fact, didn't deserve it.

So, in essence, for many a marine who fought in Vietnam (I included), a Purple Heart or a medal didn't mean a whole lot. What was important in our minds was to "win" the war and return home with some kind of "favorable" recognition from our families and our fellow American citizens. That, for the most part, failed to happen, and in fact, when we returned home, some of us were spit upon by our fellow American citizens because these people didn't believe in the war in Vietnam and took their hatred out on returning servicemen.

We didn't like their actions then, and to this day, we still are pissed at what they put us through. The only reason some of us didn't strike back, and we could have kicked ass and done some severe damage, was because we love our country. We love it so much that we would not stoop that low and hurt our fellow Americans physically, like they hurt us mentally. We put our lives on the line to protect our country and our way of life—and will do it again in a heartbeat. We truly love America and its way of life. And it damn well didn't matter if we were white, black, green, or yellow. We all fought together, and many of us died for our nation, and even if we stand alone, "*we stand proud.*"

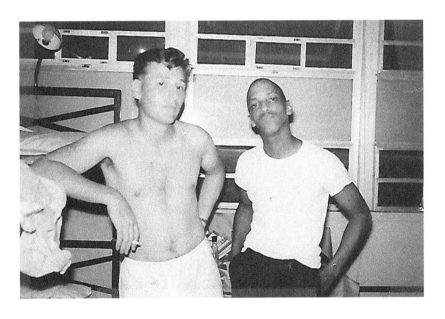

"CLOSE BUDDIES AT MARBLE MT......CHRIS FABRIS AND BERNIE THE BROTHER."

Medevac—Rescue of Children

MY FIRST ENCOUNTER WITH KIM (My Friend You), her brother Lanh, and Aunt Thien was during a most memorable medevac mission that occurred in mid-July of 1965.

One of our squadron's medevac crew chiefs whom I had made friends with had promised he would select me as a volunteer crew member the first time an opportunity occurred. Two days after his promise, one of his flight crew members was having a bout with sinus headaches, and the staff sergeant crew chief radioed me at the Engineering Office, and asked was I available, and I assured him I would somehow make myself available. He made true to his promise, and I was bored logging flight time; I was excited at the opportunity.

Sinus headache had worked for the crew member, so I used it as an excuse with my direct report and did a fine job of playacting. I didn't win an Oscar that morning but was good enough to be ordered to my tent to sleep off my dreadful headache.

Instead of walking to my sleep tent, I double-timed it over to the Flight Office and, as soon as I arrived, was ordered to man the medevac chopper because an emergency had just occurred. A leader of a Vietnamese ranger patrol unit had just radioed into our Flight Office requesting a UH34D medevac helicopter be dispatched and flown per his coordinates to pick up a party of seventeen children that his patrol unit had recently discovered hiding in the jungle.

The ranger leader stated many of the children were in immediate need of medical attention. He reported it didn't appear any of the children had been shot or wounded but suffered from a two-week journey in the jungle. He said the kids had jungle foliage cuts all over their bodies, and they were suffering from numerous insect and small rodent bites.

Minutes later, the Vietnamese ranger called back to our Flight Office and stated the seventeen children had escaped a VC raiding party two weeks back, about fifty miles north of Da Nang.

While the medevac crew was scrambling to board the helicopter, our copilot checked with intelligence and was informed a VC raiding party had, in fact, burned out a small village of approximately two hundred people, about fifty miles north of Da Nang, two weeks back, and killed several of the adult villagers.

The officer in charge of dispatching aircraft from MAG-16 that day informed the ranger leader that he was aware of the small village that had been attacked by VC two weeks back, that MAG-16 would honor his request, and that a UH34D medevac helicopter would be dispatched immediately to fly to his requested location.

On this particular medevac mission, two navy corpsmen were assigned. And they began instructing the cabin flight crew on what duties they were to perform in helping the children as soon as they climbed into the helicopter.

I didn't pay that much attention to the two corpsmen balking off demands because, as a volunteer crewman, my duties on medevac missions were normally always the same. They were to take orders from the helicopter crew chief and assist at his command. If the sick or wounded were aboard, the crew chief would direct volunteer crewmen to assist flight corpsman in attending to the medical needs of those individuals.

Since I was six foot two and weighed almost two hundred pounds, I normally was assigned to assist in performing some type of lifting duties aboard the medevac chopper. At the corpsman command, I would assist in lifting the wounded and placing them in positions as directed. On a few occasions, I was instructed to lift a brave one who had fallen into our helicopter, zipped up in those ugly dark-colored body bags. On those occasions, normally the flight trip back to base was a quiet one.

While flying as a volunteer crewman on medevac, the assignment I liked the most, but came only twice, was when I was ordered to man one of the M60 machine guns that was mounted at both door openings of the helicopter.

The only time I got the opportunity to fire the M60 was back in May around the time of my birthday, and our medevac chopper was being fired at by a VC sniper that was hiding in a field that contained about twenty water buffalos. The crew chief gave me the command to fire the M60 because our aircraft was taking hits from the sniper, and our primary gunner was using the head.

Following orders, like a good little marine, I gave the M60 a couple of short burst but to my recollection never hit the sniper. I did, however, manage to hit a couple of water buffalos. I saw about a half a dozen of them lying dead from the air, and due to my love for animals, this bothered me a long time afterward, and still does.

The South Vietnamese ranger patrol leader radioed in again and warned us that there was heavy VC movement to the south of his unit's position and that his men would mark the LZ for our medevac chopper by employing orange smoke grenades. He ended his conversation by saying we were about to evacuate seventeen half-starved children and that to bring along plenty cans of C rations.

Our medevac helicopter soon taxied to its launch position. Directly after the pilot's check off procedures, the helicopter was airborne and flying per the ranger's directions. Our medevac crew consisted of our pilot, copilot, two navy corpsmen, a crew chief, three flight crewmen, and a volunteer crew member by the name of Cpl. Donald Clark, your author.

As soon as we were airborne, the South Vietnamese ranger radioed our copilot and again informed him of VC movement directly adjacent to our landing zone that was currently being marked by his men with orange smoke grenades. Our copilot requested that the South Vietnamese ranger leader form a landing zone defense perimeter at the marked zone.

The ranger leader agreed and moved into action. Within ten minutes, the ranger radioed back to the copilot and stated that it was all clear on the ground and that it was safe to land at the marked orange smoke grenades.

The chopper took a deep right downward turn, and the pilot began his quick decent where the rangers had marked with orange smoke grenades. All was going smoothly, and our chopper was about fifty feet from landing, and all of a sudden, we began taking hits into our fuselage from small arms fire. Our M60 door gunners didn't know which direction to return fire because it appeared we were receiving gunfire from all four directions.

Our crew chief really proved his worth and took control of the chopper's cabin. He kept us calm and alert. We all felt safe under his direction. Then, suddenly, our chopper took a hard turn left and upward. We were climbing fast, and then, all of a sudden, our aircraft slowed down, and we all heard a weird sound come from the engine.

Meanwhile, as we were attempting to climb, bullet holes were appearing into the sides of our helicopter at an increasing rate. The weird sounds from the engine grew louder, and suddenly black smoke began to extrude from the engine compartment and engulf the belly of our chopper. All of us inside began choking, and the helicopter began to slowly descend.

Yours truly tried very hard not to panic during this ordeal, and our crew chief was doing a great job of keeping calm in the cabin, but our aircraft continued to take hits from ground fire. Each time a round penetrated the chopper's magnesium body shell, it made a sound like "ping."

The crew members who manned the M60s were blasting away, with short bursts in every direction. It appeared they had been through this drill many times before and really had their shit together. I felt safe in their company and noticed their feet slipping on empty ejected M60 shells. I located an empty C ration box and quickly began scooping up the ejected shells and dumped them in the box. This action provided solid footing for the door gunners, and they appeared to appreciate my actions.

Our crew chief was constantly talking to the copilot through his helmet mike, and it was evident something was terribly wrong by his actions. The crew chief suddenly turned off his headphone, stood up, and shouted to his cabin crew that the chopper was about to go down.

The crew chief again shouted that the helicopter will be "auto-rotating" downward and that it appeared it will experience a soft landing and land on target. All while the crew chief was talking, the two door gunners were quickly dismounting their M60s from their stands and gathering up ammo belts.

The crew chief looked over at me and could tell I was scared shitless and calmly came to me and asked if everything was okay. While breathing very heavy, I asked if our chopper was about to crash and burn. He smiled and informed me that autorotation meant the chopper would be descending at a controllable speed due to the activity of the two rotor blades, and that all was good. He then gave me the thumbs-up and told me to be prepared to exit the aircraft when it landed with my M14 at the ready. Words can't explain how relieved I felt after he gave me those thumbs-up. As a result, I felt real good inside.

Prior to the crew chief providing me with the "thumbs-up," I had become so fearful of our chopper crashing that I had begun uncontrollably peeing all down my leg. The urine was so warm on my leg that, for a brief moment, I thought maybe I had been shot. The biggest fear I had now was to not allow any member of the crew to see my wet pant leg.

As the chopper continued its autorotation descent and was about to land, I began frantically searching for my M14. Finally, I located it but had the most difficult time sliding the ammo magazine in place. I had never been in a serious firefight before, and words can't describe how nervous I felt. I tried hard to pull myself together and kept saying these words my parents taught me. "The will of God will never take you where the grace of God will not protect you." That phrase was extremely comforting, and, instantly, I felt I could handle this fearful situation.

Our crew chief was a staff sergeant and was on his second tour in the Nam. He was so cool and calm during this entire landing episode. His calmness, gave me strength, and courage; and I was very fortunate to have him as our chief.

He called for our attention and began to count from ten to zero.

One of the door gunners informed me that when he gets to zero, our helicopter will have touched down. During his countdown, I noticed the other members of our crew frantically strapping themselves into their seats, so I followed their lead and strapped myself into my seat and bent over and held my head low between my legs, just like they were doing.

During the crew chief's countdown and when he reached six, one of the door gunners broke silence, and said to another crew member, "Corporal Jeffrey, what would your mama do at a time like this?" And, suddenly, there was laughter inside the belly of our chopper. It may have been nervous laughter, but it was laughter just the same, and it was soothing. It really helped.

While I was bent over, I began to pray aloud, and a door gunner setting next to me quietly said, "Corporal Clark, you're not going to die, so please shut the fuck up." He further said, "The pilot will not let you die. He will autorotate this big-ass bird softly to the ground. It seemed liked it took forever, but finally our chopper touched down, and, luckily, it landed in the middle of a small rice paddy. The water smelled awful, but it was soft and only about six inches deep.

As soon as we landed, we began taking hits to the fuselage of our helicopter by small arms fire. We were being shot at from one direction, and our two door gunners opened up with their M60s, and much of the incoming small arms fire ceased for the moment. I assisted the portside gunner by helping feed rounds into his weapon.

The crew chief ordered us four marines out of the chopper and had us spread out in a defensive position around the helicopter. Meanwhile, the copilot was in constant communication with the ranger leader in regards to retrieving our cargo of seventeen children.

There would be a pause in the gunfire, and, suddenly, it would start up again. When the gunfire stopped, the surrounding jungle terrain became quiet, and when the gunfire started up again, the noise of the jungle became increasingly louder.

While lying in monkey grass in the prone position, I couldn't help but to think what would my actor hero do in a time like this. For some strange reason, this thought kept entering my mind.

Our crew chief kept talking in hand signals, and for the life of me, I didn't have a clue as to what he was saying. Apparently, I had failed to attend hand signaling classes during jungle training, and I think most marines with my MOS failed to attend. I had faith in our crew chief and figured if there was something I really needed to know, somehow, he would get the word to me.

Every few minutes a couple of rounds would fly overhead, and we would hear what appeared to be enemy chatter. The enemy chatter appeared to be about fifty yards out. The more the enemy talked, the more little voices began talking to me. These little voices began asking me all sorts of dumbass things. I tried hard to turn them off.

I noticed the three other marine crew members who were laid out in monkey grass surrounding our helicopter. They appeared so cool, calm, and collected. Hell, they were calmly lying in their positions, as if they were about to take an afternoon siesta. They didn't appear to have little voices talking to them or to allow these small-framed black pajama-wearing bastards frighten any of them.

Our crew chief signaled for two of us to crawl over to him. I and one of the door gunners responded, and we arrived at the same time. The crew chief softly said he saw movement and ordered us to take our weapons and fire off about a dozen rounds at a thick palm tree about thirty yards out.

We opened up and blasted away. He with his M60, I with my M14 set on semiautomatic. After firing, we heard a loud voice shouting in the targeted area. After examining the area behind the thick palm tree, we witnessed traces of blood leading back into the jungle. It certainly appeared either I or the door gunner had hit one or some of the enemy but without a body; the only confirmation was the blood trail.

I was happy the crew chief chose me to be a part of that action, because it marked the very first time I got the opportunity to fire my M14 at a target during an actual combat situation in South Vietnam.

Yours truly was getting kind of used to this war stuff and sort of getting his shit together. Perhaps the prayers my parents taught me helped out, or the calming words of our crew chief did the trick, but I was amazed at myself for how calm I was carrying on during the loud noises of war activity. *At this particular time, at this very moment, I suddenly felt like a United States marine.*

All of a sudden, all of the shooting stopped, and I began to see our pilot and copilot stirring in the cockpit and constantly talking over the flight radio. Our crew chief ordered us back into the helicopter and began talking over the radio.

Our pilot informed us that friendly forces were arriving and to place our weapons safeties in the "on" position. As soon as he issued that order, the South Vietnamese ranger leader appeared along with six of his rangers. They had much to do with silencing the gunfire. I was told they shot and killed half of the enemy that was firing at our helicopter and that the other half ran and hid off in the jungle.

The rangers told us about a dozen of the enemy firing at our chopper—and that they were able to assist in our firefight once they fought off another contingency of the enemy which totaled around twenty. In summary, these rangers saved the day.

When it had become safe to move about and the firing had finally stopped altogether, one of the corpsmen shouted at my direction and said that he needed my immediate assistance. I followed him, and we managed to wade through some smelly rice paddy water and to reach the cargo we were sent to rescue. The cargo the ranger leader requested we rescue consisted of sixteen children and one young adult female who led their escape from a VC attack of their nearby village.

The corpsman, I, and another crew member began lifting the children out of the water and into the medevac chopper. We moved extremely fast, and in no time, we had the children and the young female inside the helicopter.

While we were lifting the cargo into the belly of the chopper, the crew chief and his crew were busily at hand working to repair the shot- up engine. Luckily, they carried the right spare parts in order to perform the quick fix because the crew chief was hastily radioing the pilot and informing him the repairs had been performed and the aircraft was available for lift.

Meanwhile, lifting the children from the rice paddy into the chopper was going smoothly with the only exception of when we attempted to lift a young teenage boy into the chopper. The reason we had such difficulty with lifting him in the aircraft was his younger sister was tightly clinging onto him, and for the life of her, she wouldn't let go of him while we tried lifting him into the chopper.

It was terribly awkward attempting to lift two people at once that I and the corpsman accidently dropped both the boy and the girl into muddy rice paddy water in our first attempt. We were finally able to break the two apart and managed to successfully lift them into the helicopter. But the mud bath I suffered during that ordeal, I'll never forget.

I faintly heard a young lady who was already aboard the chopper call out the names of Lanh and Kim as she rushed over and hugged the two that caused my mud bath. I later learned the young lady's name to be Thien.

We would "not" have successfully completed our medevac mission, and I would not be alive to write this story if it were not for the bravery and fierce fighting of the South Vietnamese rangers. They were laying down protective cover fire that had the enemy fleeing in all directions, thus, making it possible for our aircraft to land safely.

God was certainly with us that day, because none of our helicopter crew of nine was killed. Only one of our crew was wounded. He was one of our door gunners, a corporal, and proud as hell to be called a Texan. He was hit in his right thigh during the latter stages of the fighting. This Texas kid was a brave and courageous *sob*, because he continued to fire his M60 even after he was wounded and, for some reason, kept shouting, "Remember the Alamo."

The corporal lost a lot of blood during the ordeal and collapsed into the corpsman's arms after we had lifted off. His blood was all over the floor of our helicopter, thus, making the floor very slippery and difficult to walk on while the aircraft was in flight.

The pretty little girl who caused my mud bath stared at me the entire flight back to Marble Mountain. Every once in a while, I would flash a Tee-like smile to her direction, she would quickly turn her head away from my direction, then turn it back again and continue the constant staring.

It was hard not to notice how this pretty little girl of about ten was still holding onto her brother. Partway during our return flight, the corpsman who helped me lift her into the chopper tried to offer her some chewing gum if only she would loosen her grip on her brother's neck. This attempt failed, and she simply would not separate from him. We finally gave up trying.

The crew chief informed me we were about to land and ordered me to break the little girl loose from her brother in order to set her in a seat and fasten her seat harness.

As I approached her, she began to cry uncontrollably. I then attempted to separate them, and she struggled to break loose from me. Finally, the crew chief signaled for me to let it be and to take my seat and buckle up for the landing.

While loosening my grip on the little girl's arms, I felt something warm on my chest area. Then the smell hit me . . . Apparently, during my struggle with attempting to break them apart, the little girl had accidently urinated all over me.

Now embarrassed, I quickly sat my piss-smelling ass down and buckled up.

Our helicopter began slowing down, and I was able to look outside and to notice some familiar surroundings. We were flying into Marble Mountain and seconds away from landing. Suddenly, I became overjoyed, and the piss smell didn't even bother me.

I was alive and kicking. I had just experienced my first serious war action while in South Vietnam, and the good Lord surely had watched over me during the ordeal. I survived without a scratch, and I was truly grateful. *Thank you, Jesus!*

> *"Trust in the Lord with all thine heart; and lean not unto thine own understanding. In all thy ways acknowledge Him, and He shall direct thy paths to safety."*
>
> —*Proverbs 3:5–6*

"DON HARD AT WORK....LOGGING HELICOPTER FLIGHT AND KEY COMPONENT DATA....IN MAG-16'S AIRCRAFT ENGINEERING TENT (MARBLE MT.)."

Little Kim—a.k.a. My Friend You

OUR UH34D MEDEVAC HELICOPTER SAFELY landed at Marble Mountain, and it was fully loaded with its cargo. With the pilot and copilot's permission, the two corpsmen and five marines aboard carefully unloaded the aircrafts cargo of seventeen villagers to the outstretched arms of awaiting hospital staff who were standing on the helicopter pad with roller hospital beds at the ready.

The rescued villagers actually consisted of sixteen children, and one young adult lady who had recently escaped an attack by VC raiders on their small village located about fifty miles north of Da Nang.

The rescued villagers were to be rushed from the landing pad to our newly constructed hospital's ER ward where they would receive immediate medical attention and undergo standard routine medical examinations.

While most of the children being attended to by our base hospital staff, they were fully cooperating. I couldn't help but to notice this same pretty little girl who was crying on board our chopper during our short flight was once again crying while she was waiting to be medically checked out at the entrance to the ER ward.

As demonstrated during our medevac flight back to base, she was crying uncontrollably all while tightly holding on to her teenaged brother. Her brother was trying to stop his little sister from crying, but it seemed the more he tried, the louder she cried.

This pretty little girl screamed and cried so loud it was quickly becoming deafening, and the little girl couldn't have been over ten years of age. As a matter of fact, her crying was so loud she was literally hurting everyone's eardrums that was working in or in close proximity to the ER ward.

Our two flight crew corpsmen had asked me to stick around and help with the children and requested that I do something to quiet the youngster. I just happened to have in my shirt pocket a few sugar mints provided to me by my blue-eyed soul brother, Corporal Chris Fabris. So I figured by offering her a sugar mint, she would calm down and stop her loud crying.

So I casually walked up to the crying little girl and offered her a mint. She first stared at me as if I were some kind of monster; then she quickly grabbed the sugar mint from my outreached hand, popped it in her mouth, slowly looked me up and down, then flashed me the prettiest smile I had ever seen on a little girl her age. But, most importantly, she ceased her hysterical crying.

The entire hospital staff working that night in the ER ward was extremely pleased that finally someone had silenced this little girl. They even went so far as to give me a standing ovation. I couldn't help but to feel a little important that evening and thanked anyone I came in contact with for their display of gratitude.

A corpsman approached me and asked for my assistance with the crying little girl's older brother who had carried her all the way from the helicopter landing pad. Apparently, the kid had collapsed from total exhaustion as a result from carrying his little sister. He also looked hungry, and it was possible that lack of nutrition had something to do with his problem as well.

I assisted in lifting the young lad from the hospital's floor, onto a hospital rolling bed. It was a good thing I hung around because the sight of her brother passing out caused his little sister to start crying loudly again, and I was there with a shirt pocket full of sugar mints to silence her, yet again.

When the corpsmen rolled her brother into the examination room the pretty little girl ran over and stood close to me. I reasoned, with her brother momentarily out of action and since I had provided her sugar mints, I was the only friendly face she saw in the hospital, which is why I'm getting all of this attention.

As stated earlier, I assumed the little girl ran over to me because she figured I had more sugar mints, but as time passed on, I realized she came over to me because she was frightened and figured I would protect her in some kind of way.

We sat down on a nearby sofa. I pointed to a few children's books lying on a table she could look at, but she wasn't at all interested. She only wanted to snuggle up close to me, close her pretty little eyes, escape her mind from all the war activity and medevac commotion she'd recently experienced, and simply get some sleep. I further reasoned she felt safe sleeping close to me.

She took only a few minutes to fall asleep, and as she slept, I thought back through my life and tried to remember some of my most frightening moments during her age. What quickly came to mind was being chased by my neighbor's large boxer dog. The dog was only playing with me, but I didn't know it then and was scared out of my mind each time he chased me.

How minor my most frightening moments were as compared to what this little girl had been experiencing lately. And the mere thought that she had been escaping from VC these past two weeks was mind-blowing. While covering her with a hospital blanket, I thought, *What a brave little girl.* Hell, I didn't blame her from earlier crying her little heart out.

She slept well over a half an hour, and while she slept, I didn't leave her side. I simply sat there watching over her like a father watches over his daughter. For some strange reason, I felt, for the first time in my life, that I was needed by someone. And I felt this strong desire to somehow forever protect this little girl. I didn't have the slightest clue as to why I felt this way. I just did and didn't even know this pretty little angel's name. Nor did I know if she had living parents.

As she continued to sleep, I wondered if she spoke English and was trying for the life of me to remember her name . . . the name that I heard someone say, when I was experiencing my mud bath, when I and the corpsman were struggling to lift her out of the rice paddy into the medevac helicopter. Her name had seemed to escape my memory.

By this time, it was approaching midnight, and she opened her pretty little eyes and sat up snuggled beside me, then reached her pretty little hand out to request a sugar mint. And I said a couple of simple things in English to her, and she failed to respond. This is when I realized she couldn't speak any English.

Her teenage brother had completed his medical examination and located us and sat down on our sofa. I asked him how the exam went, and in almost perfect English, he responded, "the examination went well, but the room was cold." I was blown away at the fact he was speaking to me in proper English.

He saw my amazement and began to laugh. Then he informed me that he was practically fluent in the English language. I was totally blown away that he could speak my language that well. This poor-looking kid just didn't look like the type that was capable of speaking proper English.

After he ceased laughing, he went on to inform me he had taken English classes each year he attended school and that he liked speaking the English language. He further explained it came in handy when he worked parttime during the day as an interpreter for GIs in a small merchant shop in Da Nang.

He also stated that his English-speaking talent came in extremely handy when he worked evenings interpreting for American GIs when they would call upon him to negotiate sexual rodeo pricing with the working girls in the red-light district of Da Nang. He said he made most of his money in this fashion.

He further explained that his little sister didn't take English classes in school and that she knew only a few words. *He told me his first name was Lanh and his little sister's first name was Kim.* He lowered his eyes and softly told me his parents were killed during the VC's recent attack on his small village and that he wishes to leave it at that. I respected his wishes and didn't pursue any questions pertaining to his parents.

Lanh said his name meant "quick minded" and that his sister's name of Kim meant "golden." Then Kim leaned over and whispered something into her brother's ear, and then she began to softly giggle. He told me his sister wanted to "thank me" for providing her with the sugar mints and also watching over her while he was being examined, and she was sleeping.

I told Lanh to tell Kim it was not a problem watching over her, and I'm glad she enjoyed the mints. Lanh told Kim what I had said, and he further stated he was sorry that he and his sister caused me to get mud soaked as we were attempting to lift them up into the chopper. I told Lanh no problem and that I probably needed a bath anyway. We laughed.

Little Kim whispered in Lanh's ear once again, and Lanh told me his sister wants to know my name. *I paused a moment and leaned down and softly told Kim my name was My Friend You.* As soon as I said those three words, her eyes lit up, and she broke out with the cutest little giggle. Then she repeated the words *My Friend You* over and over again.

She struggled a little when saying the three words at first, but the more she said them, the easier it became for her. Apparently, these three words were the only English words she could pronounce. But each time she said, "My Friend You," her pretty little eyes would light up, and she would break out into joyous childish laughter. It was simply a beautiful sight to see her and to hear her say, "My Friend You."

Lanh said that in his language names of people meant something, and so he asked me the meaning of the words *My Friend You* so he could explain them to his little sister. I thought for a moment, and for the life of me, I didn't know why in the world I told little Kim my name was My Friend You in the first place, let alone know the meaning of the three words.

In a serious tone of voice, Lanh asked me the meaning of "My Friend You" a second time; I thought for a moment, then *told him to tell Kim that the meaning of "My Friend You" was that I would be her friend forever, and she would be mine—and that I would be that big bad marine who would "always" protect and watch over her.*

Lanh told Kim what I said; and as he was telling her, she looked up at me, flashed the prettiest smile, and began to giggle. She whispered in Lanh's ear again, and Lanh told me she had asked him how I would protect her. *I told Lanh to tell her that if she ever finds herself in danger to simply shout out our special three words* My Friend You, *and I would suddenly appear to protect her.*

Lanh told little Kim what I had said, and they talked to each other a few minutes. Then suddenly she stood up, smiled at me with those big beautiful dark-brown eyes, and loudly shouted, "My Friend You. My Friend You," and kept saying it.

It was clear that I was confused, and I turned to Lanh and asked him to explain to me why little Kim was calling for me. I told Lanh, "Your sister is not in any danger at this time. Therefore, at this time, she doesn't need my protection. So why is she calling out My Friend You?"

Lanh said that Kim was calling out for me because he had told his little sister that members of the hospital staff were looking for her to perform their medical examination on her. He explained that Kim was afraid of the medical exam and feels she was in some kind of danger and that if she shouts out, "My Friend You," the big bad marine would appear and protect her from this danger.

His explanation made sense, and now I fully understood why she was calling out, "My Friend You." I couldn't help but to laugh. Then I explained to Lanh, who explained to little Kim that, when I said "in danger," I meant "in danger with some bad guys, like the VC."

Lanh spent five minutes explaining to Kim what I had explained to him, and by her actions, Lanh had made it perfectly clear to her. Kim acknowledged to Lanh that she totally understands my meaning of "in danger." Then all three of us began to laugh, and laughed some more.

After our bout with joyous laughter, Little Kim whispered something into Lanh's ear, and he told me that Kim was asking me could her name also be My Friend You. I asked Lanh to ask Little Kim why she wanted the name My Friend You. Lanh asked her, and he told me, "She wants the name My Friend You so she can protect you when the bad guys come around."

When Lanh told me what Kim had said, it instantly brought tears to my eyes; I tried hard to conceal them, but a few escaped. Fighting back tears of joy, I told Lanh to tell his sister that "From this day forward, my name is My Friend You, and her name was My Friend You. My Friend You will be the way by which Kim and I will greet each other, and I will always protect her, and she will always protect me."

He translated everything I said to Kim, and as usual, her pretty brown eyes lit up, and this time, she came over and gave me a girlish hug. The hug made it official, *from this day forward, Kim and I officially had a special way by which we greeted one another, and a special relationship that parallels the relationship of a father and his daughter.*

As I sat there watching Kim attempt to hide from passing corpsmen walking the hallways of the hospital, I began thinking about how I could somehow adopt little Kim and take her stateside to my parents' home once my tour of duty in South Vietnam was completed.

My thoughts were interrupted by a female nurse asking me what the little girl's name was and whether she completed her medical examination. Evidently, Kim sensed what I and the hospital nurse were talking about because during our conversation she had gotten up from sitting beside Lanh and walked over, sat down beside me, and, to my surprise, snuggled up close to me, as if I were her protector.

The hospital nurse witnessed Little Kim's actions and began asking Lanh to assist her in translating a message to her. I spoke up and asked the nurse which room number should Kim come to for her exam, and the nurse said she should come to room number 4. I told the nurse I would personally bring Kim to room 4 in about five minutes. The nurse thanked me and departed down the hallway.

Little Kim closely watched the nurse as she disappeared down the hallway, and I noticed Kim had a puzzled look on her face. I asked Lanh to attempt to find out what was bothering her and tell me his findings. He and Kim held a brief conversation. Upon completion, Lanh said his sister felt something was wrong, but she can't rightfully figure it out.

I told Lanh to tell Kim that there was nothing wrong and that I simply told the nurse that I would see to it that Kim showed up for the exam. After Lanh translated what I had said to Kim, she told him to ask me how many sugar mints did I yet have. My reply was plenty. My answer prompted Little Kim to strike up a deal. She told Lanh to tell me that if I provided plenty sugar mints, she would go with the nurse for the medical examination but only if I and Lanh go to protect her.

Lanh and I promptly agreed to her deal, and I silently said to myself, how bright for a ten-year-old to think up such a thing. I further thought that not only was this little ten-year-old a pretty sight to behold, but she's a brainy one as well.

We located room number 4, and shortly thereafter, Kim's painless medical examination was completed. As predicted, the doctors found she suffered from numerous plant leaf cuts and various types of insect bites. They also noted she was in immediate need of proper nourishment and body hygiene.

While the hospital staff was administering Kim's medical examination, this provided Lanh and I a few minutes of private time together, and as soon as we were alone, Lanh asked me what my real name was and said he wanted to know it in case he attempted to contact me in the near future.

I told him that I sincerely wanted to be his friend and Kim's protector for life, and that my full name was Cpl. Donald Clark—and that the meaning of the word *Donald* was "ruler."

On a small notepad, I spelled out my full name and provided my work phone number and told him he could call me at that number at any time. He told me he would call me as soon as they place them in a temporary home and that he hopes their temporary home will be close to my base so that I'll have the opportunity to visit him and his sister.

I was thrilled to hear Lanh say he was going to call me once he was settled into his new home and that he wanted me to visit him and Kim. Then suddenly I became afraid with the thought there was a possibility he and Kim would be split up and be placed into separate temporary housing.

By this time, the nurse was walking Little Kim over to where Lanh and I were sitting, and when they came within twenty feet, Little Kim broke loose from her grip, ran, and leaped into my arms. When the nurse got close enough, I asked her if Lanh and Kim would be placed in the same temporary home. She said to ask base admin this question and that she would request they be housed in the same residence. I thanked her in advance for her actions.

Soon as the nurse walked away, a pretty young Vietnamese woman walked up and sat down directly across from where we were and didn't take her eyes from our direction. Her stare down was making me a little nervous, so I asked Lanh if he knew her, and he quickly said yes and that she was his mother's younger sister.

This made her his aunt, and I asked him her name. He said her name was Thien and that she was everything her name signified in his language, which was "heavenly." Thien had been cleaned up, and looked absolutely beautiful. She didn't look at all like she did several hours back when she was being lifted out of the muddy rice paddy. As I remembered, Thien was the young lady who cleverly managed to mastermind the children's escape from the VC.

While she sat staring me down, in return, I closely gave her a thorough observation and thought to myself, *Not only is this young lady a beautiful person to look at, but she is also brave and courageous.*

Couldn't help but to wonder if Thien spoke English, so I asked Lanh. He said he thought she spoke a little, but for me to ask her. Soon afterward, Thien and I locked eyes; just as we did, I figured I would jump at this opportunity to ask her if she spoke English.

Just when I was about to ask Thien, Little Kim interrupted and began pulling on Lanh's shirt sleeve and mine. She then whispered in Lanh's ear, and he turned and said his sister successfully completed her medical exam and that she now wanted the sugar mints I had promised her.

I told Lanh I would be more than happy to provide Kim the mints but was about to ask his aunt Thien questions concerning her English aptitude. Lanh told me, "I know for a fact she speaks some English, but now that I have given it some thought, I think now is not a good time for me to have that discussion with his aunt."

He provided the reason for his statement, and it was, "My aunt is still grieving over the death of three immediate family members by the hands of the VC during the village raid two weeks back, and until her mourning period is finished, she'll most likely not be answering any English-speaking questions or, for that matter, answering any questions at all." He then asked me, "Do you fully understand?"

I acknowledged to Lanh that I fully understood and further said I thought mourning the death of her family members was very honorable. I asked Lanh, "How long would Thien remain in mourning?" He said he didn't have that answer and that only Thien knew. He further said, normally, the mourning period lasted about ten days.

Little Kim interrupted us again and held out her little hand for some sugar mints. I only had a few left in my shirt pocket but was more than happy to give them to her. While chewing her mints, she would smile, and I would go so far as to say it was worth a million tons of sugar mints to see that angelic smile appear on that pretty little face of Kim's. She was a total darling.

By this time, a member of the hospital staff walked over to where we were sitting and informed us I had to leave the hospital and that he had to escort Thien and the children to their sleeping quarters for the night. I hugged Kim and Lanh and attempted to say goodbye to Thien, but, as usual, she avoided eye contact and was totally focused on the children.

It began to rain when I arrived back at my tent that night. As I began to bed down, my good friend Tee came to my bedside and quietly told me he heard about the trouble we faced trying to rescue the children in the jungle. I told him how frightened I was during the entire ordeal and that I figured he must have experienced this type of situation often, as much as he volunteered. Tee just laughed it off.

We then began to discuss all the praying that took place among my medevac crew members. I told Tee how each crew member had "thanked the good Lord" that none of the crew on board was killed.

Then, suddenly, I lost it and broke down and began sobbing like a newborn baby. Tee sat there holding my hand by my bedside for a good five minutes and allowed me to let it out. I had waited until I was in the company of a close friend before I let my emotions explode. I thanked my dear buddy for allowing me to go off on him like that, and he said he understood. And I knew he, in fact, did understand. Tee had flown on at least five times as many medevac flight missions as a volunteer crewman, as I had.

Tee made sure I had completely drained my emotions; then he softly said that he and the guys had been "praying for all of us," then he quietly hit the sack.

Yours truly hit the sack as well and tried hard to go to sleep but failed to sleep a wink. It wasn't because of the rainfall outside. I normally sleep soundly when it rains outside. The reason I couldn't get to sleep was easy to figure out.

I couldn't fall to sleep, because I was fascinated with that pretty little Vietnamese girl and was unable to shake her character from my mind. This little girl was so special, and I kept hearing over and over her pretty little voice saying in her own special way, "My Friend You."

Tee slept adjacent to my bunk, and when I got up and was dressing the next morning, he came over and said he noticed I was tossing and turning in the sack much more than usual last night. I told him I was having a hard time trying to get to sleep.

Tee said I must have fallen asleep at one point, because, several times last night, he overheard me talking in my sleep. I told him the reason was the events that occurred the day prior. I stated that I had met some incredibly brave children during the medevac and had been introduced to one special little girl. She was about nine or ten and had the prettiest smile and that I couldn't shake her from my mind. I told him I didn't sleep well last night, because I couldn't get that pretty little girl's face out of my mind.

I explained to Tee that, for some mysterious reason, I was attracted to this little girl and that the first chance I got that day I would go to hurry over to the hospital to check on her. Tee looked at me with a puzzled frown on his face. He then finished dressing, smiled as he passed by me, and went on his way.

While walking to the Engineering Office tent, I was informed by my corpsman buddy that the young lady by the name of Thien stayed awake last night watching over the children who were sleeping soundly. He said his fellow corpsman tried to give her a sleeping pill to help put her to sleep, but she refused to swallow it and simply sat up on the corner of her bed and watched over the sixteen children throughout the night.

During the following day, I was extremely busy logging aircraft flight time and was unable to get off work until well past 5:00 p.m. As soon as I was released from work, I swiftly walked over to the hospital to check on Little Kim, her brother Lanh, and the rest of the rescued children.

While walking to the hospital, I began a little soul-searching and attempted to figure out why I was attracted to this little girl. After kicking this subject around inside my head, I ended up with a dead-end conclusion. I ended my thoughts on the subject by reasoning the good Lord placed Kim in my life to protect and watch over and to simply leave it at that.

Upon my arrival at the hospital, Little Kim came running down the hallway practically dragging poor Lanh along with her. She had such joy in her heart, and it was all pure and sincere. The first thing she did when she reached me was close her pretty eyes, pause a few seconds, and shout out the words, "Hi, my name is My Friend You." I would say, "And my name is My Friend You." Then Little Kim would giggle and, of course, stretch her cute little arms out in hopes of retrieving some sugar mints.

We practically always began my visitation session by me asking Lanh how everything was going, and he would respond by saying, "Everything is going okay." Then I would follow that up by asking Lanh, "How has my pretty little girl been doing?" And he would say to her what I had said; and she would put a smile on her face, lean her shoulders back, and shout out, "My Friend You, okay?" And she would end it up with that cute girlish giggle of hers.

For some reason, I began telling Little Kim and Lanh about my parents during this visit, and as soon as I opened the subject, Lanh said something to Kim, and she left. I inquired as to where she was going, and Lanh told me he sent her to get him a drink of water at one of the water coolers down the hall. He said he did this because he didn't want her to hear about my parents, because that would get her to asking about their parents.

Lanh's actions caught me by surprise, so I asked him, "Did Kim, in fact, know about the death of your parents?" He said, "Yes, but Kim doesn't want to face reality concerning the fact her parents were killed, and I'm trying to avoid the topic as much as possible." I apologized to Lanh for bringing up the subject matter, and Lanh told me it wasn't my fault but that he would prefer not to discuss anyone's parents around Kim.

Then Lanh suddenly broke down and began crying. Not knowing what to do to ease his pain, I simply just sat there and watched over him as he cried. Thank goodness Little Kim was taking a long time with his drink of water, because Lanh must have cried a solid five minutes. He then ceased crying, straightened up, and quietly said they loved their parents very much.

As soon as Lanh expressed his love for his parents, Little Kim popped her pretty little head from around a hospital bed and was running toward us with Lanh's cup of water. When she arrived, half of the water had spilled onto the floor; and the second half was spilled when she came to an abrupt stop, leaned her shoulders back, and shouted, "My Friend You," and giggled. She was so full of life.

My visit with Lanh and Little Kim turned out to be a joyous one as usual. We laughed a lot, and Lanh even tried to teach me a Vietnamese song. I tried to get Kim to say Donald, but she insisted on calling me My Friend You. And she insisted on me calling her My Friend You. When I would call her Kim, she would shout back, "My Friend You." She was simply fascinated by those three words.

The following day's visit, we ate candy, drank soda pop, and simply enjoyed the four hours we were together. There were times we just sat there and simply did nothing. We settled down onto a hospital sofa for a good hour and did nothing but watch the hospital staff busily at work. We three were at peace at being around one another. We were an odd union, but to us, it didn't seem to matter. God had somehow joined us together, and we didn't fight it; we simply enjoyed it. We enjoyed every single moment we were together.

That evening, I returned to my tent, lay in my bunk, and dreamed of Little Kim as if she were my daughter. And I would dwell on this thought throughout the night and would vision her and me back at stateside, just hanging out and taking it easy.

Our base chaplain and I had discussed my desire to adopt Little Kim. The chaplain, a navy commander, told me it was difficult to adopt children from South Vietnam; and since I wasn't married, it would be almost impossible. I told him I would seek out a wife. He just chuckled and wished me luck. I could tell by his actions he thought I was crazy, but I was sincere about my desire to adopt this little girl. And, God willing, I will somehow find a way to do just that!

I was determined to see Little Kim, Lanh, and the children as much as possible while they were on base; and it seemed as though the workdays would never come to an end, and when they did, I would hurry to the base hospital to check on them.

As soon as I would arrive at the hospital, I would search for little Kim; and each time, she would be holding on to her brother, Lanh. When she would see me, she would scream out, "My Friend You," and she would always display the prettiest smile on her pretty little face.

Only when I got within ten feet of them would she let go of her brother and run up to me with that smile a-beaming and her pretty little hand extended out, looking for sugar mints. With a smile as pretty as that, I better have brought some sugar mints, and as always, I had my fatigue shirt pockets overflowing with them.

The medevac'd children had been on base for four days, and by now, I was providing sugar mints to all sixteen of the children. The supply of sugar mints that Corporal Chris was providing just wasn't enough, and I had to start purchasing sugar mints from our base PX store. On the fifth day, I bought out the PX store supply and had to supplement the sugar mints by purchasing jelly beans. I simply had to keep Little Kim and the children happy, and if candy was the answer, then candy it would be. By providing candy to all the children, I quickly became very popular with them. I would even drop by the hospital during my noon break to check in on the children and, of course, provide Kim and the rest of them some sweet treats from the PX. They soon began looking for me during the noon hour, and this made me feel like someone special.

It seemed as though Thien and the sixteen rescued children remained in base hospital care much longer, but they were only there for six days. On the afternoon of the sixth day, Tee and I arrived at the hospital to greet our newly found friends with pockets full of candy, and were informed the children and Thien were no longer there and that they had been bused off to an orphanage.

My corpsman buddy informed me of the name of the orphanage the children were sent to and that it had been recommended by the ranger officer who stumbled upon the children hiding in the jungle. He further stated the ranger officer was cousins to a brother-and-sister team who operated the orphanage in West Da Nang.

I prayed that night for God to help me locate the place where Little Kim was sent so I could continue to visit her. I was fond of her brother and all the other rescued children, but Kim held a special place in my heart. And, as I fell asleep that night, I knew God would allow me the opportunity to see her again and hear her sweet little voice shout out our three special words *My Friend You.*

That following morning while eating breakfast in our mess hall, Tee and I were discussing methods of how we could locate the children's orphanage, and Corporal Tee came up with the grand idea of tracking down the South Vietnamese ranger.

We both figured that tracking down the whereabouts of the South Vietnamese ranger should be relatively easy, and, once achieved, we can get from the ranger the address of his cousin's orphanage where the children were bused to yesterday.

What a brilliant idea of Tee's, because the ranger's location was determined easily early that morning. We made contact with him, and he readily provided the address and phone numbers of his cousin's orphanage. He further provided the names of his two cousins who had recently opened the orphanage.

The two cousins' names were Tuyen and Trang. The ranger said Tuyen operated the home, along with the help of three lady assistants; and her policeman brother, Trang, provided financial support and helped out in many other ways.

141

The ranger further stated that his two cousins Tuyen and Trang's parents were also killed by VC and that they decided to make their parents' home into an orphanage in their parents' honor. He said they hadn't yet named the orphanage but that the home was located about a dozen miles northwest of Marble Mountain.

After hanging up from talking to the ranger, I shouted out with joy because, *once again, my good Lord had smiled down on me and provided me the opportunity to reunite with Lanh and Little Kim, and she would again receive sugar mints from that big bad marine she called My Friend You, who was always going to protect and watch over her.*

"Jesus, friend of little children be a friend to me, take my hand and forever keep me close to thee."

"HELICOPTER DON WAS ABOARD AS A VOLUNTARY CREW MEMBER DURING THE CHILDREN RESCUE MISSION"

Purchasing Guitar Strings

AFTER WORKING HARD ALL WEEK long, the sound of Saturday liberty call was a sweet welcomed sound for most marines and navy personnel at our base at Marble Mountain. Those of us who were fortunate to be awarded liberty normally headed off toward Da Nang and highly looked forward to the grand excitement we hoped to experience while visiting the city.

Military intelligence had warned our base and nearby bases that enemy activity was increasing in Da Nang and its surrounding villages. And they had been providing cautionary warnings to remain alert at all times.

Even as we caught taxicabs into Da Nang, we were receiving additional words of caution from base MPs and senior NCOs who were also headed to town on liberty, and they were drop-dead serious about their admonitions. They made it perfectly clear never once forget where you're at and why you're there.

Military intelligence nor NCOs didn't have to keep reminding Tee or me. We firmly adhered to their warnings and remained on high alert each time we went on liberty into Da Nang.

Our dear friend Chris traveled into Da Nang with us on this particular liberty, and we really enjoyed his company. We referred to Chris as our blue-eyed soul brother from Chi Town, and if a firefight erupted, you would want old Chris to share your foxhole because this guy wasn't afraid of anything or anybody. He simply loved to fight and was damn good at it.

Chris had recently flown on a medevac rescue mission as a voluntary crewman, and the UH34D he was flying in was shot down, and the chopper's door gunner was seriously wounded. Chris immediately stood in for the wounded door gunner, and several crewmen aboard that aircraft said after they had returned to base that they might not have safely returned had it not been for the heroic manner in which Chris manned that chopper's M60 in laying down cover fire.

He would hang with Tee and me every chance he got, and we got along great. I think old Chris recognized the "country" in both Tee and me, and he sort of enjoyed being around that. He had grown up hard on the cold streets of Southside, Chicago, and it was comforting for him to hang around a couple of down-home square type of guys, like Tee and me, from time to time.

When our taxicab reached Da Nang, old Chris wanted to hit the red-light district and spend two dollars on a cute working girl while we wanted to do other things. So we departed from Chris. Tee skipped over to a nearby music record store, and I walked until I located a telephone booth.

Two weeks had slid by since the medevac rescue mission where I was introduced to Little Kim, her brother Lanh, and their young aunt Thien. I had been telephoning the orphanage home Little Kim and Lanh were staying daily since the day they were shipped there and was never able to reach Lanh.

Fortunately, I was most always able to speak to Tuyen, the owner of the orphanage, who spoke fluent English. Tuyen would serve as Little Kim's interpreter, which enabled me to chat with Little Kim (via Tuyen) almost on a daily basis. And she would tell me the reason Lanh was unavailable was because he was out working.

Tuyen would keep me up-to-date and tell me how things were going at the orphanage. Then she would put Little Kim on the phone, and Little Kim would most always shout out, "Hi, My Friend You." Then she would ask me (via Tuyen) when I was to go visit her and provide her more sugar mints. Then little Kim would always end our little conversation with her cute girlish giggle.

With Tuyen serving as my interpreter, I would explain to Little Kim that I would be visiting her right now if only I could. I would inform them that the area where the orphanage was located had been classified "off-limits" to American GIs. And that, as soon as the "off-limit regulation" is lifted, I would be over to visit them as soon as I was awarded liberty. And I'd also be bringing plenty of sugar mints.

As always, we would end our phone conversation with Little Kim shouting, "Bye, My Friend You!" And I, too, would say, "Bye, My Friend You." As soon as I said goodbye to Little Kim, Tuyen immediately came back on the phone and said that she really understood why her home was off-limits and that she had heard locals discussing increased VC movement in her area on several different occasions, and that it was causing her great concern for the safety of the children.

Then Tuyen would begin to cry. Hearing Tuyen softly crying over the phone was disturbing, but some locals wanting to use the phone were getting pissed at me for talking so long, so I could only spend a minute attempting to calm Tuyen down. She heard the locals shouting at me on the other end and told me that she appreciated my calming words and that she would be all right.

Glad to hear that Tuyen would be okay, I then finally exited the phone booth. As soon as I walked down the street a ways, I ran into a couple of marine buddies I had recently met on base. They had been in-country for almost a year now, and all they wanted to do was to go straight to one of the popular bars and get wasted. Their reasoning for getting drunk was it relieved them of the many war-related horrors they had witnessed or were about to witness.

These guys had every justifiable reason for getting drunk, but drinking alcohol and getting wasted simply wasn't my schtick, so I quickly parted ways with my marine buddies and walked over to the record store to join back up with Tee.

After listening to some new released soul tunes, Tee and I left the store, and as soon as we hit the payment, we ran into two more of our marine friends on base, and after briefly talking to them, we learned they were in search of finding a couple of nice young working girls and getting their rocks off.

Normally, they would spend two dollars for a quickie and be satisfied, but our two buddies said they had done without for an extended period of time and that they were going to pay for an hour worth of sexual pleasure. Normally, an hour's worth of sex with a pretty young working girl would cost five dollars. Tipping was always in order, and many of the guys would tip their girl if they had a good time.

Many of the working girls whom GIs socialized with sincerely liked the GI, but some of the working girls only pretended they enjoyed the GI's company. In some cases, these working girls actually hated the GI and were VC.

There were several documented episodes where pretty young working girls collaborated with the VC and caused a GI to be killed or seriously hurt, which is why most American GIs touring Da Nang on liberty were armed, just in case they stumbled upon Victor Charlie.

Tee and I never had getting a two-dollar quickie from a working girl on our agenda while we were on liberty in Da Nang. We concentrated mainly on shopping. Tee mainly shopped for soul music albums, while I normally shopped for souvenirs to mail back home to Mom or sheet music to be used while playing my guitar that I purchased while stationed in Okinawa.

We also didn't drink alcohol, so we never hung out at the bars and taverns. I guess you can say Tee and I were boring to be around while in Da Nang. And because of that, we normally ended up by ourselves, doing our own simple, boring thing.

During this particular hot afternoon in late July of 1965, I went along with Tee to another one of his record stores to listen to the Motown sound, but after an hour or so in the store, my ears began to hurt, and I told Tee I needed to leave. His mission today was to buy records.

My mission while on liberty was to buy a set of new guitar strings so I could continue my quest to become a good guitar player. I was playing with the guitar's original strings, and they failed to produce a decent sound. It was time to substitute them for a brand-new set.

While growing up, my parents would say, "Son, if you indulge in a task, try to be as good as you can." In following their teachings, I wanted to master playing the guitar and started taking the Les Paul home study course to guitar playing while stationed in Okinawa. I had planned on continuing my pursuit to mastering the guitar while being stationed at Marble Mountain.

Six marines in my sleep tent had guitars, and every one of them was damn good at plucking the instrument. I wanted to play better than anyone in my tent, so practicing on my guitar in the evening became my passion.

After leaving Tee at his favorite record store, I must have walked over a mile in search of a shop that sold new quality guitar strings. While resting on a bench, my eyes came upon this little shop nearby that had about six new guitars hanging from the ceiling.

As I entered the small store, I noticed the guitars hanging from the ceiling were made with good craftsmanship and appeared to be of fairly good quality. I reasoned, if this shop carried quality guitars to peddle, then maybe it would also have quality guitar strings to peddle as well.

As soon as I entered the store, an elderly Vietnamese man approached me and began speaking in his native tongue. I didn't have a clue as to what he was telling me, and he didn't know what I was saying.

I tried hard to explain to the elderly man my need to buy a new set of guitar strings. I kept pointing to the guitars he had hanging from the ceiling and practically shouting my request to buy new strings.

During my attempt to explain my need to the elderly man, I faintly heard a familiar voice say, "Sir, do you need my assistance in talking with the store merchant?" Then from the corner of my eye, I noticed a young Vietnamese teenage boy approaching me from the rear.

Then suddenly without saying a word, the young boy and I embraced. We must have hugged each other for a good three minutes. This hugging activity was blowing the elderly storekeeper's mind.

Lanh finally said, "Corporal Don, how are you doing?" Then Lanh explained our situation to the store merchant. Then he said his little sister, Kim, always talked about me and that she really wanted to see me. I told Lanh that hopefully I would be able to come to the orphanage and visit Little Kim soon—and that, at that time, I was on a mission to purchase a new set of good-quality guitar strings for my guitar I played during my leisure time back at the base.

Lanh spoke to the elderly store owner. Then he said the store merchant did have several brands of guitar strings to sell. Then the storekeeper reached behind a counter and brought out a display of about eight different brands of new guitar strings.

I asked Lanh to ask the elderly merchant which guitar strings contained the best quality. The merchant pointed to the strings packaged in yellow. Lanh told me the merchant wants to sell the yellow package because they have been in his store a long time.

Lanh and the elderly merchant engaged in about a three-minute heated discussion in their native tongue, and, finally, Lanh said the guitar strings contained in the green package were "really" the best quality. I thanked Lanh for the tip and asked him to ask the old man the price of the strings in the green package.

Asking the price of the guitar strings contained in the green packaging caught the old merchant by surprise. The old man looked at me as if trying to figure out how I knew the strings in the green package were the best quality. Lanh and the elderly merchant engaged in another discussion, and, finally, Lanh said the price he was asking was four dollars, but they were normally two dollars.

I told Lanh to tell the old man that the price of four dollars was too high and that I was only willing to pay two dollars. I then pulled two dollars from my wallet and laid them on the store display countertop.

Lanh told the merchant what I had said, and the merchant looked madly at me; then he spoke to Lanh. Lanh told me the old store merchant said two dollars was not enough money and that I had to pay more money, or no deal. Then the old store merchant began placing the guitar strings back on his store shelf.

I replied, "Okay, I would buy them for three dollars." Lanh spoke to the store merchant and told him what I had said, and he told Lanh to tell me, "It's a deal, Marine." Then the old man flashed a big-ass grin on his face.

Reluctantly, I paid the three dollars, and the store merchant packaged up the guitar strings. I asked Lanh how much of the three dollars did he receive, and he informed me the old man would most likely give him twenty-five cents for his interpreting assistance. I then pulled out a fresh new dollar bill and handed it to Lanh and thanked him for his assistance.

Still elated to find Lanh in the store, I asked him, "How long did you work today, and what exact time did you get off?" Lanh smiled at me and stated he can get off any time he wanted to and that he set his own hours to interpret for the elderly store merchant.

So I asked him if he could leave now, and Lanh said he would check with the store merchant. They talked; then Lanh turned to me and sadly said the old man really needs his interpreting services the next two hours because a GI was coming into the store for a large instrument purchase. I told Lanh to remain and help out the old man and that hopefully I would see him the next time I visited the orphanage.

Lanh and I embraced each other while saying our goodbyes, and he told me that he couldn't wait to tell little Kim that he had seen me this afternoon. I told Lanh I had to rush and catch up with my friend Tee. Then I exited the store, elated that I had seen Lanh and that I now know where to locate him during daylight hours in Da Nang.

It had been well over an hour since Tee and I had separated. Since Tee was on foot, I figured he couldn't be too far away. Almost each time Tee and I came to Da Nang together, we ended up frequenting the same area of town. He would most always end up in a store that contained soul record albums, and I knew where the three of them were located.

Tee loved music, especially soul music. He would hang around in the record store and listen to each soul record album in its entirety prior to making a purchase. So I figured all I had to do was walk by the record stores that Tee frequented, and I would most likely find him.

After walking by two of the records stores Tee regularly frequented and failing to locate him, I began experiencing hunger cramps in my stomach. So I hastily walked a few blocks to a place where most US servicemen ate at while on liberty in Da Nang. The place was called the Hamburger Café. They served good burgers in this place, and I couldn't wait to wrap my lips around one.

After entering the café and grabbing a seat, I impatiently waited for one of the table waitresses to take my order. She finally came to my table, and I ordered a large hamburger, french fries, and a large soda. I gave the tiny waitress a shiny half-dollar and asked her if she could "rush" my order because I was starving. She smiled and graciously took the half-dollar and hurried to the kitchen to place my order.

Within a matter of five minutes, the waitress had returned, and I was munching on a juicy burger and fries. The half-dollar given to her did the trick. While eating my burger, I heard a familiar voice shouting the words, "Guitar strings, Corporal Don." I looked up, and there was Lanh holding up the package of guitar strings I had recently purchased.

Lanh told me that he had been looking for me to provide me the guitar strings I'd purchased from the old store merchant. Evidently, I left the elderly merchant's store in a big hurry, and in my haste, I had accidently left my guitar strings in his store, like a dumb idiot.

All while Lanh was talking to me, I was thinking to myself, *What an honorable young guy to run all over Da Nang looking for me to hand me the guitar strings I had bought.* I pulled out two dollars and gave them to Lanh to show my appreciation for what he had done. If I had more money on me, I would have tipped him even more.

As he reached up for the dollar bills, I couldn't help but to notice how he kept his face turned to his left side. It appeared he was turning his face in this manner in order to conceal something. I asked Lanh what was wrong. Then I kindly asked him to turn the other side of his face toward me.

Reluctantly, Lanh turned his head to the right, and I clearly saw what he was attempting to conceal. His right eye was badly swollen and turning blue. His right cheek bone was also badly bruised, and his bottom lip had suffered a deep cut.

After carefully checking Lanh's facial wounds, I reasoned he had been in some kind of fight and figured he was a little embarrassed about it, and so I didn't inquire about it. I figured he would tell me all about the episode when he was damn good and ready.

The waitress seated Lanh next to me, and he also ordered a large burger and fries. Once seated, I was able to see some additional bruises to Lanh's arms and legs. I reasoned the fight must have been rather brutal, and the more I observed his wounds, the madder I got at myself for not being there to help him.

We both remained quiet until after his food arrived, and even after he had taken a few bites. Then Lanh spoke and said he had recently received his cuts and bruises from fighting with a couple of street thugs. He explained when he ran out of the merchant's store in search of me that he failed to conceal his activity—and allowed three street thugs that were standing on a nearby corner to figure out that he was on an errand for the store merchant.

Not concealing his actions resulted in the three thugs following him with hopes of catching him and taking either money or items of value that the thugs reasoned the store merchant had provided him to transport to another store location or to a nearby paying customer.

He further explained that this was how some of Da Nang's street thugs made their money, by beating up store errand runners and forcefully taking goods they were transporting that contained value or money the errand runner was carrying to provide change to a store customer.

Lanh explained how the three street thugs caught up with him at a dead-end alleyway and how they were having their way beating him and demanding any money that he might be carrying. Since they were older and bigger than he was, he said he was helpless and their punches were really hurting him.

He said that, after a while, he was unable to withstand the punishment they were inflicting on him and that he was very close to being knocked out until, all of a sudden, out of nowhere, up walked four of his close friends. He said these were working girlfriends he had met while interpreting for GIs during his evening hustle.

Lanh stated that each of his friends had a reputation for carrying razor-sharp switchblade knives—and that they were locally famous for knowing how to properly use them. He said the three street thugs challenged his four working girlfriends, and they returned the challenge by cutting up the three street thugs.

He continued by saying when his girlfriends finished cutting on the street thugs, it had become one hell of a bloody mess in that alleyway. He said he practically owed his life to his four working girl friends and that he sincerely thanked them, and even tried to offer them money, but they wouldn't accept any.

They simply hugged Lanh and sent him on his way to find the owner of the recently purchased guitar strings. Meanwhile, the waitress brought our food out, but after listening to Lanh's bloody story, my appetite disappeared, so I leaned back in my chair and checked out all the other GIs socializing inside the café.

Lanh certainly didn't play around when it came to eating. He was eating his food like it was going to fly away. While watching him eat, I couldn't help but to wonder how nice teenage boys like him managed to survive in war-torn Vietnam.

When Lanh finished eating, he raised his head, looked me straight in the eyes, and asked me if I had a family back in the US, and if I missed them. I told him about my mom (Gwendolyn), my dad (Curtis), and younger brother (Kenneth). I emphasized the fact that I sincerely missed my family dearly and that I hoped all went well during my time in his country so that I could safely return home and unite with them.

In a mature statement, way beyond his years, Lanh stood up and said, "Corporal Don, Kim and I and all of my fellow countrymen who embrace freedom hope that you return home safely. We thank all American servicemen that are fighting for our freedom in our country." Upon completing his statement, he flashed a big smile and sat down.

His choice of words simply blew me away, and all I could think to do at the time was to reciprocate his big smile. After smiling at each other for several minutes, I reached out and tightly hugged Lanh and, with tears dripping from my face, said a soft "thank you." I was so touched by his choice of words, and so proud of this little guy. I gently leaned over and hugged him again.

Our moment of gratefulness only lasted a minute, because suddenly our waitress ran up to our table in a panic and in broken English warned us of big trouble stirring outside by the curbside. We were clueless as to what she was warning us about until Lanh looked out the front window.

While looking outside, Lanh turned to me and, with a strained look on his face, told me to quickly leave the café because there was going to be trouble.

When Lanh got upset, his English-speaking skills vastly worsened, and I was having difficulty understanding what he was saying. Meanwhile, all the customers inside the café were stirring about like bumblebees and checking out the commotion that was occurring out by the street curbing.

Curiosity was getting the best of me, so I decided to look outside myself with hopes of obtaining an understanding of what the commotion was about. My eyes focused in on about a dozen thuggish-looking guys, standing outside by the curbing, looking up toward the café, and hollering something that I was unable to understand because they were speaking in their language.

It also appeared that half of them had what appeared to be large objects in their possession. I heard them hollering Lanh's name. Also standing out there and hollering Lanh's name were the three street thugs who were cut up by Lanh's four working girlfriends earlier in the day.

Their clothing was bloodstained, and they had received medical treatment because each of the three had white bandages wrapped around their arms and legs, which provided me a clear indication that Lanh's friends sliced them up pretty bad.

I attempted to calm Lanh down and asked him to translate what the thugs were shouting. Lanh said the thugs were saying they were aware he was inside the café and for him to come outside. He further said they were shouting there was nowhere he can run because they have the rear exits blocked.

At the same time Lanh was translating, he was gathering up his personal belongings, and I asked him, "Where in the hell do you think he was going?" Lanh looked me dead in the eye and said he was going outside to meet the thugs and get it over with. He further stated this situation was his problem and that he wasn't afraid.

As Lanh lunged for the front door of the café, I jumped in front of him and shoved him back into his seat. I told him the street thugs were going to gang up on him. In addition, I informed Lanh that some of them carried large sticks and that he wouldn't have a chance fighting these guys alone. In addition, I stressed that his fight was my fight and that there was no way I was allowing him to fight these clowns alone.

Emphatically, Lanh shouted at me to let him go and that he didn't want me to get hurt. He stated the street thugs only wanted to get even for the licking they suffered from the hands of his girl-friends earlier in the day and that this showdown was bound to happen sooner or later.

Again, Lanh pleaded with me to stay out of the situation, and even said that if I joined in the fight, I may stir up trouble from the town locals. Then he eased toward the door, and as he leaped for the front door, I grabbed his arm and again shouted to him that I was not going to stand by and watch these assholes beat him. Then I began searching around for a club or something to use as a weapon.

While I was searching for a weapon, Lanh quickly ran past me and out the café onto the street. He even attempted to run past the street thugs but failed at his attempt and was tackled by one of them.

While viewing from the café window, I witnessed Lanh putting up a good fight, but the street thugs were too much for him and were literally kicking my young friends behind parts. Unable to locate anything reasonable to use as a weapon, I quickly exited the cafe and began helping Lanh in the street fight.

First thing I did when I reached the fight scene was tackle one of the thugs and take the club he was carrying. I then commenced to put the club to use and crack a few heads. With the employment of this club, I was cracking head after head. And during this brief period of time, Lanh and I were winning this thing.

Then as I swung my club at the head of the gang leader, I must have swung too hard, because I lost my grip, and the large club went flying through the air. I then began hitting the street thugs with what I was born with, my fist. Lanh and I were outnumbered, and we were getting beat down. It was just a matter of minutes before we both would be knocked out.

Then I faintly heard a voice say, "Marine, we got your back." Then, all of a sudden, I heard fist hitting jaws, and teeth began flying around. I heard fist hitting heads so hard that I saw eyes began popping out of sockets. I heard bones cracking, and with joy to my ears, I began to hear our street thug opponents begging for mercy.

Shortly after the street thugs had been beaten to a pulp, I made them promise to never bother Lanh again. The thugs complied too my demand; then all twelve of them swiftly ran down the back alleyway and out of sight, licking their wounds like little bitches.

Lanh and I then turned to the two marines who helped us kick ass and to even the odds. And we sincerely "thanked these guys for helping us." It had turned out to be just two marines who helped us kick ass. They were two young lance corporals who were in town on liberty. They were part of a First Force Recon Team that was stationed about a klick down the beachhead—in close proximity to Marble Mountain.

Recon marines were well trained in hand-to-hand combat and normally worked behind enemy lines to perform top secret missions. They were specifically trained on how to put the hurt on a person. During our street brawl, their expertise was thoroughly demonstrated . . . because, for what I saw, these two marine recon guys were literally kicking the shit out of the street thugs, and they were doing it with ease.

Lanh and I were fortunate these two recon marines were enjoying their liberty in Da Nang and happened to get hungry and head over to the café at the time we were getting beat down. It's like God sent them our direction. "Praise the Lord!"

After buying the two helpful recon marines hamburgers and fries, Lanh and I said our goodbyes to them, and my liberty time was coming to an end. I told Lanh I wanted to spend my last hour on liberty talking to him, and I wanted to talk in private, and not in a crowded place like the cafe.

Lanh thought for a moment and stated there was a small park about a block away—and that we could talk there. As soon as we reached the small park and located a bench to use, we sat down, and I firmly told Lanh I was deeply concerned about the way in which he was currently making his money and that if he continued his street hustling he would end up beaten to death and thrown in the back of one of Da Nang's alley trash cans—and that Little Kim would end up not having an older brother to look after her and protect her while she was growing up in the world.

With as much emphasis as I could muster up, I continued my plea by saying that I sincerely cared about him and that I didn't want to hear about him getting hurt. I emphatically told him he would have gotten hurt real bad this afternoon if I and the two recon marines hadn't jumped in to help him fight off the gang of street thugs.

Then I walked over to where he was sitting, placed my hands on his shoulders, and caringly asked Lanh why he just didn't simply get a normal job to make his money and cease this dangerous street hustling type of life.

Upon completing my lecture to Lanh, I went and sat down on an old fruit crate, lowered my head, and began to softly cry. Lanh walked over, put his arms around me, and gave me a warm embrace. He softly said, "Don't cry, Corporal Don." But cry I did. I must have sat on that stupid fruit crate and cried like a newborn baby for several minutes. I sincerely cared about this kid and his little sister and didn't want anything harmfully stupid to happen to them in their war-torn country.

For several minutes, we both were silent; then Lanh broke the silence by saying, "Corporal Don, I'm very much aware that you care about my little sister and me, and that you are afraid something bad will happen to me which will eventually adversely affect Kim. And I totally understand why you are concerned about me hustling in the streets."

Then a grin appeared on his thin little face, and he said that maybe my attitude will change toward his life of street hustling once I allow him the opportunity to explain why he hustled in Da Nang's streets. I willfully agreed to hear him out, and he began by saying the reason that he use to hustle money in the streets of Da Nang was to help his parents out monetarily with living expenses.

But since his parents were dead, he said he currently hustled to provide much-needed money to Tuyen's orphanage. He said in the short time that he, Kim, and his aunt Thien had stayed there, they had become very fond of Tuyen and that Tuyen needed help monetarily to buy food, children's clothing, and other necessary items for her kids housed in her home.

He went on to say that Tuyen was extremely nice to all of her orphaned children, and if it wasn't for her taking care of these kids, they would probably have ended up seriously hurt, or even dead. With sincere emphasis, Lanh said he really enjoyed providing Tuyen with the majority of his street-hustling money.

While Lanh paused, I stepped up and told him that what he was doing with the money he received from his dangerous street hustling was honorable, but that I remained fearful for him and wished that he would find a safer way to make money. I also told him that by the looks of his worn-out clothing, he must not be making a lot of money from street hustling.

Lanh laughed at me and said he makes good money interpreting for GIs and working girls in the evenings and store merchants during the day. He went on to say that he makes in a day what the average kid his age makes in a month working a normal job. He stated he wears these dirty worn-out clothing to get GIs to feel sorry for him—and that the more the American servicemen felt sorry for him, the more money they would tip him for his interpreting services for store merchants and working girls.

Wanting to make sure that I completely understood, Lanh said once again that he earned the majority of his money in the evenings, interpreting for GIs who are seeking sexual pleasure from a working girl in Da Nang. He said he had contacts with some of the prettiest working girls in the city. He further said many of the working girls tip him for directing GIs to their place of business.

Lanh then stood up, proudly pulled out twenty-nine dollars from his pants pocket, and boastfully said that he made this amount of dough in just one day of hustling. He went on to say that as long as American GIs continue to arrive in Da Nang on liberty, looking for a good time, he would continue to earn good money.

He then stood tall, stuck his chest out, reared back his shoulders, and said, "Corporal Don, do you know I am one of the most sought-out interpreters by American GIs in the entire red-light district of northern Da Nang? I'm famous, Corporal Don. I'm somebody."

I reach out and hugged Lanh and softly told him that I know that he was, in fact, somebody and that I was very proud of him. He seemed to seriously enjoy my commendable remarks and just sat there soaking in my words for a few minutes.

We ended our private discussion with him informing me that he had been doing this for the past two years and that he would catch rides into Da Nang from his small village and begin his street hustling.

So I reasoned that he had been doing this about two years prior to our medevac rescue meeting. In that amount of time, he had become damn good at street hustling, and his English-speaking skills had made him popular with some of the prettiest working girls in the city.

After thanking Lanh for explaining why he hustled in Da Nang's streets, I told him he was a very good young person and that providing his street-earned money to an orphanage that he, his sister, and aunt had only been living a short while was a very good gesture. I also told him his parents, who were looking down on him from heaven, would be extremely proud of his good deeds as well.

Lanh thanked me for mentioning his parents and further stated that providing money to assist the orphanage even made his aunt Thien proud of him and that the orphans living there also appreciated his monetary support. He also stated he enjoyed giving money to

Tuyen and her older brother, who owned the home. He said Tuyen's brother was a nice man, and a Da Nang policeman.

He then ceased talking and lowered his head into his hands for a few minutes of inner reflections. Then Lanh excitingly said that his money-hustling activities on the streets of Da Nang made him feel like he had a purpose in life. He then paused and began to quietly cry.

After a few minutes of silence, Lanh looked up with eyes full of tears and quietly said he really enjoyed our talk today concerning his safety and that he was much honored that I personally was sincerely concerned about his personal safety. I could easily tell that he was earnestly struggling with his future decisions.

We hugged each other, and I told him it was time for me to begin my return to Marble Mountain. As always, I told Lanh to say hello to Little Kim for me, and he shot back with, "Corporal Don, you mean to say hello to My Friend You, right, Corporal Don?" We laughed, and he walked with me for a couple of blocks, then said he was going to head off and begin walking toward the red-light district to begin his evening interpreting duties.

There was a record music store two blocks up the street, so I swiftly began walking in that direction with hopes that my buddy Tee would be inside the store listening to and/or attempting to purchase a popular soul tune.

The closer I got to the record store, the easier it was to hear the record the store was playing on its turntable. Most record stores had outside speakers installed, and as they would play a record for a prospective buyer, the sound would come over the store's exterior speaker to entice another GI walking the street to stop in and make a purchase.

As I approached the doorway of the record store, I could clearly hear the sounds of sweet soul music blasting from the exterior speakers. When I looked inside the store, I saw my dear friend Tee standing beside the record turntable, listening to a hit soul tune. He had his eyes close and had a big shit-eating grin on his face. Tee would flash his famous grin when he was feeling happy, so the soul record he was listening to must have really made him feel happy, because he had one big-ass grin across his face.

Trying to surprise Tee was extremely hard to accomplish. I slipped into the record store and silently walked up behind him and waited for that exact moment, and, suddenly, Tee turned around and said, "Hi, Corporal DJ, I see you."

We greeted each other and checked the time to see how much time we had remaining on liberty. According to our wristwatches, we had about three hours prior to catching a taxi back to base.

Tee wished to remain in the record store and continue listening to more soul sounds. I felt hunger pains growing and decided to skip over to the Hamburger Café and sink my teeth into a juicy burger. Tee promised to join me at the front entrance to the café in about an hour so we could catch our taxi back to base.

When I walked through the door of the café, the first person I laid eyes upon was Lanh. He was interpreting for a GI with one of the most beautiful working girls I had seen in the Nam. She was simply gorgeous, and I said to myself, *What a shame this young beautiful girl is wasting her life prostituting when she is so beautiful.*

Lanh noticed me as I entered the café, and after he completed his negotiations, he joined me at my table and told me that he thought I had already caught a taxicab back to base. I explained to him I had some time to kill, and I thought the best way in which to achieve that end was to come to the café, order a large one, and chow down.

The waitress took my order, and I asked Lanh who the young girl he just interpreted for was. He told me her name was Khan and that she was his age and one of the most popular working girls in the area. He said she demanded top dollar. I said that she was beautiful and that I could easily understand how she could demand a higher price for her charming services.

Khan has a baby girl to feed and look after, Lanh explained. He further stated her parents and other family members had been killed during the war and that at the early age of twelve she had to do whatever was necessary in order to survive. He said she was raped by a group of VC soldiers two years ago and became pregnant. When she became pregnant and had nowhere to go, Lanh said his mother took her into their home and helped her along.

He continued by saying his parents had done a lot of helping young kids when they had lost their parents during the war in his country. By this time, my order had arrived, and Lanh was checking it out with hungry eyes, so I told the waitress to bring him the same as I had ordered. While waiting on Lanh's food, I asked him to tell me more about his dad and mother. I made sure to explain to him that if he felt it too painful to talk about, he didn't have to endure the pain.

Lanh thought a while about what I had said and decided to tell me about his father and mother. He was proud of them and wanted me to know some of the good things about them. While eating, Lanh began telling me about his father. He began by saying his father was considered one of the three village leaders and that his dad helped to shape most of the policies that governed their village.

He stated his father was the youngest of three brothers and that his uncles, like his father, were killed in the war. He then shifted to his mother and said that she was very supportive of his father and that she was highly respected in their small village.

Lanh spoke about the dignified manner in which his father carried himself and how most of the villagers looked up to him for advice and counsel. He said his mother was highly popular in his village and that she was practically the only woman that sat in during village policy meetings. He further stated both his father and his mother were formally educated and were teachers in their village. His father taught high school classes, while his mother taught elementary school classes.

While discussing his parents, there were several times Lanh would cease talking and deal with his emotional struggle. Discussing his parents had to have been difficult for him, and there were several times I noticed tears dripping from his face.

It was extremely difficult for me to listen to Lanh talking about his parents and not tear up myself. Marines don't tear up; they just kick ass. But listening to Lanh that particular evening, I did, in fact, drop a tear, and not one but many.

The manner in which Lanh spoke of his parents made it obvious that he loved them very much. He continued on to explain how his father tried hard to provide for his family by working his small rice field. He said that sometimes the rice field failed to turn a profitable crop yield, and this made it extremely difficult for his father to pay his bills.

As tears began to swell up under his eyelids again, he softly said that when his father's rice field did yield a good crop, the crop was often taken by force by the Viet Cong. He said leaders of the VC would enter their small village and demand that his father and the other village farmers gather up their rice crops and provide most of it to them, to feed their hungry fighters.

He continued by telling me about the time his father attempted to hide much of his rice after a good sizable yield. But that his father's neighbor, a villager who was pro-VC, informed the VC of his father's intended actions. With deep emotional pain, Lanh managed to say that a ban of VC came to their home and inflicted severe bodily injuries on his father. As a result of that beating, his father walked around their village with a noticeable limp, and afterward, he began using a walking cane.

Lanh said his father tried to avoid talking about his hatred of the Viet Cong and their destruction of his country around him and his sister. He said even though his father tried hard to conceal his feelings in their home and not get his family involved, Lanh said it was easy for him to sense how hateful his father was toward the Viet Cong.

Lanh was beginning to take long pauses and beginning to choke up. I reasoned it was becoming too difficult for him to continue discussing his parents and their situation, so I stood up and suggested he cease discussing them and that he discuss something else. He agreed, then quickly shifted his conversation to once again talking about the streets of Da Nang.

While Lanh was taking a restroom break, I managed to check the time. And it showed I had about an hour left prior to having to hail down a taxicab and begin my journey back to base to avoid being in violation of curfew. I began to look out the large front window of the café for my friend Tee. As soon as I peered out the window, there he appeared, with an armful of record albums.

I waved him down. He entered the café and ordered a soda, and when Lanh came out of the head, we said our goodbyes, and Tee and I began hailing down a taxi to begin our short trip back to base. Lanh walked outside with us and emphatically told me not to get into the taxicab that had pulled over to the curb to pick us up.

I listened to Lanh, told the taxi driver to drive on, and asked Lanh what was the problem. He said VC Corporal Don, VC. I understood, and we hailed down another taxicab. This time, the taxicab met Lanh's approval, so after embracing Lanh, Tee and I entered the cab and began our six-mile trip back to Marble Mountain.

Just prior to Lanh shutting the taxicab door, he said, "Corporal Don, you might want these." Then he handed me my newly purchased guitar strings. Evidently, I had left them in our seat at the café. This made the second time Lanh had to give them to me . . . Both Lanh and I laughed. While entering the taxi, I told Tee that I will never forget this day that I purchased guitar strings in a small shop in Da Nang.

The two most important words: "Thank you."
The most important word: "We."
The least important word: "I."

"LITTLE KIM AS A 5 YEAR OLD"

Lanh's Survival

ANY FOLKS WHO LIVE BACK in the world and live in states such as Arizona, Florida, or Nevada think it's hot in their respective state during the summer months. Their stateside summer temperatures may soar to 100 degrees on the hottest of days. While on any given day in Vietnam during summer, an afternoon temperature more than often exceeds 110 degrees.

In essence, it gets extremely hot during the summer months in the Nam. White GIs took advantage of the hot weather and tanned up. Black GIs arriving in Vietnam an almond color normally left jet-black. Personally, I favor hot weather, but the heat that I was suffering during early September of 1965 was downright brutal . . . On the second day of September, it hit 112 degrees.

In a few days, it would be time to celebrate our nation's Labor Day, and due to VC movement reported by military intelligence, only a select few of us from Marble Mountain would be awarded liberty. My name was listed as one who was granted liberty during Labor Day, and, boy, was I thrilled. I had worked my ass off this past week working several fourteen-hour days, and I couldn't wait to visit with My Friend You or to hook up with her streetwise older brother, Lanh.

Prior to leaving for liberty in Da Nang, I was informed I wouldn't be able to visit Little Kim due to her orphanage location classified as "off-limits," so I called her on the phone before I boarded a bus into town and was able to talk to her (via Tuyen acting as interpreter) and hear her cute little voice. About the only understandable English Kim knew was her newly adoptive name of My Friend You, of which she would proudly say many times during our talks.

Tee informed me that we had missed the last bus leaving Marble Mountain and traveling to Da Nang, so he got us a taxicab. Meanwhile, I had to quickly end my telephone call, and as usual, Little Kim would end our call by saying, "Bring My Friend You sugar mints." Then she would provide her cute giggle and hang up.

Corporal Tee and I boarded the taxicab heading into the city. As soon as Tee reached his destination, he had the taxicab stop, and he asked me the time and the place we were to meet on our return trip to base. We established our coordinates, and off he went to his favorite record shops.

It had been two weeks since I last saw Lanh. Our union would normally always end up with the two of us eating burgers at our favorite café. After pigging out on fries and burgers, I would normally sat back and listen to Lanh's many stories. His stories were always interesting, and to put it simply, I was "blown away" by them.

The last time Lanh and I were together, he promised me the next time we meet that he was going to tell me how he and his sister, Kim, survived the suspected VC raid of their village. Also, he was to tell me how they both ended up being escorted through the jungle and avoiding harm's way by the keen direction of his mother's youngest sister, their aunt Thien.

I instructed the taxi driver to drop me off at a portrait studio a few blocks from where Lanh worked. Three weeks back, I had dropped off a photo of my mother (Gwendolyn), my dad (Curtis), and my younger brother (Kenneth) to have painted over onto silk. The studio did excellent work and told me the portraits would be ready in a week, so I assumed they were ready for me to pick up.

When I entered the portrait studio, I couldn't help but to notice that the owner was crying uncontrollably. I asked the female cashier what was wrong, and in broken English, she informed me his oldest son was recently killed.

He was the artist that actually performed the silk paintings. I didn't know what to say to him, so I simply said nothing. He looked up and noticed me and ceased crying. Then, very professionally, he said, "Corporal, your order is ready." I paid him handsomely, and he managed to place a smile on his face. But, as soon as I exited his shop, I overheard him start to cry again. I felt sorry for this seemingly nice person, but there was nothing I could do to help him. So I hurriedly walked down the street toward the old merchant's store where Lanh was working as an interpreter.

While walking the few blocks to Lanh's job, I witnessed a fight between two marine lance corporals that was very brutal. There were three marines standing around them as they fought, and I couldn't understand why they failed to stop it. I approached one of the marines watching the fight and asked him, "What in the world is going on here, and why aren't you or your buddies attempting to stop this fight?"

He said the reason the two are fighting was a racial slur one of them called the other. I noticed one of the combatants was Hispanic and the other Caucasian. It appeared the white guy was getting the best of his opponent. I felt this fight had gone long enough and stepped in the break it up.

The three marines watching the fight shouted at me to "leave them alone, to let them fight it out." I shouted back, "Marines don't fight marines," and I ordered them to help me stop this thing. Finally, the onlooking jarheads assisted in breaking it up.

Since I was an NCO and outranked the five marines who were present, I said to them, "We fight the enemy and not each other." The Hispanic marine said, "He called me a wetback, and it was offensive." I agreed with the Hispanic but said back to him, "Can you imagine the insulting names that I've been called?" The Hispanic marine gave me a slight grin and pick up his head cover, and the five of them began walking away.

The white marine who was fighting walked back to me, and he tried to convince me that he did not in fact call the Hispanic marine "wetback" and that he was sorry all of this had happened. I simply told the lance corporal that these kinds of things happen and to get back to being the good marine that I knew he was. He thanked me, and I once again began my journey to see Lanh.

Noticing a telephone booth as I was walking, I stopped to use it and telephoned Lanh at the old merchant's store. Lanh said he couldn't get off from work until noon and asked if it would be okay for us to meet at the café at noon. I told him that would be fine and looked at my wristwatch, and the time was eleven o'clock.

Having an hour to kill, I noticed a small shop that sold costume jewelry. I didn't have a girlfriend back in the States, but I had a beautiful mother, who wrote me often, and every chance I got, I would purchase a bracelet or necklace to send to her. She would write me and tell me how she really enjoyed the pieces, so I kept sending. I brought a beautiful pair of earrings in this shop and, as always, had to haggle over the price, but finally the store owner and I arrived at an agreement.

While departing the jewelry store, I realized it was getting close to noon, so I hurriedly walked over to the Hamburger Café, where I was to meet Lanh. When I arrived, he was already sitting at our favorite booth. As I went to greet him, I couldn't help but to notice his big brown eyes filled with tears and that he was in a very bad mood. I sat down beside him and didn't know what to say, so I said nothing. I had no idea what the problem was and sat there patiently until he began talking.

About five minutes went by, and finally he looked up at me and said he was sorry for the poor welcoming but that he was planning on telling me some important episodes of his life and that, while he was thinking about them, his emotions got the best of him. I said to him that I understood and to take all the time he needed to get himself together.

Lanh leaned back in our booth and said this afternoon he wanted to tell me about his story of survival and that some of the events that took place during the ordeal were not pleasant and surfaced some sad memories. He said his story was going to take a while and asked if I was ready. I said I was ready.

It was predicted the temperature was to reach 110 degrees today, and I was glad we were sitting inside the shady café. They served good food, and the prices were inexpensive. Plus, the place was normally filled up with American GIs. I felt safe there, and that was very important.

In my attempt to get a smile across Lanh's face, I told him I would be the big spender this afternoon and that he could order anything on the menu. He did, in fact, muster up a smile and said would I order him a couple of large hamburgers and french fries. I noticed he hadn't ordered anything to drink and asked him what he wanted to drink. He flashed that big smile of his and said, "Corporal Don, a beer would be fine."

Our favorite waitress walked by and asked if we were ready to order and if we wanted the usual. I told her the usual would be fine for me and to double up on Lanh's order. She smiled and scampered off toward the kitchen.

She soon returned with our order, and before I could fold back the wrapper from my burger, Lanh had finished one of his and was halfway done eating his large order of fries. I'd grown accustomed to his eating habits by now and wasn't shocked by how fast he ate, but other GIs watching him eat from other tables were shocked and thought Lanh's eating style was amusing.

Even though Lanh was only fifteen years of age, he was far beyond those years in life experiences. He had big brown eyes and the cutest smile. His body built was thin and muscular, and he appeared to wear clothes that were two to three sizes too large. He told me he got his clothes from a store that sold secondhand clothing and that he shopped there because that was all he could afford. Again, he stressed that practically all of his money went to the lady who operated the orphanage.

Lanh liked talking, and he liked telling me about his life story, and adventures. I was a very good listener, and he enjoyed that. It made him feel special by capturing my undivided attention when he told his stories. I felt honored that he would so readily pour his heart out to me. We developed a relationship that I'm unable to describe in words, except that it was special, and we both enjoyed it.

We finally finished eating our burgers and fries. We also decided to move to the rear of the café so I could hear Lanh more easily. We got comfortable, and Lanh leaned back and began talking and telling his story.

Lanh took a deep breath and, with a trembling voice, began to explain that, on a rainy night, he and Kim were awakened in their sleep by his mother and father. They spoke firmly to them and instructed Lanh and Kim to run as fast as they could to the predetermined hiding place in the jungle directly behind their village.

Their parents had instructed them several months ago if their village ever came under attack that they were to go and hide out in this predetermined location their parents had showed them several months ago during a fishing trip.

By the tone of both parents' voices, it was easy for the kids to figure out whatever the situation was that it was extremely serious. Kim was terribly frightened and began crying and hugging her mother. Lanh said his mother held Kim by her arms and looked her dead in the eyes and said that she had to grow up fast and to stop being afraid of things.

Their parents calmly explained to them that they would join them later in the night. Lanh said his folks told them not to worry but that they must immediately carry out their instructions. He went on to say his mother was tightly hugging Kim all while they were talking and that his parents were as serious as he and Kim had ever seen them.

With tears swelling up in his eyes, Lanh managed to explain to me how his mother sincerely told him to always care for Kim. He said they all four embraced and that it was difficult to pull Kim away from his mother.

Lanh said as they broke from one another's embrace, he demanded to know what the problem was, and his father simply whispered in his ear the word *VC*. Lanh said his mother once again hugged them both very tightly and sternly instructed them to run immediately to the hiding place. His dad again ensured them they would join them later, and, without another word, they swiftly ran out into the rainy night.

Lanh said it took him and Kim about an hour to locate the hiding place in the dense jungle behind his village. The hiding place was a good mile or so away from their village—and that, after a tiring run, he and Kim arrived there without a problem; then they impatiently waited for their parents to arrive. He said they waited for them that entire night.

Lanh continued and explained how he had to fight off a wild pig and several baby piglets who had adopted their hiding place as their newly found home. The wild pigs had released their bowels in many places, thus, making the foul smell unbearable and causing flies and a countless number of other insects to crawl and buzz around.

He further explained how terrified he and Kim were as they kept hearing loud screams coming from the direction of their village. The horrific screams coupled with the continuous small arms fire kept them both from falling to sleep.

Lanh said they also heard lots of foot movement directly outside of their hiding place, but they didn't check it out and strictly followed the instructions their father had provided them which was to remain as silent as humanly possible in their hiding spot.

He went on to explain that when morning came and their parents had failed to show up, both he and Kim began thinking the worse but were too afraid to verbally share their feelings. He said they merely hid in their hiding spot terrified and listening to the many screams from their fellow villagers.

Lanh said that, somehow, he and Kim both had fallen asleep but were suddenly awakened by noises of palm leaves and bamboo stalks moving about. Suddenly, their mother's younger sister came crawling into the hiding place. There were three children along with her.

Their mother's younger sister's name was Thien. And Lanh recognized the boy and his younger sister who were traveling with Thien. He was one of his many friends in their village. Lanh said he failed to recognize the third young boy.

He explained how his aunt Thien took control of their small hiding spot as soon as she arrived and that the first order of instruction she gave was not to talk but to softly whisper if communication was required. She told them in a whisper that everyone would do as she instructed them to do and emphatically whispered that our lives depended on following her instructions.

Duc was the name of his friend who had crawled into their hiding spot and that they were the same age. Duc's younger sister's name was Cam, and she was about the same age as Kim. Duc was dead tired when he reached the hiding spot and informed Lanh that he had to carry Cam the entire way because she twisted her ankle at the beginning of their escape run.

He said the third boy was Duc's first cousin, and was ten years of age. Duc's cousin didn't talk much. As a matter of fact, he hardly talked at all. Duc had informed Lanh that, several years back, his cousin had witnessed the killing of his father and older brother. And since that incident, he hardly said a word.

While listening to Lanh's story, I became a little impatient and, out of curiosity, asked Lanh if his mother, uncle, or aunt ever showed up; and Lanh explained to me that after his aunt Thien crawled into the hiding place she immediately informed him and Kim that they were not going to show up that night and that she couldn't go into detail at the time but would explain later.

Lanh explained how he had noticed how his aunt Thien failed to look directly into his eyes when she spoke to him about his parents not arriving. He said his aunt always gave him direct eye contact when she spoke to him and that this worried him to see her avoiding direct eye contact. He said that since the bad guys were in the area and searching for them, it was not the appropriate time to elaborate on the matter.

Lanh was doing a good job of explaining this episode in the English language, and all while he was telling me his story, I became even more impressed with his courage and bravery. This was only a fifteen-year-old sitting beside me, and he's speaking to me like a mature adult. The more he spoke, the more my admiration toward him grew. What a strong young person he had proven to be, and to think I thought that I had it rough growing up in the States at fifteen. My little world of hard knocks was a walk in the park compared to Lanh's life struggles.

As Lanh continued to speak, I couldn't help but to notice a distinct strain on his face; his face grew red, and the veins in his face appeared to about to explode. Several times I interrupted him and asked if he wanted to discontinue and begin another day because it sure appeared this story he was telling me was getting the best of him emotionally. But Lanh emphatically told me that he wished to continue.

He finally did take a break, but before he ended, he looked up at me with those big dark-brown eyes and said, "Corporal Don, I have never told my story to anyone else, and it means so much to me to tell someone." With tears in his eyes, he paused for a moment, and we went to the counter to order some fries and root beer drinks.

After eating our fries and downing our drink, Lanh began again by saying while in their hideout, they constantly heard suspected VC movement outside. Thien would whisper that bad guys were searching for villagers. She warned us to be as still as possible and not to stir up the foliage under our bodies when we shifted our weight.

Lanh said they would hear rifle shots fired, loud screams, and deep moaning sounds from the direction of their village. It was obvious the suspected VC raiders were hurting fellow villages.

One of the adult wild pigs that lived in their hideout attempted to return to his home, and Lanh explained to me how his aunt Thien fought the wild pig off with a small knife. Lanh said because of the pig's loud squeals during the fight, it almost blew their cover. He said his aunt Thien was waving her knife back and forth like a crazed person. She eventually forced the wild pig to leave their hideout and return to the jungle.

Lanh paused and began to quietly weep. I put my arm around his tiny little shoulders and tried to comfort him the best I could. He trembled as he began to speak again. He told me the children sat quietly in their hiding spot and just looked at each other with tears in their tiny little eyes as they listened to the screams generating from their fellow villagers. He stressed how they all wanted to help in some way but knew they were helpless without weapons or some method to defend themselves.

Each one of them grossly imagined the horror that was currently being inflicted on their family members and friends. Lanh softly said they just sat in their hideout, holding each other tightly, and quietly cried.

After a very long pause, Lanh said a short time after the three arrived and joined him and Kim in the hideout, it seemed as though the three children and his aunt Thien were stinking worse than the wild pig's dung spread about the den.

Lanh said it took him awhile, but finally he mustered up the nerve to confront his aunt Thien about her and the children's poignant smell.

Aunt Thien motioned for Lanh to cease whispering and quietly informed him that she was very sorry about the foul smell, but due to their circumstances, she would explain it later, because this wasn't the time to be discussing body odor.

Lanh said they somehow remained still and quiet in their hideout, and that it was late into the night when his aunt Thien quietly directed them to quietly slip out of their hiding place and out into the jungle. He said the five of them adhered carefully to his aunt Thien's instructions. He said his aunt instructed him to bring up the rear and to assist her in keeping the children quiet.

It was pitch dark that particular night, and the moon was hidden by low-hanging clouds. Lanh stressed how he took great pains to ensure all the children were moving in the same direction as his aunt Thien.

He stated that his aunt led the children through the dark jungle like a trained scout, and that she had them crawl through the tall monkey grass, and she instructed them to walk softly through the bamboo thicket that appeared to be everywhere. To avoid being detected by the raiders, his aunt directed them to walk far away from paths and trails.

He said taking the off trails was most challenging and that making their way through this difficult terrain took its toll on the children, but Lanh emphatically stated they all grew into young adults during their escape that night.

Aunt Thien constantly checked on her children to ensure all of them were all right. Lanh said she was like their protector, and he stressed how they all loved Thien for her leadership ability and words of assurance during their brutal ordeal.

During the second night of their journey, it appeared they had successfully escaped the VC, and Lanh said he was unable to wait any longer for the word concerning the whereabouts of his parents. He took his aunt Thien by the arm and demanded the knowledge of the whereabouts of his parents. He told her that he and Little Kim had feared the worse and that if she knew what had happened to them, they both wanted to know, and to know now.

His aunt Thien was strong for her size, and easily broke awake from Lanh's grasp. And in a whisper, she told him that she would tell him and Kim about his mother and father when they were in a safer place.

He said he backed off and cooled down. And he reasoned that Aunt Thien must have good reason for stalling and that she would tell him about his parents in due time. He also stated how good he felt inside that Kim was traveling with him. At least he knew her whereabouts.

While walking, they came across a small sugarcane field, and Lanh described how it was crawling with lice and snakes. He said that he and Duc had to hoist their little sisters onto their shoulders as they wadded through the snake-infested sugarcane field.

He discussed how it was difficult to walk and remain quite when there were snakes and rodents crawling all around their legs. With the encouragement of his aunt Thein, they all managed to move through the cane field without incident.

I asked Lanh what they ate during their escape through the jungle. He said they ate almost anything. That they survived off eatable jungle weeds, small rodents, insects, wild berries, eatable roots, and selected tree bark. He said that Duc was good at capturing small field mice and that they ate the little critters raw because starting a fire would have exposed their position.

He further said Aunt Thien demonstrated on how to sleep under palm leaves and use them as blankets for warmth. He said Little Kim would snuggle up against him so close that it became hard for him to breathe properly. He said he didn't sleep much and that he would lie awake dreaming of the day he would reunite with his mother and father.

Lanh said he slipped out from his palm-leaf bedding to go empty his bladder, and upon returning, he noticed Duc had moved closer to where he had been sleeping. He lay back down, and his friend Duc leaned over and whispered that he couldn't hold it any longer and that he so badly had to tell him about the whereabouts of his mother and father.

He said Duc made him promise not to tell his aunt Thien that he revealed his mother and father's whereabouts. Lanh said that he promised not to tell his aunt and said that suddenly tears began pouring down Duc's face. Lanh said he had been friends with Duc a many years and that he couldn't remember a day he had ever witnessed him cry. He hugged Duc and told him everything was okay and that he was strong enough to handle the news he was about to hear about his parents.

He said that finally Duc pulled himself together and began telling him why the four of them possessed that terrible odor when they arrived two nights ago in the hiding place.

Duc said the reason they smelled so bad was due to where they were initially hiding at during the village raid. He went on to explain how his aunt Thien hid them in a head down between the two buckets.

Lanh knew perfectly well what Duc was referring to because Lanh used the head (toilet) on a daily basis. Then Lanh explained to me that as a goodwill gesture, the navy Seabees had recently built a new head (toilet) in his village. The head was seven feet by eight feet. The structure was seven feet high and was constructed by stretching screen wire around its formed perimeter to enclose its sides and that the roof was made from a piece of galvanized steel sheeting.

The navy Seabees would dig a four-feet-deep hole in the ground (five feet by six feet). From a seating platform made of wood, they would insert two twenty-four-inch-diameter steel buckets in the hold. They were placed there to catch urine and human waste. The two buckets were emptied on a daily basis, and the contents set afire.

While using the head on a couple of occasions, Thien had observed that there was spacing on the sides and in between the buckets. Her observance would soon prove to be lifesaving during the suspected VC raiders attack on her village.

Duc further informed Lanh that his aunt Thien had been captured by a couple of the attackers and that they tied her to a post on the newly built head. The attackers thought they had tied Thien securely, but Thien managed to break loose and hid down between the buckets in the head. Duc said when her attackers returned, they were unable to find her because she was hiding in a place where a human being was most unlikely to hide.

He continued telling Lanh that he, his sister, and cousin were told by their parents during the attack to run as fast as they could and seek safety. Duc said while running they saw a couple of the raiders and hid behind the head. Thien saw them and quietly instructed them on how to slide down and hide between the buckets. The three of them squeezed in between the two large buckets, alongside Thien, and remained there for several hours.

When Thien felt it was safe, they left their smelly hiding place and lit out for cover in the nearby jungle. With Duc's eyes swelling with tears, he told Lanh his aunt Thien successfully hid them, thus, saving their lives and that the three of them would be forever grateful to her for her courageous effort.

Lanh said Duc explained that from their hiding place in the head, he and his little sister Cam sadly witnessed their father and older brother being shot to death. He also said they witnessed other village members murdered. Duc said while hidden in the head, they had a bird's-eye view of the carnage and devastation that was taking place all around the village.

Duc said that many of their fellow villagers were tortured and murdered in close proximity of the head (toilet) that they were hiding under and that it took all the strength that he and his aunt Thien could muster up in order to keep Cam and his cousin from crying out as they witnessed the slaughter of their fellow villagers from their hiding place between the buckets in that head.

Lanh said that his friend Duc said that even with them closing their eyes, the excruciating screams from their tortured fellow villagers were so loud they sent chills and powerful sensations through their bodies, a feeling Duc said that, for as long as he lives, he will never forget.

Duc told Lanh that possibly a handful of their fellow villagers escaped from being murdered, because it appeared the attackers were not killing young males that they captured. Duc said he witnessed the young males being tied up and led away. He reasoned they would undergo an intensive bout of brainwashing. Then they would be forced to train and eventually fight for the VC cause.

Lanh said he informed his friend Duc that he sincerely enjoyed hearing how they escaped by hiding in the head and all, but that he had not told him anything about his parents. Lanh said that about this time, his aunt Thien had somehow overheard them talking and broke in and told Duc to take watch and that she would tell Lanh about his parents.

Lanh said aunt Thien had him wake up Kim, because she wanted his sister to hear what she was about to tell him. After waking Kim, Thien began by telling them both that due to the circumstances that surrounded them, she had to get right to the point.

Then Thien began telling them that the reason their parents failed to show the other night at the hiding place was they had been murdered by the attacking suspected VC raiders. She then told Lanh and Kim did they want to hear the details concerning their parents passing.

Surprisingly, Little Kim stepped up told her yes, and Lanh described in detail the events his aunt Thien described to them. He said that Thien explained how a suspected VC raider began asking Lanh's mother questions, and his mother failed to respond with an answer. Thien said the head (restroom) that they were hiding in wasn't close enough for them to actually hear the exact questioning but that she could tell by the suspected VCs gesturing that her older sister was not fully cooperating.

Thien said the questioning of their mother went on for several minutes, then suddenly another suspected VC appeared on the scene. She said that he seemed to be one of the leaders. He took over and asked their mother some more questions, and when their mother failed to adequately respond, the leader removed his revolver from his belt and shot their mother in her foot. They then dragged her into a nearby hut.

Thien told them the leader dragged their father over to where their mother had seconds before been shot in her foot. She said the leader began questioning their father. Thien said it appeared the suspected VC leader knew their father or knew about their father's position and reputation in their village.

Thien stated the questioning of their father lasted for about five minutes; then. all of a sudden. the leader began hitting and kicking their father. Thien told them how their father's arms and hands were tied behind him and that it was impossible for him to defend himself.

She told them their father didn't say a single word and that he took the suspected VC leaders bruising punishment like the true legend he had become in the village. Thien said the leader kept reading aloud some statement into their father's ear, and suddenly their father spit directly into the face of the leader.

Spitting in the face of the leader infuriated him, and Thien said that he shouted an order to one of his men, and soon their father's wife was dragged out of a nearby hut. Thien said her sister pleaded for the mercy of her husband. Her pleas went to deaf ears, because the leader slapped her across her face.

Then the leader ordered two of his men to let their father stand up and force him to watch as the leader pulled out a razor-sharp knife and slowly slit their mother's throat from ear to ear. She said blood poured from his sister's wound and that the leader pushed her over onto their father's lap so he could hear her take her last breath.

Thien told them how the leader laughed out loudly and soon afterward leaned over and, like a surgeon, slit their father's stomach open with the same razor-sharp knife he had used on their mother and her loving older sister.

She then explained how the leader dragged their father's dying body to within ten feet of some of the captured villagers they had lined up on the ground. He wanted the villagers to get a good look at the horror as he commenced to gut their father. Thien pointed out how their father didn't make a sound and that he didn't take his eyes off the leader and stared at him until the moment he died.

Thien told Kim and Lanh they would have been very proud of their mother and father and that they were both courageous in life, as well as in death. She explained how all of the villagers who were killed didn't have a chance to defend themselves and that it was supposedly a suspected VC spy inside their village, impersonating as one of them that got many of them killed.

She said the spy pointed out to the suspected VC raiders which villagers were anti-VC and which were pro-VC. Thien said the anti-VC villagers were killed that evening and the villages who were pro-VC were released and apparently lived to see another day.

Lanh suddenly ceased telling me about Thien and his story. Then his face turned pail, and he slumped down into our café booth and quietly began to cry. I cuddled him up into my arms like a mom would a newborn baby and quietly cried along with him. We both sat there in the corner of Hamburger Café crying like newborn babies.

Normally, I would have been embarrassed, but this thought never entered my mind, because I'm more than certain that many of the GIs that saw us in that corner could probably relate to some similar incident during their tour in the Nam. For several minutes, we continued sitting in our booth crying like little bitches. Then we embraced in earnest and simply sat there in silence.

While sitting there, I reasoned the pain Lanh was experiencing was almost unbearable and extremely difficult for one so young to figure out, so I simply just sat there beside him as his protector, and when he finally did stop crying, I asked him if he wanted to continue telling me his story. This brave little guy looked up at me with those big brown eyes and said, "Corporal Don, I must continue. I have to tell my story to someone I care about."

It was easy to tell by the look on Lanh's face that getting this episode of his life told to a person he trusted was extremely important to him. So I simply kept silent and, once again, became all ears.

Prior to continuing, we ordered more burgers and root beers and relaxed for a few minutes and talked off the subject. After the short break, Lanh was back on the subject again.

We first discussed how difficult it must have been for his friend Duc to attempt to inform him of the death of his parents. Lanh said Duc was a true friend and that he treated him like the brother he never had. He further told me that Duc's parents were two of the nicest people he had ever met and that they were like second parents to him and Little Kim.

Prior to Thien taking over the conversation concerning the death of his parents, Lanh told me how Duc informed him how the village attackers were animalistic like as they carried out their acts of murder and terror. Duc said the attackers shot most of the livestock in their village, including most of their pet dogs.

Lanh said he asked Duc if he overheard why the attackers raided their village. He said Duc told him that he overhead them saying they did this as a warning to similar nearby villages "not to cooperate with their enemies."

Lanh explained how the news of their parents' deaths had adversely affected Little Kim and that, after his aunt Thien informed them, she soon later thought it may have been a bad decision to tell this to Kim. Thien reasoned that perhaps Little Kim wasn't mature enough to handle such brutal information, because from the minute Thien broke the news to them, his little sister, Kim, hadn't spoken one single word.

Lanh continued by saying when he and his aunt Thien confronted little Kim, that Kim dropped to her knees and began to quietly weep. Thien picked her up, and hugged her very tight. Lanh said that Thien then told Kim she would take care of her, and that she loved her, very much. Kim said she loved Thien very much as well, and they hugged each other very gently and that they both began to cry softly together.

Thien called Lanh over to where they were, and she hugged both Lanh and Kim very tightly. All three of them knelt down, and Thien began to pray. Lanh said it was a most memorable time in his life—a time in his young life he would never forget for as long as he lived.

He went on to say the party of six found shelter under some palm leaves and went to sleep. They awoke early the next morning, and Thien went over to Kim and repeated what she had said last night that she would do everything within her power to see that Kim was raised safe and sound.

Lanh said he didn't get the same discussion from Thien, because being a boy it was expected of him to be strong and become a man very quickly and take care of himself. Lanh totally accepted this calling and vowed he would one day be a strong man and help take care of his sister, just like his parents and auntie.

Then suddenly Lanh paused, looked up at me, and asked me if I understood his story and if I had any questions. I told Lanh I understood his story totally and that I was very sorry to hear about the fate of his family and the numerous atrocities that occurred in his village but that I was wondering where was the military forces during this time.

Lanh said he didn't know why the military failed to come to their rescue. And that his village was only forty-five miles from the marines based at Marble Mountain. And there was a South Vietnamese Army Unit stationed thirty-five miles from their village, but on that particular day, zero military help showed up.

All of a sudden, a smile grew on Lanh's cute little face. He proudly stood up, pounded his little chest, and said with much pride that the attackers didn't get all of the villagers that unforgettable night and that he knew for certain that seventeen young people from his village escaped and survived.

Lanh said emphatically their escape was solely possible by the courage and leadership of his mom's younger sister, aunt Thien. He went on to say that with aunt Thien's leadership skill, they were able to hide out in the jungle for almost three weeks and ultimately escape capture.

He caught me by surprise when he said seventeen successfully escaped with Thien. All this time, I thought the number was six. I was only aware of Thien; his friend Duc; his sister Cam; Duc's cousin; and, of course, Lanh and his darling little sister, Kim.

Lanh said they started out as six, and the six people I mentioned were correct.

But he said the number of young villagers grew as Thien led them through the many side trails and rice paddies. He said other children who ran to safety from the attackers joined Thien's group and that, because of her kind heart, she didn't hesitate to accept them.

He went on to say that at the age of twenty-five, his aunt Thien was the oldest person in the group. Lanh said there were a total of seven boys and ten girls, including aunt Thien. He said that he and Duc were the oldest boys in the group, at fifteen, and three boys were age twelve, and Duc's cousin was nine years old, and the little club-foot boy was eight. The oldest girl besides aunt Thien was eighteen, while the youngest girl was nine.

With a proud grin on his face, Lanh said that his aunt Thien was the most courageous person besides his parents he had ever known—and that she deserves to receive the highest medal South Vietnam had to offer.

Lanh further said there was a sixteen-year-old girl in the group who had been sexually assaulted by the attackers and that she wouldn't eat anything, and refused to have Thein examine her. She suffered a deep gash on the right side of her head and that one of the boys who witnessed her attack said she had been hit in the head with a rifle butt. Lanh was instructed by Thien to keep an eye on her because it was believed she didn't have a desire to live after the assault. And as the group of seventeen walked through the jungle, she would fall back, as if she didn't care about escaping.

Lanh explained how, finally, his aunt Thien took the girl aside and firmly explained to her that all the other youngsters in the escape group had a deep desire to live and that if she kept falling behind, she might cause them to be captured. After five minutes of Thien talking to her, the girl "got the message" and didn't fall behind anymore.

As Lanh kept telling me this heart-wrenching story, I kept saying to myself, *This boy is only fifteen years old, and he has experienced things most men five times his age hadn't experienced or ever will.* It was amazing listening to him telling his story and telling it with pride and sensitivity.

This little guy was an incredible young man and had an incredible story. As I listened to him, I couldn't help but admire this lad and thanked God for dropping him into my life.

He asked to excuse himself, that he needed to use the head (restroom). During this down period, I managed to stretch my legs that were beginning to cramp up. While he was away, a soul-searching sensation came over me, of which I've never experienced before.

For whatever reason, I felt then, as I do now, that God felt it was imperative these many acts of bravery on the part of this young survival group be told to the world. It appears I've been chosen to pen their story. A novelist I am not, but somehow, someday, their story will be told. That, I pledge.

When Lanh returned and we began talking again for some strange reason, I couldn't keep from entering my mind the crazy thought that maybe Lanh was not telling me the truth and that he was somehow fabricating parts of his story.

This notion soon left my mind as I witnessed Lanh's intense facial nerve strain as he related events and the sincere emotions pulsating from his body as he talked. I quickly concluded that no human being could fake what I've witnessed from this kid's body language. Lanh's story was true and nonfictitious. Every single word he spoke was factual. Who could make this stuff up?

Out of curiosity, I asked Lanh, "Did the group of seventeen escapees come across any villages during their journey?" He said that, on two occasions, they came upon small villages. Each time his aunt Thien directed the group to remain quiet and not attempt to get anyone's attention. Lanh said they would quietly pass by the villages late at night. His aunt Thien wasn't sure if the villages they had encountered were inhabited by the enemy.

I asked Lanh, "Did the children attempt to disobey your aunt out of being hungry?" Lanh said not once did anyone go against his aunt's instructions. He then elaborated and said as they approached the villages that they would lie quietly on their bellies and allow the jungle foliage to provide cover. He said they would watch villagers working in their rice fields and that some of the children wanted to call out to the village workers and request food but adhered to Thien's orders.

He went on to say that Thien was extremely protective of her flock and cared for every one of them as if they were her own. He said she was determined to guide her group of sixteen to complete safety and that they all trusted in her to do just that.

He then grinned up at me and said, "I'll be truthful with you, Corporal Don," further saying that there was, on one occasion, a young woman caring a basket on her head came within touching distance as they were hiding by a small pond. He said the village woman was carrying food items in her basket. Like a fool, Lanh said that he tried to reach out and take some of the food items from her basket as the woman passed.

He said that he was unsuccessful in taking any of the food items and that, shortly afterward, his aunt Thien walked up and slapped him harder than he had ever been hit before. He said he was angry at his aunt Thien for her actions but realized as the day passed that if the women carrying the basket was VC affiliated, the entire group of seventeen would have possibly been captured or killed. He soon afterward apologized to aunt Thien and prayed that she would forgive him for his act of stupidity.

Lanh said he didn't remember the number of rice paddies they had to wade through, sometimes waist-deep, but it was a lot of them. He told how the older children had to lift the smaller kids up onto their shoulders above the waterline. He said their weight made the older children's back muscles ache a lot but that it was necessary.

He further stressed how at times the older children would literally be walking underwater as they carried the younger children on their shoulders. He concluded this part of his story by stating his close friend, Duc, nearly drowned by swallowing a lot of water as he carried his sister, Cam, on his shoulders.

He then said, as always, aunt Thien came to the rescue. She frantically pumped Duc's chest and managed to get Duc to cough up much of the water he had swallowed.

During their escape through the jungle terrain, Lanh stressed how they had to endure numerous insect bites. He even said that a couple of instances they had blood-sucking leeches crawling on their bodies while wading through the rice paddies. Once again, he said Aunt Thien came to the aid of those who experienced leeches; she would use her small knife and remove them.

Several times as Lanh was telling me his story, he would pause and simply stare out at the people sitting in the café. He wouldn't say a word, and his big brown eyes would be filled with tears. During these pauses, I would remain silent as well and provide Lanh this reflection time.

As I sat there, watching Lanh attempt to gain control of his emotions, I thought how unbearable this adventure must have been for these young people. What brave souls they were.

As Lanh started talking again, he said he figured they ran, walked, and crawled their way some ten or more miles through dense jungle. He or his aunt Thien didn't have a compass or a device of that nature to provide directions—but that it appeared his aunt Thien knew where they were headed.

I silently said to myself, Thien and her flock had an angel sent from God guiding them.

After another emotional pause, Lanh said with tears pouring from his eyes that his blessings were answered, because after two weeks of clawing their way through the jungle, the escape group came upon a South Vietnamese ranger unit.

The South Vietnamese rangers were the elite fighting force of the army of the Republic of South Vietnam and their unit's point man thought he heard noises in the brush ahead of him. He and several of his units men conducted a complete search of the area. After their investigated search for the noises, they luckily discovered Thien and her group of tired sixteen children hiding in the tall monkey grass.

Once Thien realized who had stumbled upon them, she cried out with tears of joy. She and the children instantly knew by the sight of the rangers, they were in safe hands and soon would receive decent food to eat and much-needed medical care.

Lanh said as soon as the rangers appeared he could hear Aunt Thien say a prayer. He too said a short prayer and quickly became happy and sad at the same time. The sadness was not having his mother and father with him while being rescued by the rangers.

The medical officer attached to the twelve-manned ranger patrol administered as much medical aid as possible to the children. He treated numerous cuts and bruises over many parts of their bodies. He also discovered the children had many small reptile and rodent bites to their legs and feet. Additionally, he said the kids suffered from dysentery and that most of the children had symptoms of malaria.

Then Lanh lowered his head and sadly said his little sister Kim was the only kid in the group who failed to appear cheerful. He said her actions were solely due to her knowledge of the death of her parents.

I asked Lanh the age of his sister again, and he reminded me she had just turned thirteen. He said she was mature enough to appreciate the sacrifice he made by carrying her through the rough parts of the jungle—and that she was forever grateful to him. In essence, she was totally aware that she and her brother had literally crawled through hell.

Lanh said during the last time he saw his parents alive, he had promised them he would take care of Kim. In honoring their request, he said that as long as he lived, he would watch over and protect his little sister.

Lanh said his sister hadn't smiled or appeared happy since she heard her mother and father had been killed. Then with joy in his speech, he said, "She has appeared happy and full of life since meeting you, Corporal Don, during the medevac rescue." He said the day I came into her life, she became a new person. He continued by telling me how important she felt by me naming her My Friend You, because her new name made her feel safe.

Obviously, I was flattered by Lanh's statements and said that his sister, a.k.a. My Friend You, was also happy to get the sugar mints." Lanh sincerely said, "It is not the mints, Corporal Don. We are just so happy you came into our lives."

His remarks made me feel real good inside. He then sat down beside me and began to quietly sob. I reached over, cradled him up into my arms, and said, "Lanh, it all will get better." He looked up at me, wiped tears from his eyes, and quietly said, "Corporal Don, why does God allow war to happen?"

I didn't attempt to answer his question. He had asked a difficult one. So I simply just sat there, staring out at space and feeling his pain, and it really hurt. Fifty years has passed, and when I think of our discussion that day, I still feel his pain, and it continues to hurt—and hurt real bad.

By the appearance of Lanh's body language, he had come to the end of his survival story. After generously tipping our waitress, I embraced Lanh and sincerely thanked him for telling his story of survival. It was obvious this little kid was totally exhausted from detailing his story.

Then, without saying a word, he looked at me and smiled. I provided him three dollars for taxicab fare. We then exited the café and separated. Lanh caught a cab to his orphanage, and I hailed down a taxi for my trip back to Marble Mountain. For the entire trip back to base, I kept thinking to myself, *What an amazing story as told by an incredibly courageous young man.*

Shortly upon my arrival back at Marble Mountain, I hit the sack. I was completely worn out but experienced difficulty in falling to sleep. Thinking about Lanh's incredible survival story was the sole reason I ended up not getting an ounce of sleep. The following day, I was extremely tired, but because of what I had experienced, this didn't bother me the least.

> *"The Lord is thy keeper; the Lord is thy shade upon thy right hand. The Lord shall preserve thy going out and thy coming in from this time forth and even for evermore."*
>
> —*Psalm 121:5–6*

"LANH – KIM'S TEENAGED BROTHER"

Lanh's Best Friends

ALL DURING THE ENTIRE WEEK, I had a difficult time performing my aircraft engineering flight-logging duties. My lack of concentration was solely attributed to the constant reenactment in my mind of my street-fighting encounter, alongside Lanh and the two recon marines, in front of the café last week.

To again "thank" them, I attempted to make contact with the two recon marines who literally saved Lanh and me from receiving a severe ass kicking from the hands of those street thugs. I made two phone calls to their command station but was unable to make contact with them.

During my third attempt to reach them, I was able to talk to their unit gunnery sergeant. He informed me that one of the marines who came to our rescue had recently been shot and that he was currently fighting for his life aboard a nearby naval hospital ship.

I explained why I was calling, and the friendly gunny told me he would inform the wounded marine the next time he would visit him aboard ship and that he would tell the second marine involved as soon as he would return from a recon mission.

Also during that phone conversation, I was able to provide their gunny my contact phone number and asked him to keep me informed of the condition of the marine who had been shot. The gunny promised to keep me posted.

Three days after our phone conversation, the gunnery sergeant called and told me the wounded marine failed to make it. There was a short pause, and I could hear the gunny softly weeping over the phone. Then he spoke and said his marine was in a better place. He then quickly said goodbye and hung up.

I redialed the gunny's number and warmly "thanked" him for getting back to me and requested the marine's home address so I could send his family a letter, detailing their son's bravery in the streets of Da Nang. The gunny told me to send the letter to him and that he would ensure the fallen marine's family would receive it.

I wrote down the gunny's base address and made a note to inform Lanh of the helping marine's tragedy when we hook up this weekend during my preapproved upcoming liberty call.

It seemed as though liberty call for this upcoming Saturday was taking forever, but finally it arrived, and I was one of the first marines off base. I know Tee was wondering what in the world had come over me, because Tee and I always went off base to Da Nang together.

This particular day, I left without Tee because he told me he wouldn't be able to leave base for another four hours. I told him I would be hooking up with Lanh at the Hamburger Café and, if he was in that area, to join up with me.

Noticing me leaving without Tee, several of our buddies on base assumed I'd met some pretty girl in town and that I was going into town alone, and without Tee, because this girlfriend had my nose completely wide open.

My good friend Tee explained to our buddies that I simply had met a local teenage boy and his younger sister . . . and I enjoyed talking to the both of them and that they both fascinated me.

Tee pointed out how the boy fascinated me by telling me stories . . . detailing true life on the streets of Da Nang and Tee said the boy's younger sister fascinated me simply by being herself.

He also told them that I met the kids during a recent medevac rescue mission and that, after spending time with them, I'd developed a sincere desire to adopt them and take them stateside. Tee ended his explanation by telling the guys the kids had recently lost their parents.

"I'm lost for words in attempting to explain what it feels like to have a friend looking after your backside in a foreign land during wartime. Tee and I did just that for one another. And we watched out for one another, not because we were ordered to or because we were black. We simply did this because we truly liked one another."

It was that time liberty call on base had sounded, and I began running to the nearest taxicab pickup station. I directed my cabbie to drive me to where Lanh worked as an interpreter during the day. As soon as the cab drove up to the elderly merchant's shop, Lanh had bolted out the door and ran toward the taxi with a big smile on his face. As always, Lanh appeared as happy to see me as I was to see him.

Lanh leaped inside our little taxicab, and we directed our cabbie to drive us to the Hamburger Café. It would be a short trip; the café was located only about three miles from the elderly merchant's shop.

As soon as our taxi turned at the corner and headed toward the café, Lanh spotted a girlfriend he knew engaged in an argument with a US sailor. Lanh requested the cabbie to pull over and stop at the scene of the confrontation.

The taxi pulled over, and before coming to a complete stop, Lanh had jumped out and bravely stood between his girlfriend and the sailor. Lanh asked them what the problem was and if he could be of any assistance. They both ignored Lanh's request and continued shouting at each other.

Having a gut feeling this thing could escalate into something more serious, I stepped from the cab and asked the sailor (who just happened to be a brother) if I could assist him, in any possible way, with his apparent problem.

The brother calmly informed me that he had bought several drinks for this girl at a nearby bar. And when he was informed she was a prostitute . . . that he propositioned her. He said this was when the trouble started, because she told him she only did "boom, boom" with white people. And that she didn't "boom, boom" with people of color. She told him if she had sex with blacks, it would damage her reputation and hurt her business.

He looked straight into my eyes and said, "You're a brother. You know how this shit makes you feel—the hurt it extricates." He said she simply had pissed him off, and he went off. I told him I know the hurt feeling he was speaking about and that I thought as he did that we had left Jim Crow back home.

The sailor said that when our taxi pulled up, he was only trying to tell the girl that all men are created equal and that one day this type of problem will disappear.

Then Lanh entered our conversation and substantiated what we were discussing. Lanh said his friend was a popular working girl in the city and that her former pimp taught her only to date white people—and never date black people.

The pimp told her if she ever dated a black person, their business would suffer.

Lanh went back to talking to his girlfriend while I ended things up with the sailor. The sailor said he was cool about the whole thing and that it was forgotten. We then did the soul brother handshake, and the sailor went on his way.

When Lanh saw the sailor leaving, he came over to me and said he didn't exactly know why his friend was told by her former pimp never to date black people—but that she was only trying to protect her business.

I told Lanh the reason her former pimp taught her not to date black people had to do with what was referred to as "racial discrimination" and that one day I would fully explain racial discrimination to him—when we have plenty of time.

After the sailor had walked away, Lanh's girlfriend began giving me dirty looks, so he provided her a quick explanation of who I was in order to avoid further racial complications. Apparently, she accepted his explanation about me, because the dirty looks soon stopped.

Lanh and I stepped back inside our cab, and he asked if I would mind if we provided his friend a ride to the café. At first I refused, and my reasoning, spoken sarcastically, was I didn't want to shame his friend because of my skin color.

Lanh picked up on my sarcasm and repeated his request by saying, "Would you mind providing my best friend a ride in your taxi." Reluctantly, I agreed to his second request, only because he said she was his "best friend."

It was evident his best friend overheard and understood my sarcastic remark concerning her riding along with a person of color, due to the mean look she gave me as she entered our cab.

Lanh asked her where she was headed, and she motioned she was headed in our direction. I quietly said, "At least the bitch and I agree on something." She overheard me and said angrily in good English that she would pay her own way.

Her argument with the black sailor coupled with my cute remarks was evidently a bit much for his friend to take, because I noticed her eyes filling with tears. I reasoned the time had arrived for me to cease being a jerk. So I kindly told her there was no need for her to pay anything and that I was deeply sorry for insulting her.

She flashed me a warm smile and said that she was also sorry for her unkind actions. She then expressed her apologies to Lanh for her unkind treatment of his friend of color.

Then, at the same time, we three began laughing, and I assumed our laughter sealed our friendship. Only during the laughter . . . did I get a good look at Lanh's girlfriend. I said to myself, *Wow! This lady is drop-dead gorgeous!*

As our cab came to a stop in front of the café, I couldn't help but to notice how nervous Lanh appeared. He was also heavily perspiring and beginning to slightly shake a little. Concerned, I asked him if everything was okay. His failure to answer me . . . was totally out of character. So I repeated myself. He still didn't respond and simply sat there, as if frozen, staring at one of the three guys standing on the corner directly across from the café.

Lanh kept his eyes focused on the three guys at the corner, all while we exited the taxi. As I was paying our fair, I asked the cabbie if he knew the three guys standing across the street. He said he did and that they were "pimps." I tipped him two bucks, and he drove away.

We went inside the cafe, and his best friend went to visit the ladies' room. Lanh and I seated ourselves at a vacant booth. After sitting there for a few minutes, I again asked Lanh why was he nervous a minute ago, outside in front of the café. He was slow to answer, so I informed him that I knew the guys he was staring at were street pimps.

Lanh asked me how I knew that, and I told him the cabbie told me. Only then did he open up and say that he feared the pimp in the white suit. He said this guy had been pimping girls for several years and that he was an asshole.

Then, surprisingly, Lanh said that up until a few weeks ago the pimp he feared was the pimp for his best friend whom we had just provided a ride. I asked for his name, and Lanh said the pimp's street name was Thao.

I then asked Lanh, "Why did his girlfriend leave him?" He said she left him because he was doing some terrible things. Then he nervously stood up and said he had to use the boys' room.

By this time, his girlfriend had returned to our booth, and I told her that I was confused by Lanh's recent behavior. I explained the Lanh I knew didn't nervously shake when a pimp was around, like what I had witnessed and that the little fella I knew wasn't afraid of anybody.

So far, I hadn't been told Lanh's best friend's name, so I asked her for it. She politely said her name was Dung and that her name means "beautiful one" in her language. I replied a "beautiful one" you certainly are, and she shot me a warm smile. As if she knew my thoughts, she quickly said, "By the way, I know what *dung* translates to in your language." And she gave me a smile.

Apparently, she felt comfortable setting with me. Because she began friendly talking and telling me she was a close friend of Lanh and his family, and that she had known him his entire life. She went on to tell how he was like a younger brother to her. And she explained that, on several occasions, Lanh had put his life on the line to help her escape some dangerous situations and that she would be forever grateful to him.

She told me Lanh told her a little about me but that she wanted to know why we seemed to be really good friends with a short time knowing each other. I told that only God knew why we hit it off, then fully explained how Lanh and his little sister and I had met during a helicopter rescue mission. I further explained that we both feel safe around each other and that I sincerely like Lanh and Kim. Then I fully elaborated on my special friendship with his sister, Kim.

Dung was deeply listening to my every word, and every now and then, she would flash a warm smile in my direction as if she was signaling her approval of my friendship with Lanh and Little Kim. She told me that she also adored Kim and asked me if I was aware of Kim's new name My Friend You and that Kim proudly told everyone she knew about her new name change.

I told Dung that I was the person who provided Kim the new name and that it was a long story as to how her new name originated. I then told Dung that, when time permits, I would enjoy telling her how Kim's new name came about. Dung said she would like to hear the origin of Kim's new name.

Suddenly and strangely, Dung ceased conversing and began seriously staring at her former pimp, who was talking to a sailor, who was standing directly in front of our booth. It appeared the pimp was propositioning the sailor, because he motioned to one of his working girls nearby to join them.

Ten minutes had passed, and Dung continued staring at this asshole—never taking her eyes off him. I tried a few times to strike up a conversation with her, with hopes of interrupting her strange behavior, but was totally ignored.

Only when I told her that I was aware he used to be her pimp did she snap out of the weird behavior. Out of courtesy, Dung apologized for her actions. I told her I was glad she came back to earth because, for a minute there, I thought she had left the planet. We both laughed.

We then switched our conversation back to discussing Little Kim, and I told her practically everything I could think of concerning my relationship with Little Kim. When I finished talking, Dung kindly asked that, if time would permit at that time, if I could tell her how Kim came about her new name of My Friend You. I completely explained how I came up with Kim's new name.

Dung found my explanation amusing but didn't understand why Kim suddenly shouted out her new name. I told Dung this was a private game Kim and I invented. I explained that when Kim joyfully shouted her new name, My Friend You, suddenly this big bad marine would appear and safely rescue Kim from danger.

Dung began laughing and said, "Fascinating." She told me she understood She said Kim shouted her new name when she felt danger approaching . . . and the big bad marine who was to arrive and save her from danger . . . was none other than me, Corporal Don. She laughed again and sincerely thanked me for telling the complete story behind Kim's new name. Then she softly said that she loved Kim like a baby sister and had known her from the day she was born.

After a short pause from my storytelling, Dung said, it was good that I know and adore Kim because what she was about to tell me totally revolved around her. As tears began slowly running down her beautiful face, Dung told me the reason she dumped the pimp was she caught him trying to rape Kim.

She said Lanh soon found out about it and that he and several of his street friends began searching for the pimp, and they soon found him at his older brother's house. She said they drug him outside and beat him up real bad, and they also cut and stabbed him in several places. She said they also beat up his older brother when he tried to help his younger brother.

I asked Dung if she was a participant in the pimp's beat down . . . Her reply was "most certainly." She said the pimp remained in a nearby hospital for two months and vowed to get even with the people responsible for placing him there.

Lanh arrived back at our booth as Dung was finishing telling me the reason she left her former pimp. I thanked her, then firmly embraced Lanh and told him he would shake nervously no more either around this pimp or any other pimp. I told him that, for as long as I remain his friend, I would protect him and Little Kim from being harmed by some jive-ass pimp. Then I asked him if he understood me.

Lanh said he understood me clearly. Then I told him it was time for me to help my friend. In fun, I asked Dung if she minded being in the company of a black person . . . because I didn't want to hurt her business in anyway. Dung said that she could care less about what her white customers thought right now. Lanh pointed out that I was in civilian clothing and no one recognized me as military. So I calmly said to them, "Let's do this."

Then, suddenly, as if an alien force had come over me, I stood up and motioned for Thao to approach my booth. Thao failed to recognize Dung and Lanh standing behind me; he figured I was an easy score, requesting him over to request a date with one of his girls he had socializing about the café.

When he got closer to our booth, he recognized them both and began shouting obscenities in their direction. They were retaliating, and they were only fighting each other with dirty words until Thao ventured close enough to take a wild swing at Dung.

At this point, things turned ugly because Dung responded by throwing a large porcelain sugar container that was part of our table setting and striking Thao squarely in the face and causing blood to splatter all over his clean white suit.

So far, I hadn't joined in on the fun . . . primarily due to the fear of being disciplined back at base. But when Thao ceased assaulting Dung and began assaulting Don . . . his actions caused the fear of being disciplined on base to grossly dissipate and the pride of being a United Sates marine to astronomically emancipate!

Without hesitation, I grabbed Mr. Pimp and slung him up against a nearby wall and began to beat him and continued to beat him until there simply was no more beat in him. Then I drug him across the floor and tossed his bloody ass out the door.

Dung followed me as I drug Thao out the door and, with a wooden walking cane, commenced to hitting him in the head. Lanh saw Dung going crazy on Thao's head and tried to pull her off him. Thao must have said something offensive to Lanh . . . because he quickly began punching Thao in his gut.

Finally, Lanh ceased punching Thao, and he managed to pull Dung away. I thought it was all over, but then came along two marine buddies whom I knew back at the base. Either feeling I warranted their help or simply wanting to kick some ass, both marines gave Thao a dropkick to the head as they were leaving the café.

By this time, Thao was completely beat down; not an ounce of fight was left in him. The fight was over and done, and many of the café's employees began running around in an attempt to clean up and restore order.

Then Dung and Lanh ran up to me and, with panic in their voices, told me we had to leave the café and leave right this minute.

As we three were exiting the café, they both began explaining that several locals witnessed the two marines kicking the pimp in the head as they were leaving the cafe and that they were afraid the town locals would get involved. Dung said if the town locals get involved, this thing would quickly escalate out of control, and many innocent people would get hurt.

I'd only met Dung today and didn't know her well at all, but I knew Lanh very well. Even though Lanh was only fifteen, this kid was streetwise, way beyond his years. I listened to Lanh, so we three swiftly fled the scene.

We ran hard for nearly a mile and spotted a park bench where we could rest. Totally shocked and stunned at my actions inside the café, I said nothing for a good five minutes and simply sat there motionless. I was normally not one to engage in a fight but reasoned that I put the hurt on Thao because of his attempt to do the nasty with sweet and innocent Little Kim.

After we had sufficient time to rest, I asked the both of them . . . . what they felt about the pimp seeking revenge and if they would ever feel safe again operating in this portion of the city.

Dung spoke up first and said Thao would certainly attempt to get revenge. She further said she knew him pretty well and that he would not only seek revenge but that he would attempt to put the hurt on us, and really bad.

Lanh repeated the same thing Dung had said and further stated that he would stay around the orphanage more to protect Kim. He further stated he believed Thao would try to get revenge quickly in order to save face—and that he would hire several thugs to assist him.

When it was my turn to speak, I said that I would contact the proper authorities at the base and attempt to place some kind of restraining order against this guy and that I was not certain of how we could best protect little Kim. They all agreed with me, as I with them. In the end, we all agreed that we had our work cut out for us.

As we were setting there thinking about what we had said, all of a sudden, Dung jumped up and said that she had accidently left her purse back at our booth inside the café. Lanh told her he would go back to retrieve it to avoid Dung from getting into any trouble.

Then I stood up and said all of us would return to the café and assist Dung in locating her purse. My reasoning was simply that we three had to face this situation of reentering the café sooner or later. They all agreed, so off we went.

While walking back to the café, we discussed what could happen if Thao was still hanging around. Dung stated that if he's still there, she would continue kicking his ass. Lanh said Thao would more than likely be hospitalized at one of the nearby clinics. I agreed with Lanh, because with the beating we put on him, he most certainly was receiving some form of medical treatment.

When we arrived at our destination, we were much surprised as to how quickly order had been restored to the café. My favorite waitress approached me and asked if we elected to be seated. I hugged her and said, "Yes, mam." While she walked us to our booth, I asked her what had happened to the guy who got beat up and whom they blamed for the disturbance.

She told us the police arrived and took away the guy who was beat up. She said he was wanted by local police for the murder of a working girl and the attempted murder of a town's official. The waitress further stated she overheard police officers saying the beat-up pimp might as well had been killed, because he was going to be sent away to prison for the remainder of his life.

The waitress then seated us, then quietly said that everyone who provided statements told the police authorities the pimp was the sole reason for the brawl taking place. She then winked at me and kindly told Dung she had her purse tucked safely away in her locker. She then kindly requested our food order.

We were so thrilled to hear that we weren't blamed for the fighting incident that we reasoned this most favorable information called for something special, so we all ordered apple pie with ice cream, and when the order arrived, we silently sat there eating our pie and ice cream with a big grin glued on our face.

After eating, we put our conversations on pause and, for the next ten minutes or so, just sat there quietly in our café booth and gazed out at the socialization taking place between servicemen, their table waitresses, and some locals.

Breaking our silence, and purely out of curiosity, I asked Lanh if there was a possibility of him getting into trouble with the town locals by being seen so often with me. He smiled up at me and answered, "No, Corporal Don, many of the town locals assumed I am hanging out with you only to hustle you." This was a reasonable answer to my question, so I quickly dropped the subject.

We finished our dessert and were engaged in some serious small talk when I noticed that about every GI sitting in the café had their eyes focused on our booth. As before, they were checking out Dung who was conspicuously sitting in a sensual position and, as always, turning my fellow GIs on.

It was also fairly easy to figure out that Dung "enjoyed" turning GIs on as she sat there sexually posing. By the way, she was turning on yours truly as well. Only a dead man could have avoided getting excited by this girl's Hollywood looks, brick-house figure, and Marilyn Monroe sensuality.

To make matters worse, she began sensually shifting her curvaceous body from side to side. And the guys were going wild. I had never seen this type of girl-watching circus before. This girl was truly that fine, and she damn well knew it.

A short working girl approached our booth and beckoned for Dung to step out and see her. After Dung talked to the girl for a short minute, she quickly said goodbye and that she was sorry she had to leave. Then she hastily gathered up her belongings and departed with the short working girl.

As always, nearly every GI in the café watched Dung strut her stuff down the cobblestone street in front of the café, and they watched her until she walked completely out of sight. I could tell by the look on the faces of all the GIs watching her that they would have paid any price for her services . . . without any price negotiations whatsoever.

As Dung walked away, Lanh and I shifted our conversation to discussing my favorite girl, My Friend You. Lanh began telling me about how Little Kim was telling everyone she knew that her name had changed from Kim to My Friend You and that she strongly demanded that everyone call her by her new name.

We continued talking about Little Kim until it had become time for me to hail down a taxicab and begin my journey back to Marble Mountain. As always, Lanh and I embraced as I was leaving, and prior to departing, I asked him if he knew the short working girl who came and got Dung. He told me he knew her and that she was a close friend of Dung's older sister, Hong Hanh. Then I quickly jump in my taxi and hurried back to base.

A few days after our pimp-stomping encounter at the café, I received a very sad telephone call from Lanh. He informed me that he had just left Dung's bedside at a local hospital and that she was found by locals last night in a back alley with two gunshot wounds to her abdomen.

There was a pause, and I could hear Lanh softly crying. Then he said Dung had been rushed by ambulance to a respectable hospital and that a notable team of doctors operated on her and that, at that time, she was in a coma. He went on to say her doctors were optimistic but not positively sure she would survive the ordeal.

Lanh continued by saying that Dung had remained conscious long enough to inform members of the hospital staff that her injuries were caused by Thao's older brother, Xuan. She was able to provide them his name and description. In addition, there were several locals who witnessed the shooting, and they gave police the same description of the shooter.

Speaking softly, I assured Lanh the attacker would soon meet justice; then Lanh quickly said, "Corporal Don will bring Xuan to justice. Keep my *best friend* alive." Then he began crying uncontrollably, and I said nothing and allowed him this moment.

When I heard him stirring around on the other end of the phone, I asked him was it possible for Dung to receive visitors, and he said she was in ICU but that he would check on it and let me know.

I also asked him if he and I could meet at the Hamburger Café at noon that coming Saturday, and with a faint voice, I heard him say, "Okay, Corporal Don, Okay."

After hanging the phone up, I slumped down in my office chair and began seriously thinking about what Lanh had told me. Then I began to cry a little myself. I didn't know Dung that well, but what I did know of her was that she seemed to be a kindhearted person who really cared for Lanh and Little Kim.

While sitting there thinking about Dung's misfortune, I reasoned there were a lot of pretty girls entering prostitution in Da Nang at this time. They were doing this as a direct result of witnessing girls who looked like them making large sums of money. Most of the money they received came from fellow GIs. For the remainder of the evening, I blamed my fellow GIs for enticing these beautiful young girls to enter the cruel world of prostitution.

I must have sat there for several hours wrongly blaming GIs and contemplating what Lanh had recently told me about Dung, and I couldn't help but to think of what this beautiful girl could have grown up to be if provided the opportunity.

As always, I thought Saturday would never come, but it finally arrived, and Lanh and I met at our favorite café at noon sharp. We hugged each other, and he told me Kim said hello. I told him to say hello to her for me when he returned home.

Then I gave Lanh a large bag of fresh sugar mints to provide to her.

When we entered the café, my favorite waitress walked up and escorted us to our booth. By the manner in which Lanh was eyeballing the food orders the waiters were carrying about the floor told me this young lad was very hungry. We then ordered a couple of their famous hamburgers, some fries, and sodas.

Our order arrived within a few minutes, and Lanh ate his meal in a matter of seconds. Without a doubt, Lanh had just set a new world record for eating and surpassed the record he set last week, by some twenty seconds.

Certain he was still hungry, I went searching for my waitress to order him a second round. When I returned, Lanh was talking to a beautiful working girl. By where she was standing, she was blocking my entrance to our booth.

This beautiful creature, like Dung before her, had nearly all the guys in the café causing quite a commotion, as they positioned themselves in an attempt to get a closer look. And, I must admit, yours truly got an eye full as well, just prior to my attempt to squeeze by her and take my seat.

During the attempt to squeeze by her, she quickly turned around and pushed me back, then shouted, "She doesn't date black guys. Could you leave?" Startled, Lanh jumped up and whispered in her ear, and suddenly like magic, she became friendly and most apologetic.

Then Lanh told me her name was Hong Hanh and that she was the older sister of Dung whom he so often spoke to me about. I told Hong Hanh that no apologies were needed and that I understood totally why she greeted me in that manner. We three laughed it off . . . Then suddenly Hong Hanh slumped down into Lanh's lap and began crying uncontrollably.

Several GIs began to mingle about our booth wondering why this beautiful girl was crying and no doubt wanting to jump to her aid, if so warranted. I quickly stood up and told them, "Everything is okay, and the girl is family." This apparently worked, because the GIs slowly began to walk back to their seats . . . but many of them kept a suspicious eye locked dead on our booth.

Hong Hanh quietly told Lanh that her baby sister passed away at 10:15 this morning. And that Dung's doctors said she officially died from a .38 caliber gunshot wound to her liver. Holding back tears, Hong Hanh said Dung was only seventeen and that she was going to be eighteen in two weeks, as she began softly crying again.

Hong Hanh began telling about the memorial service her family members were planning and requested that we both be present. When she provided Dung's memorial service date, I told her I wouldn't be able to attend due to assigned base duty and that I was deeply sorry. She understood and said she knew I would be there if I could. Lanh agreed to be there, and she provided him the details.

Then the three of us held hands, and each one of us said a little prayer. Afterward, we sat motionless for a good five minutes, thinking about Dung. Then Hong Hanh suddenly stood up, excused herself and began to exit the booth. Lanh asked where she was heading, and she said over to her uncle's home where several relatives were gathering to begin their search to find the person who shot Dung.

Lanh told her he wanted to join her families search for the killer and if he could go with her to the family meeting. She told him he didn't have to ask, because they have always considered him a part of their family. Then I held both their hands and said another short prayer. During my prayer, I thanked the Lord for providing me the opportunity of knowing Dung.

As soon as I ended my prayer, Hong Hanh leaned over and gave me a hug and quietly said, "Thanks for everything." I told her that I should be thanking her for having the opportunity of meeting such a nice person.

As we began saying our goodbyes, I said to Hong Hanh that I firmly think the reason Dung was shot was directly related to the beating incident that took place last week and that I should have stopped the beating, as opposed to assisting in it. Then I asked her if her family was aware of the beating incident inside the café.

Lanh was quick to answer for her and told me he spent two hours on the phone last night, providing Hong Hanh and her family members a detailed account of the beating we gave Thao. He also provided them information about Thao being wanted by police and that he may spend the rest of his life in prison. As he was exiting the booth, Lanh promised to keep me posted.

Several GIs swiftly gathered around Hong Hanh as she left our booth. Most of the guys were attempting to obtain her dating availability for the evening. She politely told them she was unavailable at this time but, to be sure, to check back later in the week. Then she would give them a smile and politely step around them and continue her strut out the door.

It was getting late in the afternoon and had become that time for me to catch a taxicab back to Marble Mountain. As I rode back to base, my thoughts were centered entirely on Lanh and Hong Hanh. I was particular thinking about Lanh and how the passing of his best friend took its toll on him. She was the closest thing he had to a best friend, and he loved her in that way. Then I reasoned Hong Hanh would soon take that role.

After my short ride back to base, I was extremely tired, so after a quick shower and shave, I hit the sack. But prior to falling asleep, I said a silent prayer for their complete safety and that my friend Lanh didn't try anything foolish if they came across the shooter.

Sunday mornings were always special to me, and on this particular Sunday morning, I felt extremely good. After a quick workout beside my bunk, I trotted over to my workstation. When I arrived inside the Engineering Office tent, I was warmly greeted by my best buddy, Tee. He had arrived there bright and early to begin logging flight data.

Our department was experiencing a large back log in the logging of flight data. And the reason was the increase of flight missions our helicopters were engaged in. The war in Vietnam was escalating at an increasing rate in mid-1965 which translated into an increase of our group squadron's helicopters being dispatched for both combat missions and medevac rescue missions.

Even with Tee and I working hard logging flight and component data against our squadron's UH-1E and UH34D helicopters, I still managed to inform Tee of the happenings currently going on back in Da Nang with Lanh and Hong Hanh.

Just before leaving as a volunteer crew member aboard one of our medevac helicopters, Tee stated his concern was he thought searching and capturing the killer should be left in the hands of the police. And, as he was running to his chopper, I told him that was my concern as well.

The phone in our Engineering Office began ringing off the hook, and I scrambled over to answer it because I had a feeling it was Lanh calling. When I answered, Lanh shouted, "Corporal Don, Xuan was caught by police late last night, and he confessed to shooting Dung." I was thrilled to hear Lanh's voice, and he continued by saying Xuan told police, he shot Dung because he felt she was responsible for Thao's upcoming trip to prison.

He promised to keep me informed, and I was so grateful he kept his word. I was so excited the shooter was caught that I wanted to celebrate the occasion as soon as possible, so I asked Lanh if he could hook up with Hong Hanh this coming Saturday and if he could meet me at the café at noon to celebrate Xuan being removed from the streets.

It seemed Lanh was taking forever to answer me, so I repeated my request to celebrate—still no reply from Lanh. I finally said, "Lanh, did you fully understand what I just said?" His faint answer was he understood my request, but he couldn't enjoy a celebration at this time.

After a short pause, he said the reason was Hong Hanh was accidently shot and killed by one of the policemen last night. Then, suddenly, Lanh began crying uncontrollably and said he would call back.

Stunned fails to describe my feelings after hearing Lanh's shocking report concerning Hong Hanh. Maybe the word *hurt* comes closer to describing the pain I was feeling. Or maybe there simply isn't a verb, adverb, or adjective out there that does justice to describing the gut-hurting pain I felt at that particular moment in my life, and cry I did . . . I too began to cry uncontrollably.

Later that day, Lanh called me back and provided additional details concerning Hong Hanh, but his emotions again were getting the best of him. Just prior to Lanh hanging up once more, I managed to ask him to meet me at noon at our café that coming Saturday. He said he would and hung up.

By the time Saturday rolled around, Lanh had attended memorial services for his two "best friends." And, surprisingly, he appeared to be in a joyful mood by the time we hooked up at the café.

After eating, Lanh and I ordered two strawberry shakes. While sipping on them, we began discussing Dung and Hong Hanh. At first, he told me about their memorial services. He explained how their services had mainly family members attending and that he and Kim sat with their family. He said Kim took it hard, because both Dung and Hong Hanh had attended every one of Kim's birthday celebrations and that they always bought her great gifts.

Then Lanh began talking about the girls when they were growing up in their small village. He told about their early school years and how the three of them received good grades. He didn't spend a lot of time talking about their early years. *And, without hesitation, he began telling me about how his two best friends entered into prostitution.*

He began by stating he and his two best friends shared everything and what he was about to tell me was what they had earlier told him.

He said that about a year ago Dung and Hong Hanh's father was taken captive by a group of street thugs who were suspected VC. He said their parents were one of the most respected couples in their village, and the suspected reason their father (Sinh) was taken captive was solely his vocal opposition to being a VC.

Lanh said Hong Hanh and her older brother, Trung, would search daily for their captured father, and after the third day of searching, they also were taken captive by the same thugs who held their father.

He said they took Trung deeper in the jungle and that they were attempting to brainwash and transform him so that he would take up arms and help them fight.

Then he sadly explained that the group's leader and several others in the group repeatedly raped Hong Hanh. Then, after they finished raping her, they stuck a handgun to her head and told her, if she wanted to see her father and brother alive again, she must work the streets of the city as a prostitute and bring all the money she makes to a designated location, once weekly.

He said, during these weekly meetings, Hong Hanh was provided the opportunity to briefly visit with either her father, or brother, if and only if she made a set amount of money from her work as a prostitute.

She was told to target American GIs and to provide him alcohol, with the goal of getting him drunk and hopefully causing him to discuss military secrets that she would pass on to the leader of the suspected VC group.

Hong Hanh's capturers also told her that when the GI was intoxicated, it was easy for her to rob him of his money and other valuable items such as jewelry. The suspected VC group's leader demanded she provide him any items she lifted from the drunken GI and to perform as they had instructed her, or she wouldn't see her father or brother alive again.

Out of pure curiosity, I stopped Lanh and asked him where was Dung during this time. Lanh said Dung and her mother (Linh) were away visiting relatives in western Da Nang and that Hong Hanh had called them and advised them to remain with relatives until the suspected VC uprising at their village had stopped.

Lanh continued by saying that due to Hong Hanh's beautiful face and figure, she was highly requested by American GIs and that she made lots of money.

He said her earning ability made the leader very happy.

Lanh said Hong Hanh made the suspected VC group's leader so happy that he always kept his promise of bringing either her father or brother to the designated spot to briefly meet with her once weekly.

Lanh continued by saying the suspected VC group had eventually captured some three dozen men at their village during the uprising with plans of brainwashing and transforming them into fighters for their cause.

One of the men captured at their village had somehow learned of Hong Hanh's prostitution arrangement with the suspected VC group and innocently disclosed this information to Sinh, Hong Hanh's captured father.

Lanh said Sinh became outraged when he found out the suspected VC group had forced his daughter into prostitution and that he spearheaded a bloody revolt at the makeshift prison camp where he and about fifty other village prisoners were held captive.

Lanh explained how Sinh had been shot several times in his upper body during the revolt and that he was very close to dying. There were villagers who said Sinh killed at least seven raiders prior to being shot.

Lanh explained, by this time, Dung and her mother (Linh) had returned from visiting with relatives and, after they were informed, had quickly teamed with village friends to search for their loved ones. With the help of their friends, they were able to quickly locate Sinh, and Linh frantically cared for him.

Sinh managed to tell Linh about Hong Hanh's prostitution arrangement with the capturing group just prior to dying from his chest wound.

Soon after Sinh's memorial service, Linh began searching the back streets of Da Nang, with hopes of finding Hong Hanh. With guidance from friends, Linh located Hong Hanh at a beer tavern inside the red-light district of Da Nang.

From the beer tavern, Linh informed Hong Hanh of her father's untimely death, and she also informed her of the death of Trung, her older brother. She told Hong Hanh that Trung was killed attempting to escape at a nearby training camp controlled by the group of raiders.

Dung was with Linh (her mother) when she avenged the death of Trung. And Dung told Hong Hanh that with help from sympathetic villagers, they located Trung's killer. He was tied up and blindfolded and taken to an isolated place in the jungle. Linh soon joined them, and she removed his blindfold and asked the killer if he felt good killing her son.

Dung told Hong Hanh the captured killer of Trung began crying and shaking uncontrollably and shouting he only followed orders. Then he began begging for his life and pissing in his pants because Linh pulled an American made Colt .45 from under her dress. Dung told her sister Linh ignored the killer's pleas and shoved the45 into his mouth and pulled the trigger.

Hong Hanh told both Dung and Linh that she knew the leader of the group who was totally responsible for both their father's and brother's deaths and that she had a plan on how to avenge their deaths. Linh was uneasy about allowing Hong Hanh to carry out her plan for fear her daughter would be badly hurt, or even killed.

Hong Hanh convinced Linh of her safety. So she set out in search of and located the group's leader that evening at their designated location, and as usual, he had asked her to provide him her weekly proceeds from prostituting. Hong Hanh handed him a large sum of cash.

While the suspected VC group leader was gleefully counting the large sum of money she provided him, Hong Hanh reached inside her purse and retrieved the same Colt .45 her mother had recently used and shoved it into his belly and pulled the trigger . . . Blood began pouring from his body, and he soon bled to death.

Hong Hanh safely escaped from the designated location, and she soon learned the entire group of suspected VC raiders who had been operating inside Da Nang and held her family captive had either been killed or captured by a South Vietnamese ranger unit.

It was approaching 4:00 p.m., and I asked Lanh should we consider taking this subject up the next time we met because, in about two hours, I had to catch a taxicab back to base.

Lanh told me he much wanted to finish and that, if I ordered up some food, he would be finished by the time our food order arrived. I found my favorite waitress and ordered up a couple more burgers.

Lanh explained how Hong Hanh promised her mother that she would quit prostitution, and she did exactly that. Then, tragically, Linh was shot to death that following week by the father of the raider she had recently shot and killed as a result of killing her son Trung.

Lanh explained how their mother's death practically devastated the sisters, especially Hong Hanh. She, being the oldest, felt the responsibility of providing for Dung and herself. He explained how their friends and what family they had remaining tried to help the girls financially, but it wasn't enough. After Hong Hanh paid her father, brother, and mother's memorial expenses, she was broke.

She applied for factory work and sweatshop employment, but no one was hiring. Her country was at war, and jobs were hard to find. So Hong Hanh turned to the world's oldest profession (prostitution) once again, but voluntarily this time around. He said she reasoned this was the only way for her to make enough money to take care of her fifteen-year-old sister (Dung) and pay for their living expenses. When she was a working girl, for the raider leader, she was able to keep only about 10 percent of the proceeds, and now she planned on keeping 85 to 90 percent. Reason being was she hadn't planned on working with a pimp, so she would have to pay out approximately 10 to 15 percent to various people and groups for on-street protection. In addition, she actually liked having sex with most of the friendly GIs, so she looked forward to working as a working girl again.

Lanh concluded by saying Hong Hanh had become streetwise, and she knew the ropes, and at nineteen, she had turned into a beautiful young lady who was destined to make a lot of money. Then Lanh lowered his head and, with tears filling his eyes, said she was on the right track until a young rookie policeman accidently fired his weapon in her direction when Xuan appeared to reach into his pocket for a handgun.

I asked Lanh if Xuan actually shoot it out with the policeman. Lanh said no and that Xuan was simply reaching into his pocket for his wallet in an attempt to pay the pursuing policemen off in return for his freedom.

Then Lanh began telling about Dung and how she was raped by her boyfriend at the tender age of thirteen. The boyfriend was three years her senior and the most popular boy in their village. Dung's parents filed charges with local police, but the rapist was never held accountable due to the fact that he was the nephew of a high-ranking police official.

Like most rape victims, Dung felt being rape had negatively marked her for life. At fourteen, she was the prettiest girl in the village, and boys were aware of the rape but still tried to date her and buy her nice things.

Shortly, after Hong Hanh reentered the working-girl business, Dung turned seventeen and met a fast-talking street hustler named Thao. Hong Hanh told her this guy was a known pimp, but this failed to stop her from seeing him. Dung was simply fascinated with Thao. He told her a ton of lies, and since he always had money to spend on her, she believed everything Thao said.

Lanh said Thao was responsible for Dung entering the working-girl business. Dung made Thao a lot of money, then soon dumped him when he made his run on Little Kim. Due to her outstanding beauty and brick-house figure, Dung quickly rose to be one of the most sought-out working girls in the city.

Lanh finished by saying Hong Hanh and Dung were the "two best friends" that he could possibly have in the world!

Exhausted, Lanh asked if we had time to eat again before it was time for me to catch my taxicab back to Marble Mountain. My reply was, "Let's do this."

"The Lord is my shepherd; I shall not want . . ."

—Psalm 23:1

"DON TAKING A BREAK."

Finding the Care Home

WITHIN A THREE-HUNDRED-MILE RADIUS OF the city of Da Nang, all US military installations, including Marble Mountain, had been placed on "high-alert" status for the past two weeks. Recon reported large-scale enemy buildup. Personally, the command translates to an immediate cancellation of my off-base liberty, thereby, delaying our team's search for the orphanage the children had been taken after their short stay at base hospital.

Chris learned the name of the orphanage we were looking for . . . Tuyen's Care Home. But its whereabouts was currently a big mystery. Our search team was trying very hard to locate its position . . . to the extent that some members of the team had become obsessed. We were searching day and night—and calling nearly anything and everything in and around Da Nang that resembled a place children were sheltered.

Obviously, Lanh and Kim were the two kids I personally wanted to locate and visit, but as I thought about it, during the children's hospital stay on base, I had become friends with every single one of them . . . including the young lady Thien.

Our search team consisted mainly of the marines listed below. They're also the guys responsible for safely airlifting the children back on that eventful rainy afternoon. And they donated money when applicable to ensure the children's stay at base hospital was a most memorable one.

Corporal Clark, Corporal Fabris, Corporal MacDonald, Corporal Bernie, Lance Corporal Mackey, Corporal Tellis, Corporal Williams, Sergeant Purifoy, Sergeant White, Lance Corporal Smith

Our search was turning up zero results . . . so Corporal McDonald suggested we step back and write down on paper any suggestions that may help us in our search.

Corporal Williams came up with the best suggestion when he suggested we locate the South Vietnamese ranger sergeant who made the recommendation that the children be sent to his cousin's home. He reasoned that if we could locate the ranger sergeant, we could locate the address of the orphanage. Our search team scrambled to begin calling all South Vietnamese ranger units within a three-hundred-mile radius of Marble Mountain.

Our objective was simple but not easy—because, first, we had to find someone on base who could speak the Vietnamese language and was willing to assist us in our find.

Once again, Williams provided the best suggestion. His suggestion was that I dangle a few bucks out there with the hopes of finding someone on base who spoke Vietnamese and was willing to help us in our search. His suggestion solved our objective, because, in no time, a Vietnamese base laborer who spoke fluent English answered the bell and came forth to assist us in making the calls. He, in turn, collected the fifteen bucks we had to offer. On his twentieth call, our interpreter located the ranger sergeant we were searching for.

Our paid interpreter put me on the phone with the ranger sergeant who spoke good English. I sensed the ranger sergeant was suspicious by the nature of my inquiry, but I provided him so many details of the medevac rescue mission that eventful day that he figured I was an honest guy.

I told him I was informed the children were bused from our base hospital last week to an orphanage that he had recommended—and that the orphanage was owned by his cousin, a Da Nang police officer.

The ranger sergeant began providing contact names at the orphanage. He made sure I understood the orphanage wasn't a real orphanage but simply a large home, where his cousins were caring for twenty homeless children. He also made sure I understood that his cousins did not want their home publicized and much wanted their home to remain discreet. I ensured the sergeant whom I totally understood and wouldn't disclose its location to anyone. I told him that only a Corporal Tee would accompany me to visit the children. The ranger sergeant ended our phone conversation by saying he would make a call to his cousins to determine a good time and that he would call me tomorrow.

We hung up, and true to his word, the ranger sergeant called me the following morning and provided the home's address and phone number of his policeman cousin. He then stipulated that it was mandatory that I call his police cousin prior to taking a taxicab to their home.

After thanking the ranger sergeant, I quickly dialed the policeman cousin. As soon as he answered the phone, I asked if he spoke English, and he spoke perfect English. I then took about ten minutes and explained my entire situation.

The policeman appeared to quickly grasp my reasoning for wanting to visit the children. He said he had to call his sister to clear everything and that he would call me back tomorrow. Before he hung up, he emphatically stated I was only to bring Corporal Tee with me. He then slowly said their care home for orphan children was sort of a secret, and they want it to remain that way. I told him Tee and I understand and that we'd treat their home with the upmost secrecy.

The policeman called back that evening and told me his sister wasn't thrilled over us wanting to visit her care home, but she understood my reasoning. He said we were to visit only during daylight hours. I told him we agree to her terms and if it would be asking too much to obtain their names.

He said he was named Trang and his younger sister's name was Tuyen. I thanked him and asked for a good time to call his sister, and he said, "Right now." We hung up, and I dialed her number.

A female voice answered the phone in Vietnamese, then, in perfect English, said, "Hello, Corporal Don." I asked if she was Tuyen, and she confirmed and said her older brother had earlier called in regards to our request to visit the children. I confirmed and asked her when was a good day and time. Tuyen said, "At this time, I can't provide that information, but if you call back tomorrow, at the same time, I can provide you this information." Totally elated, I told Tuyen I would call back tomorrow at this same time, graciously thanked her, and hung up.

This young marine, then jumped up and let out a man's size *yell!* Everyone present in the aircraft engineering tent thought that I had gone completely crazy. It's impossible to express in words how elated I felt on that particular afternoon. Corporal Tee was present, and I informed him of my conversation with Tuyen.

Tee was elated as well and began calling the other nine members of our search team who soon joined us, and we spent the remainder of the day . . . celebrating our successful "Search and Locate" operation. With coffee in our mugs, we toasted Tee . . . who said we locate the ranger sergeant, we locate the children.

After work, Tee and I continued our celebration at the NCO Club on base. Neither Tee nor I drank alcohol, but that special evening, we both ordered a couple of beers. When we began to get lightheaded, as a result of our beer consumption, we reasoned it was time to hit the sack and sleep it off.

The following morning, I called Tuyen, and she informed me that Tee and I could visit her home come Saturday. I warmly thanked her and told her we would be there bright and early on Saturday.

Saturday, at (0600) 6:00 a.m., Tee and I were standing tall in formation in front of our work tent and were awarded liberty. A short time after, our cab driver drove us to Tuyen's home. When our taxi pulled to a stop, we were greeted by Trang, Tuyen's older brother, who looked sharp dressed in his policeman's uniform. Trang walked Tee and I up a slight incline to the front door of their care home.

It was a fantastic day to finely meet Tuyen and a better day to finely visit the children who came pouring out of the home to genuinely greet us. I heard that cute little giggle, and as soon as I turned around, leaping into my arms was none other than My Friend You. Kim smiled up at me, then held her tiny little hand out for some sugar mints, of which I had brought plenty. God is good!

"Walk with the Lord . . . and . . . you'll never be lost."

"DUNG, THIEN AND HONG HANH."

First Care Home Visit

THE CHILDREN'S JOYFUL SCREAMS SUBSTANTIATED the fact they were happy to see Tee and me walk onto their front porch and visit their Care Home for the very first time.

Even the home's owners, Tuyen and Trang, appeared happy, along with Thien and Tuyen's lady assistants. What a grand reception. We were treated like royalty, and needless to say, we felt real good inside.

Tee was literally mobbed by the children when he walked through the front door. The kids loved him . . . his kind personality . . . unselfish generosity. To put it mildly, the children treated Tee like a "rock star." And he loved it.

Tuyen introduced us to her three assistants and began showing us around.

I was busy trying to stop Little Kim from reaching into my jacket pocket and retrieving sugar mints that I'd brought her. Kim suddenly stopped her sugar mint hunt, because her aunt Thien was hurriedly walking in our direction.

Surprisingly, when she reached us, she gave me a big hug and, while fighting back tears, said she was happy to see me again. I told her we were thrilled to find her and the children in such a nice place.

Then I asked how she liked living in the care home. Without hesitation, Thien said she loved it and that the owners and their three assistants were great to live and work around. She further said Kim and Lanh get along great with the other children and that she needed to talk with me later about Lanh.

In response to Thien's remarks, I told her that I liked everyone at the home as well and that I'm thrilled to know she's satisfied with her current arrangement.

And that I look forward to discussing her brave little nephew.

She smiled, and I noticed a few of her front teeth missing. She saw me looking at her teeth and quietly said missing teeth . . . directly related to the episode inside her village. I told her I would like to meet with her and learn more about that courageous escape and guiding the sixteen children to safety.

Tears began to slowly swell up in her eyes, and she told me it would be some time before she can talk about that episode in her life but, when she would be able, I would be the first person she would tell about it. I explained that I was sorry and didn't intend to make her cry . . . and she said okay, and we left it at that.

In an attempt to change the subject, I told Thien it appeared Kim had grown taller since the rescue mission. Thien said several months had passed since then and that Kim did appear to have grown taller.

I motioned for Kim to stand closer to us, and assuming she had been learning English in school, I leaned down and asked her if she knew she was growing taller. I also told her that I was hearing she was telling everyone she knew that her new name was My Friend You.

Kim looked at me as if she didn't understand a word I had said. So I asked Thien if she was being taught English in school. Thien explained that because of the war, Kim's school had been temporarily closed and that Kim only spoke English when she shouted the three words *My Friend You*. I said to Thien that I thought she knew that I was the person who taught Kim the three English words *My Friend You*. Thien laughed and said everyone in the home had attempted to figure out the origin of Kim's new name.

Thien told me she never knew I was the person who introduced Little Kim to the three words *My Friend You*. Thien then looked up at me and said that she was confused about Kim's new name. She explained that Kim told everyone in the home her new name is My Friend You, and she also told them the big bad marine who would rescue her from bad guys is also named My Friend You.

Understanding the apparent confusion, I began thoroughly explaining to Thien the origin of Kim's new name, and I further explained why Kim also called me . . . the big bad marine . . . My Friend You.

Thien emphatically thanked me for providing a thorough explanation and said she was very happy I explained the three words. She said she was no longer confused, then said she was going to educate the children and the entire staff in the care home as to what I had just told her, because everyone living there had been as confused as she had been.

Thien said she wanted to talk about Lanh. She began by telling me Lanh had told her about our discussion sessions at the cafe. She said he also made her aware of our fighting scenes with street thugs and lowlife characters.

She asked me if I was aware that Lanh was placing himself in danger each night he hustled, interpreting for GIs and prostitutes. Beginning to cry, Thien ended by saying, "Corporal Don, you must help me to get Lanh to stop street hustling because he eventually will be badly hurt."

We ended with me promising her I would try to stop Lanh from hustling in the evenings for GIs and working girls. She warmly thanked me and said that Little Kim feared for her brother's safety as well. I told her I understood.

Trang came to where Thien and I were talking and told me Tuyen was looking for me in order to take Tee and me on a brief tour of their care home.

Tuyen and Tee walked up, and Tuyen began escorting us through their lovely home. While walking through their home, Tee and I couldn't help but to notice how neat, clean, and orderly everything appeared to be. When the tour was finished, we expressed our sincere appreciation for touring their lovely home.

We ended up on their back porch, and Thien walked out to see if we desired a cold glass of tea. While waiting for Thien to bring our tea, Tee and I told the brother and sister that we were wondering how they were paying for all the expenses associated with their care home.

Trang said it's no secret the necessities of a child like food, clothing, and shelter cost a lot. With emphasis, he said they would overcome the financial challenges, because "caring for abandoned children was what God had instructed them to do."

He then began to explain how they were meeting their care home's financial obligations. He began by saying their parents had placed a fair amount of money in a trust fund, and the monies were available to them in case of an emergency. He said their parents recently became casualties of war and they inherited their home and the trust fund. Trang said all monies associated with their trust fund were spent in less than five months in support of their care home.

Tee asked how was Tuyen paying her three assistants. Trang said the three ladies assisting Tuyen were childhood friends and were not receiving pay. Their family members were also casualties of this war. When they saw Tuyen providing shelter for abandoned children, they moved in the home to assist her.

Trang continued by saying the care home was, at the time, financially supporting itself from mainly four sources:

1. By receiving donations from police buddies.
2. Tuyen and her assistants baked bread, cookies, and cakes, and offered them for sale.
3. Thien and the female children washed clothes and performed ironing services.
4. A boy named Lanh donated money daily that fed the children. He translated price negotiations between GIs and working girls in the evenings, and interpreted for an elderly store merchant during the day.

Trang didn't know how long Lanh's donations would continue. They're trying to stop him from his evening work, but Lanh realized the importance of this funding.

Trang ended our back-porch discussion by telling Tee and I that everyone living in their home were like one big happy family. They sincerely care for one another and were simply trying to survive in these extremely hard times of misery and war.

> *"The will of God will never take you where the
> grace of God will not protect you."*

"CAREHOME DONATORS – DON AND CHRIS."

Care Home Donations

THE TAXICAB TEE AND I caught to ride back to Marble Mountain was extremely small and uncomfortable. Riding in this little monster was causing both Tee and me to cramp up from our neck bone to our butt bone. We reasoned the grand time we had spent with the children and the care home staff was well worth this miserable taxicab ride.

In order to keep our minds totally off the uncomfortable ride back to base, we began reflecting on the great time we had earlier today visiting the children's care home for the very first time. During our discussion, there was one element that continued to surface . . . their need for monetary assistance.

Tee and I reasoned the care home would vanish if Tuyen and Trang didn't seek monetary assistance from another source. To continue to operate their care home based on money obtained from a fifteen-year-old boy hustling in the streets was "an accident waiting to happen." What if Lanh gets sick . . . . ? The children would go hungry.

We both felt their current monetary providers should be applauded for all their unselfish giving, but in order for Tuyen and Trang to continue to operate their care home, some additional funding was necessary.

Tee summed it up by saying both Tuyen and Trang had a lot of pride, but the children can't eat pride; therefore, "we had to find a way to donate to their care home."

As most always, Tee and I were in total agreement and felt we should discuss the possibility of setting something up with our team. We began tossing dollar amounts and donation intervals around as we continued our ride back to base.

As our taxi ride came to its end, we agreed to assemble the team directly after tomorrow's mass service. Our team consisted of the below list of marines who were stationed at Marble Mountain and attached to helicopter squadrons in MAG-16.

Corporal Clark, Corporal Fabris, Corporal MacDonald, Corporal Bernie, Lance Corporal Mackey, Corporal Tellis, Corporal Williams, Sergeant Purifoy, Sergeant White, Lance Corporal Smith

Tired from our ride, I quickly hit the sack. And during my sleepless moments, I lay awake thinking about the fact we barely know anything about the care home owners, Tuyen and Trang. Yet Tee and I are going to ask team members to give them a portion of their pay. The largest amount of money any one of us made was $600 a month. And the reason it had climbed that high was we were receiving hazardous duty pay and flight pay. If the aforementioned pay was not added to our regular NCO pay, we would only be paid around $300 monthly.

During sleep, my mind would shift, and I would dream of happy children inside their care home, benefitting from our donations. I'd hear that cute girlish giggle of Kim's and see Lanh hustling in order to feed the children. Then, suddenly, I heard my tent sergeant . . . screaming, "Rise and shine, marines."

I quickly showered and dressed for mass services, then hooked up with Tee. He had informed each of our team members of our plans to meet after mass. We decided to meet in the sleeping tent Tee and I occupied. During our session, we could listen to the latest soul gospel albums Tee had recently purchased.

While Tee was blasting Andre's latest gospel tune, each of our team members began locating a comfortable spot. Chris Fabris (our team's blue-eyed soul brother) said he wanted to hear about our first visit to the care home.

Tee and I were happy to tell them about yesterday's visit. We told them about the children's enthusiastic behavior. We also said the care home owners and their staff personnel also appeared to enjoy our visit.

We then explained the reason the place was called a care home, and not an orphanage. We thought it was proper to thoroughly explain Trang's security and safety concerns in case one of them are next to visit the home.

Finally, we began explaining the reason we wanted to hold the meeting. We explained how the home was currently receiving financial assistance, and we made sure they understood that Lanh's money may be short-lived. Tee and I wasted no more time in flat-out telling them that we felt the only way the care home can continue was by receiving donations from another source and that the six of us should be that source.

We tossed it out there for their complete observation, and after a number of short discussions, Sergeant Purifoy said he was ready to sign up as a donation giver and asked how he was he supposed to do this. The other team members followed the lead of Purifoy and asked Tee and I how much do we feel they should donate.

We warmly thanked each team member for their support and said we figured if the six of us donate each time we're paid, which was monthly a total of $120, that this would amount to a total amount of $720 monthly. We also told them that if together we donate a monthly total of $720, we would easily become the care home's number one source of financial assistance.

Our team voted on the $120 amount that each of us would provide. Each team member agreed to this amount, and MacDonald stated if a team member found it difficult to provide the full amount of $120, that would be okay, and he could simply donate what he felt that he could.

As soon as MacDonald said this, Bernie spoke up and said if we can we sheneek additional team members. We all agreed, and Bernie said that he had been talking to a friend from Chicago who had recently been assigned to MAG-36 about helping our children, and he seemed interested in becoming a team member. Bernie said he was still being processed into our squadron and that, once all would be complete, he would bring him to our next meeting.

Williams asked Bernie his friend's rank, and Bernie said he had recently been promoted to E7 gunnery sergeant. Williams said that an E7 should be able to donate a little more than $120. I spoke up and said we will all begin with $120 a month, and if one of us could feel we can increase that amount, then we should discuss it. We all agreed to my statement.

Sergeant Purifoy said we are the marines who initially helped rescue the young lady and the sixteen children and that we daily visited the children during their short stay at base hospital. In essence, our core team had a special bond with the children that a newcomer wouldn't have. So he felt we should maintain our six-man team for a while before bringing new members on board.

We discussed Purifoy's statement and came to the conclusion that maybe our team needed to establish some written bylaws in regards to its existence and that the next time we meet, we would vote on them. We agreed.

Then I spoke up and said, "Guys we're making this thing too difficult." I said, "Let's not plan any bylaw meeting right now and simply begin donating our agreed-upon amount of $720 a month this Friday which is payday." They all agreed with me.

After fully discussing everyone's concerns, we concluded with providing our $120 a month to Corporal Tee. And Tee would ensure the donated amount reach the owners of the care home no later than seven days after it had been collected and that I would serve as Tee's backup in case he couldn't perform the passing of the funds from our base to the care home within the seven-day period.

We ended our "donation meeting" with electing me to call Tuyen to explain our team's donation proposal, and we would meet tomorrow in my tent at 1800 hours so I could report if whether or not our donation plan was accepted. We agreed, and when we were about to break up, Chris and Bernie spoke up and stated they would like to accompany Tee and me to the care home when we go that coming Saturday.

We all agreed, and I was designated by the team to present our donation proposal to Tuyen first thing tomorrow morning. Our team meeting came to an end, and as usual, Sergeant Purifoy led us in prayer. The team members left to go to their sleep tents, and after a few minutes of discussing our meeting highlights with Tee, I grew sleepy and decided to hit the sack.

As soon as I arrived to work the following morning, I called Tuyen, and when she answered, I immediately began telling her about our team's donation proposal.

After thoroughly explaining the proposal, I stopped talking and asked her if she had any questions and what she thought about it.

Tuyen began softly crying and said she was thrilled to hear such a fine humanitarian gesture on the part of our team and said she can't wait to tell her brother about our proposal. She continued and said Trang handled the financial side of their care home business and that she'd explain our proposal to him the moment he would arrive home from work.

She said, as a result of some recent developments, she's absolutely sure Trang would be as touched and as appreciative as she was over the proposal. Then she said that God had answered her prayers.

I told Tuyen, "Our team members would be impatiently waiting to hear Trang's reply." She asked me, "Should Trang call you at work, or at your sleep tent?" I told her, "I would be working late, but I don't know how late. If Trang doesn't reach me on my work number, let him call my sleep tent. If he can't get ahold of me there, let him ask for Tee."

My supervisor, Master Sergeant Snyder, at 1930 hours, told his seven engineering clerks to cease logging and call it a day. We began working this morning at 0630; we were tired. Sergeant Snyder recognized our situation and shut down our operation in order to avoid a logging mistake.

Recently, it was suspected an aircraft engineering clerk in our squadron reportedly battling fatigue erroneously logged flight time against a key component (servo unit) attached to a UH1E helicopter. While flying on a medevac rescue mission the following day, this same UH1E was forced to land in enemy held territory due to the malfunctioning of its servo unit . . . resulting from that tired aircraft engineering clerk's logging error.

(It was actually time for the servo unit to be replaced, but the clerk's logging error showed this wasn't the case.)

Luckily, the downed UH1E had a mechanically minded crew chief on board who masterminded the repair of the faulty servo unit; thereby, allowing the downed aircraft to lift and fly safely out from the dangerous enemy-held territory and ultimately successfully completing its planned rescue mission.

(Your author was the tired aircraft engineering clerk who erroneously logged time against the UH1E's servo unit. My payback happened to be when I was flying aboard the UH1E as a voluntary crew member, and it landed in enemy territory as a result of that faulty servo unit, and it's taken me over fifty years to fess up.)

Master Sergeant Snyder was about to shut down power leading to our Engineering Office tent, thus, enabling me to receive outside telephone calls when, suddenly, my phone rang, and Trang was on the other line. Trang was so grateful and excited about our donation proposal that he was shouting, and I could barely understand him.

Sergeant Snyder saw me talking on the phone and held up three fingers. This meaning I only had three minutes left to talk to Trang. I figured three minutes wasn't enough time to speak with Trang, so I managed somehow to get his attention and asked him to call me back tomorrow. But before he and I were disconnected, I asked Trang if he approved of our donation proposal. Trang shouted yes, that he and Tuyen both approve. At this time, Sergeant Snyder said, "Power off," and my phone shut down.

That following morning, I called Trang as soon as I entered my workstation. And when he answered his phone, Trang was still much elated over our team's offer to provide monthly donations amounting to $720. I told him our team of six would attempt to recruit additional donors on base and that he could expect the donation amount to grow even more.

Trang said his prayers must have been answered, because, this past week, he had been trying to find a way to tell Tuyen that the majority of his police buddies had approached him and said they were experiencing financial difficulty, thereby, causing them to discontinue their donations to the care home.

Trang continued by saying most of his countrymen were experiencing hard times as a direct result of their civil war. Then he sadly said that two of his police pals who were donating were gunned down last week in a fight with pro-VC activists. Trang ceased talking, and I think I heard him softly crying over the phone.

He began talking again and said our team's donation amount was substantially greater than the amount his police buddies were providing, thus, enabling his sister's care home for children to continue.

I told Trang that Tee and I will be coming to the Care Home if we're awarded liberty this Saturday, and that we would be bringing our team's donation.

We ended our phone conversation with Trang saying they will be looking forward to seeing us this Saturday and that our marine team . . . were God's angels. We then hung up.

"Fear not, for I am with you; be not dismayed, for I am your God. I will uphold you with My victorious right hand."

—Isaiah 41:10

"DON'S SLEEP TENT DUING RAINS."

Fifth Care Home Visit

O N OUR FIFTH VISIT TO see the children, Tee and I decided to ask our taxi driver to stop at a small fruit stand we had seen while previously riding to the care home.

There were about a dozen customers at the fruit stand when we walked up, and it was a good thing we wore civilian clothing because on two different occasions we were asked by locals were we military. Our reply was we were civilian workers. And we would attempt to speak with an African accent.

When they heard us say civilian worker, they would give us a good looking over; then they would give us a warm smile. We could tell by the manner in which we were asked this question that these people asking were serious GI haters.

We bought about three dozen of the finest bananas, and we even provided one to our cab driver who had been so kind as to wait.

The children were thrilled to get our bananas, and I noticed that Little Kim wasn't with the children when they greeted us at the care home's entranceway. I didn't have to look for her, because she was standing behind the front door, waiting to jump out at me. She gently took my hand and led me to where her school supplies were located. Kim located a tablet-size picture book and placed it on a small table. The picture book contained pencil drawings that she had drawn.

The book contained over fifty pages of various pictures Little Kim had drawn. I could tell by her body language that she was extremely proud of her drawings. She slowly flipped through each page. She showed me at least ten drawings of Lanh, several of her parents, three of her aunt Thien, a couple of her friends, and a one of a little brown puppy dog.

When Kim flipped the page to the puppy she'd drawn, I noticed tears swelling up in her eyes. I said to her, "Your puppy," and she replied, as always, "My Friend You, My Friend You," and suddenly Kim began crying uncontrollably. I didn't know what to do. I couldn't communicate with her, so I simply just held her and hugged her until she stopped crying.

I later learned while talking with aunt Thien that the little brown puppy was a birthday gift from her father and that she had to leave it behind when the VC raided her village.

When Little Kim's emotions came under control, she continued to show me more of her drawings. She didn't say a word as she slowly turned each page and would continuously look up at me as if attempting to get my reaction. I would smile and express how pleased I was of her work.

After viewing her last drawing, she smiled and slowly placed the book back on the table. She then brought out a small box and motioned for me to close my eyes, and when she had me open them, there was a live tiny green lizard with large red eyes peering up at me.

Little Kim had captured it outside, and it was her secret possession. I laughed and took the box she had the lizard placed in and punched a few holes in it so the small reptile could obtain fresh air. I could tell by the looks Kim gave me that she wasn't happy with me punching holes in her box. In sign language, I tried to explain why I punched the holes, and I think she understood my reasoning. As always, Kim and I had this unique method of communicating with each other.

Each trip I made to the orphanage, Little Kim would show me one of her prized possessions. During this visit, it was the lizard. The last time I visited, she showed me four large cat-eyed marbles. Each time I visited Kim, she made it a ritual to show me a special item that was dear to her. And, as always, after displaying her prize, she would look at me with those big beautiful brown eyes as if to say, "My Friend You, isn't this item unique? Isn't it unique, My Friend You?"

Tee and I had been at the care home for nearly four hours, and we were about to say our goodbyes and catch a taxicab back to base when Little Kim gave me that cute little giggle and reached her tiny little hand out for some sugar mints. I was so wrapped up into looking at her pictures that I had completely forgot I had three small packages to provide her.

Tee and I warmly said our goodbyes to the children and the care home staff and walked out to our taxi, and back to Marble Mountain we drove . . . all the time I was thinking about that Kim and her little brown dog.

A beautiful smile on the face of a beautiful person
is a language understood by all persons.

"YOURS TRULY – WASH DAY."

Last Care Home Visit

THE BIG RUMOR ON BASE was future liberty visits into Da Nang were soon coming to an end due to the notable rise of enemy activity in the area. Therefore, when liberty call was approved for Saturday, practically everyone on base that was awarded liberty took it and headed for Da Nang.

Our team originally planned to deliver the monthly donation to Tuyen the first Saturday of each month. But due to the many rumors, we decided to take our first donation to her a week early. And as many team members as possible would make the trip.

After checking Saturday's duty roster, we saw that Ray and Mac had pulled duty and wouldn't be able to visit the care home tomorrow. They provided us with small gifts to take to selected children. This is when I learned I wasn't the only jarhead handing out sugar mints. We spent Friday evening hanging out in Ray's sleep tent, playing a silent card game called bid whiz.

The following Saturday morning, Chris, Bernie, Tee, and I were the first group of jarheads to board taxicabs headed to the big city. During our taxi ride, we had a fun time discussing the jubilation demonstrated two weeks back by Tuyen and Trang when they were told about our donation pledge.

Yesterday, I called Tuyen to tell her about our planned arrival today. I also told her the reason we were coming, and that while we're there, we should discuss an alternate method of providing the monthly donation, as opposed to hand delivery.

Tuyen agreed, and said to be careful during our trip, because they were hearing the same rumors. I told her we should discuss this rumor situation in detail, when we arrive. She agreed, and again, told me to be careful, just like my mom.

Halfway into our trip, I told the guys I was going to start legal proceedings to adopt Little Kim. Tee said he couldn't help but to notice the father-daughter-like affection Kim and I had for each other and that I had his total support. Chris and Bernie provided similar words of support. Their support meant a lot to me.

I told them about my conversations with the base chaplain concerning adopting Little Kim and that he told me I was fighting an uphill battle because I wasn't married. Bernie began telling me about his sister who was looking for a husband. He then tried to find a picture of her. Then Chris shouted, "We're here."

As our taxi made its turn onto their street, we saw Trang standing by the curb. When our cab pulled to a stop, Trang opened our door and hastily paid our fare, greeted us, then began hurriedly walking us up the slight incline to their care home.

As we walked toward Trang's home, I noticed how we were on the receiving end of "dirty looks" by Trang's neighbors. We weren't in our marine uniform, so why couldn't we simply be friends of the family? I asked Trang about it, and he said not to worry about it, and nervously laughed it off.

When we approached the front steps of Trang's home, we noticed a young boy about twelve years of age crawling from under the porch. Trang greeted the boy, then asked his name and asked the boy to tell him a little about himself. The boy didn't speak English, so Trang translated for the four of us.

The boy said his name was Trung and, while living off the streets of Da Nang, he ran into a nice person by the name of Lanh. That last week, Lanh had him followed him to this home. He said, when they arrived, Lanh introduced him to his aunt Thien. And she fed him and gave him blankets to sleep under.

He continued and said he'd slept under the porch the past five nights and that Thien had been regularly feeding him. The boy said he hadn't seen much of Lanh and was told by the older kids living here that Lanh was busy working as an interpreter so that he could make money to help buy food for the home.

Trang acknowledged the fact that Lanh was helping to buy groceries and that all the children living here thought a great deal of him. Then Trang asked the boy did he have family, and with tears dripping down his cute little face, Trung said his parents and two older brothers were killed two weeks back and that he didn't have any relatives living nearby.

Trang asked Trung was his family killed by VC. Surprisingly, the boy's reply was an emphatic, "No, sir." And he went on to explain that he was visiting the home of his best friend who lived around the corner when, all of a sudden, bombs began falling from the sky and exploding all around them. He said he was scared and began running as fast as he could from his friend's house toward home when one of the bombs exploded inside their home, killing all of the four people inside, including his best friend.

The boy now had tears pouring from his eyes, yet he continued and said when he ran around the corner to his house that he saw his home had also taken a direct hit from one of the bombs and that the bomb blast had killed his entire family, including his pet puppy.

He said he saw the large silver-colored aircraft responsible for the bombings flying overhead and was later informed by some town elders that the aircraft responsible for the bombings were from the United States.

The boy told Trang that staying here was keeping him off the streets and that he'll never forget the kindness both Lanh and his aunt Thien had shown him.

Trang walked over and embraced the young boy. Trang said he was deeply sorry to hear about his family and that he and his younger sister owned and operated this care home. He said he was welcome to stay as long as he wanted.

Trang also told Trung he wanted him to walk inside with us and that he would introduce him to his sister Tuyen and that they would move him from under the front porch to a bed inside the home. The boy was extremely grateful.

The six of us were about to walk up the steps to the care home's front door when Trang suddenly stopped and said, "Children suddenly showing up here is beginning to occur more and more." Tee asked him if he knew why. Trang's reply was, "Apparently, the word has spread about the care home." Bernie asked, "Is that a good thing or a bad thing?"

Trang told Bernie it was both and said "on the good side, they're able to help more children. But on the bad side, they have limited funds and are unable to adequately satisfy all the needs of the new children." He said, in addition, the VC recruited young people at most orphanages, which was the sole reason they opted to call their place a care home. Bernie assured Trang that he got the picture.

Tee and I spoke up and told Trang our team would ask additional marines to donate when we return to base. We made sure Trang understood that, currently, there were only six on our team and that we're more than positive we can increase our number, thus, helping to solve his "bad side" problem. We could tell that Trang was sincerely moved by our gesture to increase the donations.

Finally, we had reached the care home's front door. Tuyen opened the door, and every single one of her children bolted from the inside and began screaming and hugging the four of us. The children went wild with excitement to see us. And the four of us felt real good inside.

As I watched Tuyen and her three lady assistants attempt to get the children under control, I reasoned that it had been quite a long spell since four of our team members had visited the care home at the same time. It actually took several minutes before Tuyen and her girlfriend assistants gained complete control of the jubilant children.

Once Tuyen got the attention of the children, she explained that she had some important business to discuss with the four of us and asked them to quietly return to their rooms until our business was complete. The children adhered to Tuyen's request and reluctantly scampered back into their rooms.

As I looked around, I failed to see Little Kim, so I asked Thuy why she wasn't with the other children, and she told me Kim had come down with a bad cold and was in her room being cared for by Aunt Thien.

Soon after the children vacated the living room, Tuyen told us Trang had slipped out the rear door and had driven around the corner to get something. So we began discussing alternate methods of getting our donations to the home instead of hand delivery, and we began tossing ideas around. About ten minutes went by before Trang returned. He drove into their driveway, driving a shiny new police car.

Trang parked the car and entered their rear porch door carrying three large bottles of sparkling red wine. Once inside, he asked Tuyen and her three assistants to provide the each of us a glass in order to conduct a toast.

Prior to the toast, he asked Tuyen to go and find Thien so that she could share in the celebration. Tuyen told him Thien was nursing Kim's bad cold and that she'd not toast or do anything of that nature until Little Kim felt better.

After hearing about Kim's condition, I asked Thuy to take one of my packages of sugar mints and give to Thien to provide to Kim. Thuy gladly took them to Kim's room. When Thuy came out from Kim's room, I asked her how Little Kim was feeling, and Thuy told me she felt a whole lot better because she had sugar mints to ease her pain. We both laughed; then Thuy told me Little Kim's fever had broken and that she had thanked me for the sugar mints.

I thanked Thuy, then asked Tee the meaning of broken fever. Tee explained its meaning and said it appeared Little Kim would be well soon. Tee's words were music to my ears; now I was truly ready for Trang's celebration toast.

Trang made sure our glasses were full of wine. Then he began his toast by telling us how "thankful" they were of our team's support. We then took a drink; then Trang proclaimed that each penny of our team's donation money would be spent on sheltering, clothing, and feeding the children.

As we all were about to take our second drink of wine, we suddenly heard what appeared to be small arms fire. We followed Trang to the front porch area and were hoping the noises were that of firecrackers exploding, denoting a birthday or wedding celebration.

When we reached the front porch, we noticed scrambling on the part of their neighbors and began hearing the city's loud safety sirens. The sound of those safety sirens closely resembled the sound of those WWII air raid signals.

The sirens were sounding off about every thirty seconds, and they were causing nearby neighbors to panic, and we four marines were beginning to get a little nervous as well.

In view of the fact that each of us four had witnessed vast amounts of horror during our time in the Nam, we weren't feeling nervous in that way; we were feeling nervous because of the "unknown."

In essence, we were asking, what was the noise that sounds like small arms fire, and why were these stupid sirens blaring in the wind? Trang was communicating to his station headquarters via his two-way unit but wasn't receiving any solid information.

Meanwhile, the four of us began checking our hand weapons to ensure they were lock and loaded. Chris and Bernie were armed with Colt .45s, while Tee and I carried Smith & Wesson .38s.

Trang saw us checking our weapons and tried to convince us that everything was all right and that our weapons would not be necessary. During the same time, Tuyen was emphatically reminding us to remember that we're standing in a care home for children and not on some battlefield.

We tried as best we could under these circumstances to explain that we're fighting marines first and care home humanitarians second and that we know exactly where we're at and that we'll do everything possible to avoid using our weapons, but if anything went down that required us to defend ourselves, defend ourselves we did.

They understood our situation, and we decided to hold a brief meeting while standing on their front porch. Chris was the ranking NCO in our group and would act as our speaker. Trang represented the care home and opened the little meeting by stating how sorry he was about this whole thing.

Chris said we can, one day, come back to finish toasting but that, for now, we need to leave for Marble Mountain as soon as possible. We all agreed, and Trang and Tuyen began hugging the four of us.

The moment we ceased hugging, the safety sirens stopped blowing. Tuyen then requested that Trang, her three assistants, and the four of us assemble back into her living room. Tuyen also requested that one of her assistants go and get Thien from Kim's bedroom.

Tuyen told Thuy to provide each of us an empty glass. Then she asked Trang to go get his wine. Tuyen told us she was not going to allow some crazy sirens spoil this special occasion and that we are all going to finish the planned toast.

Soon after Bernie, Chris, Tee, and I reentered the living room, Thien came walking up with a big smile on her face and told us Little Kim was feeling much better and that her fever had all but disappeared. Then she ran over and embraced Tee.

The news that Kim was feeling better immediately made me feel better, and for a moment, I completely forgot about the recent safety siren episode. I asked Thien if I would be able to see Kim before I left and that I was soon to leave. She told me, "Kim is dressing as we speak, and she will be coming out after the toast."

Trang stood up, got everyone's attention, and said Tuyen had requested we finish our toast, but, first, he apologized to the four of us for the prior chaotic confusion, and that he was told by a friend at his police station the city was conducting a safety drill and that it had been poorly constructed.

Bernie asked Trang if his friend told him about the apparent gun firing that seemingly was occurring down the street. Trang said the noise we thought was gunshots was a nearby faulty circuit breaker exploding and breaking down.

Trang then looked around the room, checking to see if the ten grown-ups standing had an empty glass. He then began filling our glasses with red wine. When he finished, he nodded to Tuyen, and she presented us with the first toast. As her brother had done prior to the commotion, she thanked our entire team for sacrificing our personal needs and supporting her care home.

Tee presented the second toast and thanked the entire care home staff for allowing our team the privilege of helping the children and that for not looking upon helping these kids as if we're sacrificing anything.

Chris lifted his glass and said our entire team sincerely enjoyed helping the children and that we looked forward to increasing our monthly donation amount.

I was next, and my toast was almost identical to theirs.

It was Bernie's turn to toast, and he said, "When growing up, I witnessed my mother financially struggle to raise me and my two sisters." Furthermore, he witnessed an Irish family who lived next door helped his mother financially. Bernie ended by emotionally saying "he'll never forget that Irish family's kind financial gesture and what it did for the survival of his family."

After our toasting ceremony, Tuyen informed us the children had been working hard this morning and that they had prepared a nice little treat for us to enjoy. She then shouted out to the children and told them they could come out of their rooms and join the party.

Suddenly, the bedroom doors flung open as the kids came marching out. They were marching and high-stepping as they began circling the four of us. The kids were being directed by Thien, and she seemed to sincerely be enjoying this occasion. Then, all of a sudden, they stopped marching and stood at attention.

All while this was happening, I looked for Little Kim to come dashing out but didn't see her anywhere. Then I felt something tap me on my arm; when I turned around, there Kim was standing, smiling up at me, and looking like a little princess while dressed in her new sailor outfit that Tee had bought for her.

Little Kim's bad cold hadn't stopped her taste for sugar mints, because after giving me a warm hug and shouting, "Hi, My Friend You." She stretched her cute little hand out in search of sugar mints, and it just so happened I had a jacket pocket full of them.

Tuyen's three girlfriends and Thien took up their positions alongside the children as they were about to provide us four the treat they had been practicing all week in the form of a song.

Tuyen strolled over to her piano where she was to accompany them. Then about thirty-three children ranging in the ages of eight to sixteen began singing, along with Thien and the three lady assistants.

English language was used by the group to sing our treat—a popular tune the four of us were all too familiar entitled "The Marine Corps Hymn." While they sang, every single one of us had tears running down our cheeks. Their rendition of our song was that moving, and when they finished, the four of us quickly stood and gave them a hearty standing ovation.

After our song treat, Thien came over to where Tee and I were standing and asked when was the last time we seen Lanh. I told her we hadn't seen him in two weeks but that I talked to him over the phone almost daily and that I spoke to him last night and he appeared to be doing fine. Tee sensed she was about to cry because she was overjoyed to hear Lanh was safe. So he embraced her and gladly provided a dry shoulder for her to cry on.

I reasoned Tee could more than handle Thien's questioning and politely slipped away in search of Little Kim to ask her was she actually singing our treat song in English. And if her answer was yes, my next questions would be when and from whom she learned enough English to sing the treat song.

When I looked around, Kim was running toward me, and just when I was about to ask her about her singing in English . . . Trang suddenly stood up and requested that we hastily step out on the front porch to discuss some important information he had just received over his two-way.

The last one to arrive at Trang's meeting was Tee. He walked up looking a little pissed. Tee reasoned that time spent listening to Trang would shorten time spent talking to Thien. As Tee walked up, he surprisingly began apologizing for his late arrival to the meeting.

Trang excused Tee, and when he began talking . . . Bernie blurted out, "Trang, what is the problem this time? A faulty sewer line?" Bernie and Chris began chuckling until Trang's reply. He calmly looked at Bernie, then looked down at his notepad and emphatically said, "VC, high activity in the western section of Da Nang and its surrounding countryside. VC recruiting young men and women."

Chris used Tuyen's phone and called to check in at base command. He was told a curfew restrictive order had recently been issued, and we were ordered back to Marble Mountain.

Meanwhile, Trang had received another call on his two-way unit; this time, he was ordered to report to duty as soon as possible. Trang told us about this situation and suggested since he was driving a police car that he drive us to Marble Mountain.

Trang didn't get an argument from any of us, and we reasoned by him driving us to base that this would allow us to spend a few more minutes with the children while he dressed into his uniform and prepared himself for duty.

When I reached down to pick up my jacket, the envelope containing our first pledge donation, amounting to $720, fell to the floor. During all the excitement occurring today, we had completely forgotten that we had this envelope to provide to Tuyen and Trang.

Without any ceremony or fanfare, we simply handed the envelope containing our first donation pledge of $720 to Tuyen. She gladly accepted it with tears of joy filling her eyelids. Tuyen looked up and said, "Thank you, marines."

As the four of us were standing on their front porch steps, saying our goodbyes, Trang hastily walked up and said, for our safety, he recommended we leave at once and begin the drive to Marble Mountain.

Thien gave Tee a long hug and me a short one while telling me Kim had fallen to sleep. I gave Thien my last package of sugar mints to give Kim as a reward for being a good girl. Then we quickly said our last goodbyes and began to hastily climb into Trang's awaiting police sedan.

Our short ride back to Marble Mountain was quiet and uneventful. When we arrived, each of us hugged Trang and thanked him for driving us safely to base. We exited his sedan, checked in at security, and made a beeline direct to Ray and Mac's sleep tent to provide them a complete update of today's events.

In return, Ray and Mac told us that Marble Mountain was put on high-alert status and liberty had been suspended for all military personnel.

When Tee and I arrived at our sleep tent that early mid-October evening, we joined the other fourteen marines who occupied our tent and spent the remainder of the evening cleaning our rifles and checking our gear.

We were doing this in complete darkness due to a standing "lights out" order. We're trained to perform these functions in darkness, so no problem.

Communications in our sleep tent was to be performed at a strict minimum—in a low whisper. There are twelve-man bunkers on each sides of our sleep tent, and we began late-night drills last week to determine how quickly we could man them.

The rumor going around base was that it was eminent a VC strike was to occur on one of these peaceful fall nights. In essence, the smell of battle was in the air.

Perhaps Mr. VC was unaware . . . It's times like these . . . marines lived for . . . So bring it!

It was difficult falling to sleep tonight, and I reasoned it resulted from the phone call I received at work this morning from Tuyen.

She called at 0830 hours to tell me, within the past twenty-four hours, VC activity was seriously increasing in and around the township where her care home was located. She also said three of her older boys were confronted by suspected VC, and they tried to entice her boys to join them and fight for their cause.

I asked Tuyen if she informed Trang of this, and she said he was already aware of this suspected VC infiltration.

The problem with suspending liberty was it kept me from going to Tuyen's care home and visiting Little Kim and listening to how sweet she would say her new name, My Friend You, and the elation she would have on her face as she would look up at me with those big brown beautiful eyes and stretch her cute little hand out for sugar mints.

While other marines on base were trying to sleep but nervously thinking about an eminent VC attack, I was trying to sleep but nervously concerned about the safety of Little Kim. In addition, I was deeply concerned about the overall safety of all the children and the staff who occupied the care home.

Then my thoughts would turn to the many fun times I had with Little Kim (My Friend You), and I would soon fall off to sleep with a smile on my face.

"If you can't keep trouble from arriving, you needn't provide it a chair to sit on."

"TUYEN IN FRONT OF HER CAREHOME (ORPHANAGE)."

Attack Preparation

ALL FIVE HELICOPTER SQUADRONS ASSIGNED to MAG-16 were addressed by their respective commanding officers the morning of October 25, 1965. Their message was relatively the same which was basically for "all marine aviators to continue performing their assigned duties with ultracaution" and that Marble Mountain had been placed on the highest-alert status.

The above statement was issued as a result from information handed down by military intelligence. They informed our group squadron commanding officers an attack on our base by suspected VC was eminent.

Our six team members huddled up, directly after hearing the warning from our commanding officer. Bernie said, "The so-called big rumor is no longer just a big rumor." Mac stated, "He could actually feel tension in the air and that it was so thick he could cut it with a knife." Bernie and Mac's comments were how we all felt as we disbanded and went our separate ways to our daily workstations.

Tee and I had a short walk to our Aircraft Engineering Office tent where we both had been working twelve-hour days. When the number of flight missions by our helicopters increased, our workload of accurately logging time against both the aircraft and its main components increased accordingly.

Our engineering clerical staff only consisted of four marines. Our supervisor was Staff Sergeant Manny and his staff of three worker bees who performed the aircraft logging duties were Lance Corporal Ross, Tee, and yours truly.

Staff Sergeant Manny told us our squadron's highest-ranking NCO, Master Gunnery Sergeant Snyder, had called for our squadron's NCOs to muster this afternoon in front of our squadron's maintenance hangar 2. Time for the muster was 1700 hours, and Sergeant Manny told us to be on time.

At 1700 hours, our squadron's ranking NCO, Master Gunnery Sergeant Snyder, began taking our squadron's NCO roll call. And by the drop-dead serious tone of sergeant Snyder's voice, you would have thought we were about to engage in war with the Soviet Union. He was normally an easy going, jolly fellow, but not on this occasion.

The tone in Sergeant Snyder's voice was that of a fighting marine. Many of the NCOs present were stunned by the manner in which he was speaking. We had never heard him talk this way before, and it was jolting.

He said military intelligence had documented proof the VC was heavily engaged in a citywide recruitment campaign. He demonstrated on how they were trying to recruit fighters and said the VC was currently recruiting both men and women to help them fight for their cause.

Sergeant Snyder's statements were very effective, because when he began wrapping up, I, along with practically every NCO listening, was ready to kill every VC on the planet and then some.

Soon after Sergeant Snyder completed his opening remarks, he stated he would field questions during the second phase of his message. Before he was able to begin the second phase, a nerdy sergeant E-5 raised his hand and asked, "What is our current MAF man power strengths in the RVN?"

Without hesitation, Sergeant Snyder signaled for Staff Sergeant Manny to display a chart that quickly answered the nerdy marine's question.

Marine Amphibious Force (MAF) strengths in RVN not including Seabees:

Location:	MAF marines on the ground	arrived in July
Da Nang:	15,204;	5,743
Chu Lai:	6,949	395
Phu Bai	2,052	178

Qui Nhon	1,644	1,651
Other	115	2
Total	25,964	7,969

Sergeant Snyder told us to study the chart Sergeant Manny displayed; then he explained some of the recent history of the war. He told the assembled NCOs that last month (July 1965), President Johnson announced that the US would increase the number of its forces in South Vietnam from 75,000 to 125,000.

He then began informing us of some recent combat activity involving marines, RVN, VC, and North Vietnam regulars.

1.   He said that the day before, a coordinated two-day sweep effort involving Third Recon and an ARVN unit began southwest of Chu Lai. Results: six VC killed and forty-six captured. One USMC killed and two wounded. He termed this Operation Drum Head.

2.   He summarized Operation Trail Blazer which took place earlier in the month. It was a six-day series of ambushes by the Third Recon Battalion. It began from a patrol base about fifteen miles southwest of Da Nang. The purpose of the operation was to determine the extent of VC concentration in the main valleys leading from the mountains into the Da Nang TAOR and to determine the probability of enemy attack from that area. Seven VC were killed in the operation, and five enemy complexes of training camps and workshops were destroyed.

3.   He continued by saying during the same time frame, two companies from 3/3 launched Operation Triple Play, a two-day search-and-destroy effort conducted twelve miles north of Chu Lai. The results: sixteen VC KIA; eighteen VCW, with only two marines wounded.

4.   Sergeant Snyder finished his discussion concerning recent combat activity around our base by telling us the final numbers had been tallied from Operation Star Lite. He proudly stated several NCOs in attendance had partici-

pated in this battle. He said military intelligence projects the actual enemy KIA total ran much higher, but because of the large number of caves and tunnels that were sealed or destroyed, it was almost impossible to arrive at an exact number, but the best projection was the VC had suffered 1,430 KIA. He sadly said 45 marine KIAs and 203 WIA.

As Sergeant Snyder was completing his two-hour session, a staff sergeant E-6 asked if we will get attacked here at Marble Mountain. Soon as this request was made by the sergeant, every NCO attending the session began to talk and mumble a similar request. Sergeant Snyder brought us to attention and firmly said we would remain that way until we learned not to disrupt this meeting. We stood at attention well over five minutes until he said, "At ease, men," and stated he would address the sergeant's question.

Without hesitation, he told the sergeant, "Yes. According to military intelligence, Marble Mountain is a target, and the primary target by the VC will be our helicopters. We must protect them from destruction at all cost." He then quietly said our meeting was adjourned and that we're to fall out and double-time back to our assigned workstations.

HMS-16 was the helicopter squadron Tee and I were assigned. HMS-16 was an aircraft maintenance squadron, and the helicopters it maintained were primarily those undergoing their periodic maintenance checkups or those being worked on as a result of sustaining combat damage. HMS-16s helicopters were normally deployed on missions primarily as backup aircraft for the remaining helicopter squadrons making up MAG-16.

Resulting from the enemies increased activity in and around Da Nang the past several weeks, HMS-16s helicopters had been dispatched for both combat missions and medevac rescue missions almost as frequently as the other four helicopter squadrons making up MAG-16.

Tee and I really enjoyed our squadron's increased flight activity because it made the odds that more favorable that we would be provided the opportunity to fly as one of the chopper's volunteer crewmen. When Tee or I was chosen to fly in one of our choppers (UH34D or UH1E) as a volunteer crewman, we received additional pay . . . This was my motivation, but I know for a fact it wasn't Tee's. He simply loved being in the air and jumped at every chance provided to him.

As prior stated, Tee and I carried the same MOS (6491), and we both enjoyed performing our duties of an aeronautical engineering clerk. But logging flight time against an aircraft and its key components for an extended period had a tendency to become a "boring."

But flying as a volunteer crewman aboard a UH1E helicopter engaged in a combat mission or helping to perform a lifesaving function aboard a UH34D helicopter during a medevac rescue mission was normally viewed as the opposite of "boring" and seen as exciting and adventurous.

If Tee or I was lucky, during one of these volunteer crewmember flights, we were provided the opportunity to fire our weapons at a target different from what we were accustomed to seeing on our base firing range.

I experienced this opportunity a few times. As stated earlier, the first time I was afforded the opportunity to fire my M14 rifle as part of the flight crew was during the rescue of Lanh, Little Kim, Thien, and the remaining fourteen children.

We were ordered by our crew chief during that eventful medevac mission to lay down cover fire. Trust me . . . it's not like the movies where the good guys clearly see the bad guys as they commence to pick them off one by one. It's not like that at all. I couldn't see a damn thing that rainy evening as I was blasting my ass off.

On another occasion where I was afforded the opportunity to fire my trusty M14 was again during a medevac rescue mission. This time, the UH1E's copilot directed me to put my M14 on semiautomatic and to fire at an open field. It was around midnight, and when it gets dark in the jungle, it's really dark. As I followed the copilot's order and began firing my M14 . . . I remembered how my tracers (every fifth round) made it appear to resemble that of fireworks.

I was gleefully enjoying my self-made firework display until Victor Charlie wanted to join in on the fun and began to fire back at me. I'm not sure who won the fireworks contest, but thank God no one aboard our chopper was hit that night.

On the other hand, my close friend Tee was provided this opportunity to fire his weapon at the enemy on a number of occasions. But as close of friends as we were, Tee nor I never discussed whether or not we thought we had hit anyone. Marines normally kept that shit to themselves and hardly ever talked about killing someone . . . That part of the war was personal and was dealt with that way.

The high-alert status on base was turning out to be "just that" because, all during the morning hours, I witnessed several rifle squads from the nearby Third marines dig in and quickly build five-foot-deep sandbag bunkers in several strategic locations surrounding Marble Mountain's perimeter.

These marines were quickly becoming combat ready, and by the serious look on their faces, they were digging in to plant some serious mayhem on our enemy. I had been in-country and stationed at Marble mountain some six months but had never witnessed anything like what was currently happening both in and around our base.

These grunts had that black shit smeared all over their faces. And even black marine grunts that were as black as midnight had their faces smeared with black paint. It was a sight to see, sort of reminded me of Halloween.

Practically all the aviation marines on base were talking about how impressed they were by the professional manner in which their fellow infantry marines were going about the tasks of taking up defense positions along the base's perimeter. These guys were going about the business of preparing for warlike precision clockwork. Their professionalism made me proud to wear the same uniform.

Master Gunnery Sergeant Snyder held the position of chief aircraft maintenance NCO and worked in our aircraft engineering tent. His desk was only a few feet from my workstation, so I had the opportunity to overhear a lot of confidential information. I kept hearing both officers and noncommissioned officers telling Sergeant Snyder, it was certain our base was going to be hit.

As the workday was winding down, I somehow mustered up the nerve to step in Sergeant Snyder's office and directly asked him when he thought the VC were going to hit Marble Mountain.

I must have caught him at a good time, because, to my surprise, Sergeant Snyder told me to have a seat, and prior to answering my question, he told me that my direct report, Staff Sergeant Manny, was high on my work. His statement caught me completely by surprise and lost for words. So I told him I enjoyed my work and was happy to hear my logging efforts were not going unnoticed.

He then began to address my original question by asking me a question. He lit a large cigar and calmly asked me what I thought about the VC. At first, I thought he was just having fun with me, but by the serious look on his face, I tried hard to provide him a well-thought-out answer.

I told him I thought the VC was an intelligent and well-organized fighting force. I further said that I was told they had won several firefights against our allied forces, so they must be pretty skilled in the art of warfare. I ended by telling him I didn't understand how they were sustaining the war effort against the mightiest country known to man.

He nodded his approval to my reply and said, "Corporal Clark, you are dead-on. The VC and the Vietnamese regulars from up north are, in fact, a fighting force to be reckoned with." He said, "Their fighting units constantly display the ability to mount well-coordinated hit-and-run attacks." He thought for a long while and slowly said, "Corporal Clark, this is a political war, and the US could win it in a few days if our hands weren't tied."

Our interesting little talk came to an abrupt end as a gunnery sergeant stepped into his office and said his presence was immediately needed in the squadron's command office. He apologized to having to end our conversation.

In return, I quickly thanked him for his time, and as I was leaving his office, he stopped me and said, "Corporal, always remember this one thing as long as you wear that uniform—and that is to never underestimate your enemy." He went on to finally say, "You do that young man, and they won't be hauling your ass back to the States in a body bag." Again, I thanked him for his words of wisdom and left his office.

As soon as I left his office, I located Tee and informed him of my encounter with Sergeant Snyder. Tee said he was highly surprised Sergeant Snyder took the time to talk to me because he had always thought that Sergeant Snyder was a true "redneck" from Alabama and didn't particularly embrace the idea of having soul brothers in his marine corps.

My reply to Tee was, "I think you have Sergeant Snyder figured all wrong. True, he is ice-cold around nonperformers, but he is solid around marines of all color that perform." Tee winked at me and said he had already figured I would say something like that and flashed me his famous smile.

Prior to allowing Tee to leave, I asked him if he still had a friend who worked in the intelligence unit of MAG-16. Tee began telling me his friend's name and that he was a career marine who was recently promoted to warrant officer.

Tee then said his friend most likely would not reveal any information that pertained to our war effort in Vietnam. Tee had read my mind, and I told him I understood all of that but that we should give it a try, anyway. Then I asked Tee to contact his warrant officer friend and ask him had he heard any information pertaining to orphanages or care homes being overrun by the enemy.

Tee said he would give it a shot and ask his friend. I then told Tee we should assemble with our team of six as soon as possible. Tee went to retrieve Chris and Bernie while I went looking for Ray and Mac. We met in Ray and Mac's sleep tent, and Tee opened by telling us about his last phone conversation with Thien.

Tee told us he had talked to Thien about a week ago, just prior to our base's communication lockdown, and she told him VC were heavily recruiting near the care home but, other than that, everything appeared to be okay.

I told our team members I had talked to Tuyen about a week back, and during our discussion, she was concerned about the safety of the children. She feared some of her older kids were being targeted by the VC to join in their cause. And like Thien said to Tee, Tuyen ended our phone conversation by saying that, at that time, everything appeared to be okay.

I told our team how I was not satisfied with her ending comment and called her immediately back up and asked her what her plans were to secure the safety for the children, and she said that she would get back to me after she had a chance to talk it over with Trang. Prior to hanging up, I asked her to have Trang call me. Then she hastily hung the phone up.

The team members figured the reason Tuyen was trying to hang the phone up so quickly was she feared her calls were being monitored by the VC. I told our team that Trang called me later that day and verified there were reports of heavy VC activity in close proximity to their care home. Trang said he was keeping in close contact with Tuyen and that the children were safe and that he would keep me posted. Trang made these comments a week ago just prior to the communication lockdown order, and I hadn't heard from him since then.

Chris, Bernie, Ray, Mac, Tee, and I all felt the children could possibly be in harm's way, but by being restricted to base and unable to make phone contact, there wasn't anything we could do about it at that time. I ended our team meeting in Ray and Mac's tent by saying I was "unable to make contact with Tuyen or Trang, coupled with the suspense of not knowing Little Kim's status or the safety status of all the children was driving me crazy and keeping me awake at nights." the entire team applauded my ending statement. Then our session ended.

Our team held hands for our customary prayer session and as usual Bernie led our team in prayer. After that, we broke up and went our separate ways. Tee double-timed over to the Group Intelligence Office to discuss the things we had earlier discussed with his warrant officer friend.

Since we had about three hours of daylight left, I hurried back over to the Aircraft Engineering Office tent in an attempt to make a dent in the huge backlog of logging aircraft data. Due to VC's increased activity around Da Nang, there were twice as many helicopter flight missions. This equates to twice the amount of aircraft logging duty. Tee and I were working twelve- to fourteen-hour days in an attempt to keep up with this increased workload.

In the past two weeks, many of our helicopters were arriving back at base with damage to their main fuselage and other key components. Our UH1Es and mainly our UH34Ds were taking hits from increased rifle fire. Each aircraft's damage activity had to be properly recorded. The data was recorded in the corresponding aircraft's logbook, and this was performed by Tee or me.

When Tee or I typed the damage report and inserted it into the aircraft's logbook, this data triggered our mechanics and/or avionics personnel into action to quickly performed the necessary repairs, thus, enabling the aircraft to fly again.

In wartime, the logging process of important aircraft information needed to be performed as soon as possible. In most cases, the logging or recording of key data was performed the moment the aircraft was grounded.

As a result of the aforementioned, I was working extremely long hours and found myself beginning to sleep at nights on a squeaky old cot inside our Engineering Office tent. A few nights, Tee would sleep over with me, because by the time we had finished our daily logging, it had become too late and dangerous to walk back to our sleep tent.

Instead of four aircraft engineering clerks logging this past week, we were limping along with just two. Our fourth team member, Lance Corporal Spelling continued to experience dizzy spells as a result of a snakebite and was ordered by base doctors to remain in sick bay until he got well.

Tee was mostly absent this past week due to his popularity as a volunteer flight crewman. The crew chiefs in our squadron loved having Tee flying in their choppers as a backup crew member. Tee loved to fly, so he was all in, but, honestly, I felt Sergeant Manny should have disallowed it.

I thought it was obvious to disallow Tee from flying doing this peak logging period, because it only left Staff Sergeant Manny and myself to perform the logging duties for about twenty-four helicopters that were constantly being dispatched and arriving back at base shot up.

Finally, I got up the nerve to approach Sergeant Manny and voice my staffing concern, and I was politely told to stand down and simply to work harder. Sergeant Manny told me that Tee realized by him flying, he was leaving us to do his work. Then he asked me what was more important. I answered him and never brought the subject up again.

As I left Sergeant Manny's desk area, I felt like a damn fool. I reasoned here Tee was up in the air, putting his life on the line in an effort to help win this stupid war, and here I am, safe and sound, down here on the ground bitching about a little work. I'm unable to put in words how small I felt as I left Manny's desk area.

I decided to sleep the night in the Engineering Office because I had worked past our "lights out" curfew. So like several other aviation marines working late at night, we didn't give it a second thought to bed down in our work tent.

We felt safe sleeping in our work tents because there were infantry marines constantly patrolling our work tent area, and the professional matter in which they went about their business would make anyone feel safe. These men were preparing for battle, and by the look on their faces, they were much prepared.

"Fear not, for I am with you; be not dismayed, for I am your God. I will uphold you with My victorious right hand."

—*Isaiah 41:10*

"CAREHOME CHILDREN."

VC Attack on MAG-16 at Marble Mountain

I**T WAS THE MORNING OF** October 27, 1965, and the rumors that Marble Mountain was going to be attacked had been increasing at an increasing rate these past few days. Our squadron commanding officer requested and received a substantial increase in our base's perimeter defense.

Infantrymen from the Third Marine Division were picked to guard our base. The majority of them were trucked in from nearby Chu Lai, and the remainder arrived fresh from stateside. They immediately began the task of establishing an airtight perimeter defense, and these guys positively did not mess around. They appeared to be put on this earth to do nothing but to simply kick ass.

All of the helicopter squadrons in our group were experiencing increases in the number of combat sorties and medevacs. My best friend, and coworker (Corporal Tellis), was quickly becoming the most popular and sought-after volunteer crew member in our entire group.

Most of the chopper crew chiefs were requesting Tee to fly aboard their chopper when they were in need of another crew member. It was easy to determine why Tee was so popular . . . It was his great personality. In addition, Tee was courageous; the crew members could always count on Tee to watch their backs.

Tee and I were the only two experienced engineering clerks assigned to our squadron, the Third engineering clerk in our squadron was a rookie PFC. About everything he logged, Tee or I had to check out to ensure its accuracy.

When Tee was off flying as a volunteer crew member, I was left with the chore of performing the squadron's logging duties. The rookie PFC did his best to assist me, but for the most part, it was yours truly who perform the bulk of our aircraft's flight logging duties.

As a result of the heavy workload, I began working eighteen-hour days. And the many hours working in the Engineering Office began resulting in me falling asleep these past few evenings and awakening past the curfew hour. Thus, I would simply sleep overnight in the engineering tent on top of an old hospital cot.

I felt entirely safe sleeping overnight in our office which was due primarily as a result of the presence of many patrolling Third marines. They set up numerous guard stations all along the metal planking where our choppers were tied down and parked.

In addition, I didn't want to be walking around late at night in the work tent area that was adjacent to our parked aircraft with all those mean-looking Third marines manning their defense positions, locked and loaded.

Tee sincerely expressed several times how sorry he felt that I had to work so late as a result of his flying as a volunteer crewman. I told my old friend there was positively no need for his apology. Then I jokingly told him that I was sure he was gunning for the record of logging the most flight hours by a volunteer crew member aboard a helicopter in wartime.

Tee flashed his famous smile; then he jokingly asked me if I knew what the record was for a volunteer flight crewman.

I told him it's not his fault he was sought after to fly as a volunteer crew member by all of those crew chiefs.

Then jokingly asked him, "How much money are you paying those crew chiefs to request you all the time?"

Realizing it was getting late, we hugged each other and said our goodbyes; then Tee went hurrying off to join another flight crew to fly on yet another mission.

While observing Tee running to his chopper, I also noticed Master Gunnery Sergeant Snyder walking directly toward me, so I quickly began to square myself up a little.

He said he was running late to a meeting and that he was aware I was sleeping in the Engineering Office tent for the past several nights. He said he knew why I was doing it and sternly said for me to cease doing it. He said if our base was attacked at night, the enemy's primary target would be our helicopters, and they're parked next to this Engineering Office tent.

As Sergeant Snyder began hurrying off to his meeting, he stopped and said, "You get the picture, right, Corporal Clark?" My reply was, "Yes, sir," and thanked Sergeant Snyder for the warning and as usual ran off to the Engineering Office tent to begin my evening's load of flight logging. As I was approaching my workstation, I reasoned I had planned to cease sleeping here on my own accord after that night.

While I began logging and absorbing the discussion I recently had with Sergeant Snyder, I began reflecting over the last few nights of sleeping over in this Engineering Office tent and began realizing what a big fool I had been.

Here I had been sleeping in the Engineering Office at night which was located only 130 feet from where our group squadron's helicopters were parked. There were UH1E and UH34D helicopters parked on the perforated steel ramping.

The more detailed I thought about how foolish I had been these past several nights, the more frightening I was becoming. Helicopters from all squadrons in our group utilized the perforated steel planking as takeoff and landing pads.

There were several office tents erected on the planking adjacent to the parked aircraft for obvious convenience reasons. Our Engineering Office was erected on the steel planking and located close to the aircraft parking area because it provided ease and quick access for pilots and associated crew members to drop off their flight logs. Our Flight Office tent was situated next to my Engineering Office tent.

Additionally, the Engineering Office was where our aircraft maintenance officer and his top NCO staff were housed, thus, providing the ability to report aircraft malfunctions to applicable personnel immediately and quickly getting the reported malfunctions repaired.

Tee came to the Engineering Office directly after landing and helped me, the rookie, and our supervisor, Sergeant Manny, with some flight logging. At 1900 hours, Sergeant Manny, the rookie, and Tee all stood up to call it a day. Sergeant Manny asked me if Sergeant Snyder cautioned me about working so late and sleeping over. My reply to Sergeant Manny was he certainly did and that I was about to leave.

Tee demanded that I leave with him and began lecturing me about sleeping over in our Engineering Office. After hearing the lecture from Sergeant Snyder, I was in no mood to hear it again, so I told Tee I realized I had been doing a stupid thing—that I was totally aware I had been sleeping in a tent in close proximity to our helicopters and that our helicopters would be the primary target if our base was attacked.

I further explained to Tee that I had a ton of work to do that night and that night would be the last time I would stay up late and possibly sleep over. Because of my voice tone, Tee could clearly tell I didn't want to discuss this any further.

After he had gathered up his personal things, Tee asked me for the last time if I needed his help in logging so I wouldn't have to work late. I told him I could certainly use his help tonight and would highly appreciate it. Just as I said this, a lance corporal appeared and said, "Corporal Tee, your presence is requested immediately in the squadron's Flight Office."

Tee and I assumed he was being called to join a flight crew. I walked him to the doorway and said, "Tee, don't worry about me . . . What you're about to do is much more dangerous than logging flight time . . . " He agreed. We did the soul brother handshake, and just prior to Tee running to the Flight Office, the lance corporal returned and shouted, "Did you get the word that at 1900 hours all workstations were to be vacated?"

I asked him if he knew the reasoning behind this order. And he said he believed it had to do with minimizing foot movement around the matting area where our aircraft were locked down, thus, allowing optimum defensive coverage by the infantry guards who were manning the defensive bunkers on our base's perimeter.

Prior to departing, I told Tee for the second time "to be careful." He voiced the same, then went running toward the Flight Office tent. I turned and walked back to our Engineering Office tent with firm intentions of alleviating some of our flight logging backlog when I ran into my supervisor, Staff Sergeant Manny.

Sergeant Manny stopped me and asked if I heard about the vacate order for all workstations at 1900 hours. My reply was I'd heard about the workstation vacate order and that I was wrapping things up and would be leaving soon.

Sergeant Manny looked me firmly in the eyes and emphatically said, "Corporal Clark, I've also been noticing the long hours you've been putting in, and my marine corps appreciates that kind of work ethic, but right now I'm giving you a direct order: do not work late tonight. Do you clearly understand me, Corporal Clark?" I soundly said, "Yes, sir." He smiled at me and said, "Thanks."

As Manny left, he shouted over his shoulder that I was the last person working in the Engineering Office, so he asked me to lock it down when I leave. I told him I would lock things up as he left our work tent, then checked the time and figured I had a good two hours of flight logging remaining before I had to stop and honor the "vacate workstation" order.

While logging aircraft and associate component flight time in their appropriate logbooks, I began to nod off to sleep and would nervously awaken with the total awareness that if my ass is caught at my workstation past 1900 hours, I would be in serious trouble and could possibly face a court-martial.

I ate more than usual at the mess hall that evening, and like most people, when I eat a lot, I tend to get sleepy afterward. So I walked over and heated our office coffeepot and drank a few cups in an attempt to stay awake.

My conscious kept telling me to fold it up and dee-dee my ass back to my sleep tent, but my other conscious kept telling me this was a golden opportunity to use the Engineering Office phone and call the care home and check up on the safety of Little Kim, her brother Lanh, and the rest of the children.

Due to the telephone lockdown security order on base, I hadn't been able to talk to Tuyen or her brother Trang in two weeks. Not hearing from them and not knowing the safety status of the children at their care home was literally tearing me apart.

There had been an increase of frightening rumors floating around our base concerning VC movement in and around Da Nang. There were several rumors about how the VC were about to attack some large target and that they were recruiting young people in and around Da Nang to assist in their cause.

These rumors were sort of like old news, but what made one of them hit home in particular was there was a documented report of a young man forcefully taken from a popular boy's home in West Da Nang and later found tortured and slain, reportedly because he refused to fight for the cause of our enemy.

When I learned of this report, that afternoon, I disobeyed our telephone security order and attempted to call the care home; I just had to see if everything was okay. My hands were shaking so badly while dialing the phone number that I literally was unable to dial the correct number. After I made well over a dozen attempts, I eventually gave up and stopped trying to make the call.

I began trying everything to maintain. I poured cold water from my canteen over my head. I popped several aspirins in my mouth in an attempt to calm my nerves. I drank several cups of hot coffee, said a prayer, and tried to dial Tuyen's phone number again. While dialing, I glanced over at the clock on my desk and noticed I had approximately one hour left prior to 1900 curfew hour.

After dialing Tuyen's phone number a half-dozen times, I finally switched and began dialing Trang. I tried calling Trang at the two numbers he provided me, but for the past week, his phone numbers were blocked and not accepting calls.

By not being able to get through to them, I began thinking the worst and assumed something had seriously gone wrong. But due to this sudden lack of communication, I had no idea what the problem was or if there was a problem. I stopped dialing and poured another full canteen of cold water over my head. Then I sat down in my office chair and commenced to cry like a newborn baby.

I cried for a very long time, then suddenly stopped and commenced to pray.

The patrolling infantry guard heard me praying and asked me if everything was okay . . . I told him it wasn't, and the brother dropped his M14 from his shoulder and asked me if he could join me in prayer. We both knelt down and silently prayed for a good five minutes. When we finished, he said some words in a different language and kindly informed me that he was a Muslim.

We both stood up. He checked his M14 and placed it back over his shoulder, and we both felt real good inside. He checked his wristwatch, then reminded me I had about twenty minutes remaining prior to the curfew. Then he saluted me and hurriedly left.

After our prayer, I was simply dying to hear Little Kim's sweet young voice utter her famous three words: *My Friend You*, and it began to appear that on this night my wish was not to be granted. And after ten or more strenuous minutes of concentrated phone dialing, I decided to give my tired fingers and worn-out nerves a break.

Figuring I had about seventeen minutes remaining, I suddenly began getting mighty thirsty and quickly began searching through our office fridge for something to drink. I reasoned my tired-out nerves was driving my thirst, and like a dummy, I had poured all of my drinking water contained in my canteen over my head in an attempt to keep awake.

Fortunately, I located two bottles of light beer that belonged to Staff Sergeant Manny. I figured if I consumed one of these babies, he wouldn't miss it. The problem was I didn't just drink one but ended up drinking both bottles of beer.

I quickly tried to think up an excuse to offer Manny when I faced him tomorrow but failed to arrive at anything believable, so

I decided to act tomorrow as if I knew nothing about the situation when his beer theft discovery was made.

While sitting at my desk, trying to dial Tuyen one last time, I suddenly found myself cradling my head in my arms and getting terribly sleepy. I reasoned it must have been due to Manny's beer I had consumed. I tried rolling the empty cold beer bottle over my forehead, but sleepiness was getting the best of me.

I really fought hard to stay awake but was unable to and, in an instant, was fast asleep. I had some weird dreams and awoke shortly afterward partially due to #2 nature calling and partly due to fear of violating the 1900-hour workstation lockdown order. My stomach began cramping, and figuring I didn't have time to make it back to my sleeping tent's head (restroom), I made the decision to scamper off to the head nearest our office tent. The nearest head was only twenty yards away from my workstation which was a big relief because I really had to go. I ran as fast as I could to the head, not embarrassed one bit, because totally on my mind was sitting down and dropping some serious #2 bombs.

After reaching my destination, I realized I had left my M14 back at my office chair. But I reasoned I really had to go, and what can happen this "one time"?

Once inside the head, I began removing my shirt and trousers—not because I was freaky but because most heads were extremely hot inside, and if you were sitting down in one for any length of time . . . perspiration would literally pour off you if you were fully clothed. Stripping down made the dump a lot cooler and somewhat bearable.

My wristwatch showed I had approximately nine minutes remaining before the 1900-hour lockdown order, so I reasoned I would squat for three minutes and take two minutes to gather my things from the office and three minutes to sprint back to my sleeping tent. No problem, figuring . . . I would have a minute to spare.

Darkness was beginning to fall, causing it to become extremely dark inside the head. All the heads were constructed by Navy Seabees and constructed identical on our base. Their exterior was made of mesh wire screen construction that would severely rust when it rained. Since it rained often, the screening exterior would turn to a dark-brown rusty color, thus, making it almost impossible to view occupants inside, even during daylight hours.

However, occupants inside our head could easily view people standing on the outside without being detected . . . whether during daylight or nightfall. Slabs of sheet metal made up the roof of our heads, thus, making it extremely hot inside because when the sun shined from above, it would penetrate the sheet metal, thereby, creating an oven effect inside, which was why most of us removed our shirt and trousers when sitting down.

Due to darkness inside the head, I was having a hell of a time locating a roll of toilet paper. I had brought a worn-out magazine with me just in case there wasn't any, but I was seriously hoping there would be some because magazine paper is a bit rough on one's bottom parts.

Luckily, a marine PFC entered the head to take a leak in the second seat, and by him opening the door, I was able to spot a fresh new roll of TP. The PFC did his business, and while leaving, he quietly told me he was part of a unit guarding the many helicopters parked on the nearby steel planking. He then asked me if I was part of the guarding unit. I said I was working in the Engineering Office. He told me the base was on lockdown; everyone was to report to their unit at 1900.

I thanked him and told him I would as soon as I was finished taking care of this business. I then commenced to grunt and drop a couple of bombs. After smelling and hearing my eighteen-inch payloads hit bottom, the PFC ceased providing warnings, quickly gathered up his things, and exited the head.

After a few minutes of serious grunting, I quietly stopped to listen to some marines approaching with their mess gear clanging together rather loudly.

For some mysterious reason, I do my best thinking while sitting in the head. And on this particular evening, I was thinking how stupid it was a few marines walking around the base with noisy mess gear banging around when in fact the base was on high alert and tightly locked down.

As I thought again about them making all of that noise, their actions simply didn't make any sense to me. Not taking time to wipe my ass, I quietly slid off my stool seat and laid my sweat-soaked body out onto the head's sandy piss-soaked floor. I then quietly slid my white skivvies (undershirt and undershorts) from my dark almond-colored body and placed them under me and commenced to lay there buck naked and quiet.

As I lay there, quiet as a mouse, I said to myself if Tee or any of my fellow marine buddies opened the head door and found me lying here like this, I would have a ton of explaining to do.

The mess gear they were carrying suddenly fell to the ground, and I began to hear talking that sounded Vietnamese. *Are these guys base employees?* I raised my head up and took a peek through the rusty screening, and I saw four young Vietnamese males wearing little clothing closely huddled at the rear of the head. *Are base employees possibly playing a game . . . maybe hide-and-seek?*

They must have remained squatted there about five minutes. Then suddenly they scampered away.

Possibly they vacated their hiding spot next to the head, because of the smell generated from the eighteen inchers I had recently dropped. *Or possibly they vacated this spot out of fear of getting caught for stealing GI mess gear.*

Only at this time did my military antenna surface, and finally it hit me . . . These little guys running around with only a black piece of loin cloth covering their private parts were not base employees at all . . . *These little fellas are VC!*

So in world-record time, I grabbed my clothing and ran the short distance back to my Engineering Office tent. Shortly after entering my workstation and putting on my trousers, I began to hear extremely loud explosions and numerous spurts of small arms fire.

Realizing we're under attack, I quickly located my M14 rifle and grabbed eight magazines of 7.62 mm ammo. I then went to the rear of our office tent to thoroughly check out my M14 and to set it to auto.

Cautiously, I quietly pulled back our rear tent flap and peeked out. All I could see was a large amount of dark-gray smoke that was swiftly rising up toward the sky. Then, suddenly, I began hearing a lot of footsteps of people running around on the metal planking that had recently been installed in our work tent area.

The explosions and rifle fire began to highly intensify, and the noise of people shouting out orders was getting louder. As the smoke began to clear, I focused in on the sandbag bunker that I recently helped build to the rear of our work tent just for occasions like this.

There were about a dozen work tents that had been erected on the metal planking. The metal planking was laid down by the Navy Seabees to enable our helicopters to take off and land. It was also the area in which our aircraft were parked when not in use. And each work tent had a sandbag bunker constructed directly behind it, adjacent to the metal planking.

Several loud explosions went off in succession, and I said a brief prayer, then bolted from the rear door of our work tent and ran a dozen feet and leapt into our sandbag bunker. There weren't any marines occupying my bunker, so I quickly tried to position myself so that I would be able to see anyone attempting to enter the bunker. Then I got as low in that bunker as I possibly could and nervously waited.

While waiting, I began thinking about what could be occurring at my sleeping tent bunker. It was the bunker my friend Tee would probably be in, and I knew Tee was wondering where in the hell I was. I dropped that subject from my mind as rapid rifle fire intensified, and loud explosions began going off at an increasing rate.

Meanwhile, trip flares were being set off all around me, and the illumination from the many flares enabled me to see that, out of the twelve sandbag bunkers that had been constructed behind their respective work tents, there were only two bunkers occupied by marines. There was the bunker I was huddled down in and the bunker directly next to mine. There were three marines occupying this bunker, and evidently, they had spotted the enemy because they were blasting away with their M14s.

I tried hard to see what the three marines were firing at, but the dark-gray smoke was hampering my vision. Then, suddenly, I heard a lot of footsteps running toward our two bunkers. I aimed my M14 in that direction but didn't begin firing right away for fear the running footsteps might be those of fellow marines.

I looked over at the three marines and noticed they were firing away in the direction of the running footsteps, so assuming they had a better view and assuming they were firing at our enemy who were attacking our base, I too fired off a few rounds in the direction they were firing at.

Not able to clearly see what I was firing at bothered me, so I stopped firing. Then, all of a sudden, I saw five or six Vietnamese boys running barefooted directly toward my bunker's direction. I nervously popped in a new magazine and commenced firing in the runner's direction.

None of the runners fell to the ground as they sprinted by my bunker, so, apparently, I muffed my chance to chalk up a confirmed kill. Then I came back to reality, even if I would have dropped one or two of those runners . . . I couldn't claim any kills in this area, because I was not supposed to be in this area. If I put in a claim, I reasoned I could face a court-martial for disobeying the outstanding 1900 hour workstation vacate order.

While juggling the aforementioned in my mind, suddenly, both of my hands began to uncontrollably shake, and it seemed there was nothing I could do to stop the shaking. I tried pouring cold water on them from my canteen. Hell, I even tried slapping them up against my rifle butt until they became sore with pain.

Nothing I tried was working, so here I am, sitting all alone in this lonely ass bunker, shaking like a little bitch while a major attack—carefully orchestrated by our enemy—was occurring all around me. I can't find the words to express how humiliated this felt.

Then, all of a sudden, I began quoting the Lord's Prayer . . .

"Our Father, who art in heaven, hallow be thy name. Thy kingdom come, on earth as it is in heaven. Give us this day, our daily bread, and forgive our trespasses, as we forgive those who trespass against us. Lead us not into temptation, but deliver us from evil, for thine is the power, the kingdom, and the glory now and forever. Amen."

Just when I finished saying, "Amen," a fellow marine, a sergeant E-5, leapt into my bunker and asked me if I had engaged. By this time, the entire upper portion of my body was shaking, and I tried hard but was unable to communicate with the sergeant. I tried to answer his question by nodding my head up and down.

The sergeant quickly crawled over to my position and, without providing me a warning, hauled off and slapped me across my face harder than I had ever been slapped before. Shortly afterward, I ceased having speech problems, and my hands and body completely stopped shaking. On the one hand, I was mad as hell for getting bitch slapped by a total stranger, but, on the other hand, I was thrilled to death by its sudden positive outcome.

The sergeant never said a single word before, during, or after the slap. He simply slapped the shit out of me and, when finished, held up two fingers as if flashing me the "peace sign" that I had witnessed the hippies do so much on television back in the states. All I thought to do was attempt to emulate his gesture, so I held up two fingers and flashed him a Tee-like smile.

The sergeant then motioned to me to check my rifle and, in sign, told me to take up a defense position at the rear end of our sandbag bunker. Small arms fire was going off all around us, and a round would hit the inside of our bunker every now and then, so I crawled on my belly as low as I possibly could to the rear end of the bunker.

The sergeant crawled to the other end and, using sign language, motioned for me to keep my eyes focused to the rear and that he would keep his eyes focused to the front. He seemed to know his shit, so I followed his every direction without question or hesitation.

I figured the sergeant was from the infantry unit assigned to guard our choppers, because I had never seen him before, and I knew every sergeant E-5 assigned to our Marine Aviation Group.

While I tightly clutched my M14, with my eyes focused on the sergeant E-5 who had joined me in my bunker, I slowly began to get those damn shakes again. The mere thought that we were about to engage in combat was extremely frightening to me. And this shit was for real; it wasn't a movie script or something of that nature. This was reality, and it was happening this very moment, and there I was, a young man from Lawrence, Kansas, right smack in the middle of it.

My shakes began leaving me as I watched every move of the sergeant. I tried hard to emulate his every move. If he checked his M14, I checked mine. If he crotched lower in our bunker, so did I. If he scratched his ass, I was scratching as well. If he farted . . . I think you get the picture.

The sergeant was truly "godsent," and as I watched his every move, I sensed he was ready and prepared to kick some serious ass. Only at this moment, during this pending action, did I begin feeling, acting, and thinking like the marine I was trained as, and Thank God for sending me this buck sergeant who slapped me when he did, because God knew I was soon about to be tested.

During this short period of calm . . . the sergeant via sign language asked me how many magazines of ammunition I had. I held up five fingers, and he held up three. So I tossed him one of my magazines so he would have four, as I did.

A second wave of VC must have gotten through our perimeter, because, all of a sudden, explosions began erupting by the ramp area where our helicopters were parked. In the same location, there were several burst of machine gun fire. The only thing that separated us from where our helicopters were parked was our work tent.

Several work tents were located on the end of the ramp where our aircraft were parked. I figured our aircraft were being destroyed as a result of those explosions, and the explosions didn't appear to be incoming mortar fire. It sounded more like a satchel charge or grenade attack.

Since I didn't have my wristwatch on, I didn't know the time, but, by the looks of the night sky, I reasoned it was at least several hours past midnight. Darkness was prevalent, and due to the thick heavy smoke generated from the many explosions, it remained difficult to see much distance.

I strained my eyes trying to see oncoming VC because I reasoned that they would be very hard to see because the four I saw outside of our head were basically naked and blended in with the sand.

Parachute flares were continuing to go off overhead and light up the night sky. M60 machine gun and M14 rifle fire could be heard almost everywhere, and the noise was so loud it was almost unbearable. The sergeant and I began to hear voices of marine officers and NCOs shouting out orders all around our position. We remained hunkered down, and as ordered by the sergeant, I kept my eyes focused to the rear of our bunker.

We heard what appeared to be shots fired from an AK-47 directly adjacent from our work tent came. Marines didn't carry AK-47s, so the sergeant and I reasoned it must be enemy fire. We aimed our weapons toward the area the AK-47 shots were heard and prepared for the worst. The worst never came, because the VC that was firing the AK-47 was shot, and his brains was splattered all over a wall of one of our aircraft hangars.

Shortly after the AK-47 shot bursts, a loud explosion occurred directly in front of our engineering tent, and I reasoned the medevac UH1E helicopter that is normally parked there must have been blown up. *After the attack, I was informed our medevac UH1E was in fact blown up, and a much-liked navy chief corpsman was inside the chopper when it was destroyed.*

The explosive noises began to alleviate until there were only occasional shots fired from marines' M14s. These shots even began to subside to the point there were only one or two shots every few minutes. The M14 shots finally stopped, and all that could be heard were the shouting of orders being directed to marines from other marines.

Marines began running by our bunker, and it appeared the enemy attack on Marble Mountain on this particular October night in 1965 by a ban of near-naked VC raiders was finally coming to an end.

I reasoned that assessing damages and mopping up operations would soon follow, and I personally had to quickly figure out what action I was going to take in regards to being in a bunker directly behind my work tent that I was not supposed to be in, and how I was going to somehow explain why I disobeyed a direct order during a combat situation.

Suddenly, I became extremely afraid and actually got the shakes. While I was attempting to pull myself together, I began to search my bunker and the surrounding area for the sergeant who had guided me through this horrific ordeal, and to my surprise, he had disappeared. I thought he was the only person who could truthfully account for my actions during this attack, but he had vanished.

As quickly as he disappeared, the sergeant reappeared. And as I was about to ask him a question, we both saw a couple of short people clad in black loincloth running on the far side of our bunker. Via sign language, the sergeant directed me to back him up as he began firing at the two suspected VC characters running alongside our bunker. I also nervously fired off a couple of shots in the direction of the two runners but was certain I didn't hit any of them.

The sergeant's M14 was set on automatic as he fired off two short burst at the two running VC. I was almost certain he hit one of them, because I heard one of them cry out in pain as they continued running.

Then, suddenly, the sergeant and I began hearing nearby mumblings that were not in English. It sounded just like the mumblings I had witnessed while I was taking a crap in the head. It was chatter by our enemy. The sergeant looked over at me and gave me a look as if to say, "Get ready to engage in a firefight, Marine."

The sergeant began communicating with the three marines next to our bunker via sign language as the enemy voice chatter grew louder. Then, all of a sudden, several extremely loud explosions erupted directly behind our two bunkers, and I heard the sergeant hollow incoming 60 mm mortar fire.

The incoming 60 mm mortar rounds were landing all around us, and they appeared to be directed at our helicopters that were parked on the ramping directly in front of our bunker positions. The sergeant gave me a sign that meant to "stay put," and shortly after that, the three marines in the nearby bunker opened fire with their M14s.

The sergeant joined the three marines in firing, and since I was ordered to focus my eyesight on the opposite direction, I didn't see what they were firing at. I figured most of the marines firing had their M14s on "automatic" because the noise generated from their weapons was extremely loud.

One of the three marines in the adjacent bunker began shouting two o'clock and another chimed in with three o'clock. With them firing and shouting as loud as they could, I almost didn't hear footsteps pounding directly in front of me.

While the three marines in the adjoining bunker had their weapons a-blazing, I barely heard foot pounding in the sand, and heavy breathing quickly approaching my position. Suddenly, one of the VC came running directly to the right of me. He was running fast and was no more than five feet away from my bunker.

For some strange reason, it appeared for a moment that everything slowed down. I tried hard to focus in on the little guy, and it appeared he was not carrying a rifle or any weapon of that type. As he got closer and came scampering by, I was able to see that he was carrying some type of small explosive device. It appeared to be a satchel charge.

He was barefooted and only wore a black loincloth that barely covered his private parts. His focal point of attention was our aircraft parked on the nearby ramp because not once did he look over in my direction in my bunker. If he had, he would have, no doubt, spotted me hunched up in the far corner.

He would have also seen the sergeant firing at whatever the three marines in the nearby bunker were firing at, but his eyes were totally fixated on our ramping pad where our helicopters were parked, and he seemed to be on a direct mission to blow one of our helicopters up with his satchel charge.

When the VC carrying the satchel charge rounded the corner of our bunker, the sergeant fired off about a dozen rounds in his direction, while I fired off six. One or the both of us hit the little guy, because, with a thud, the lone enemy warrior fell to the sandy ground about ten feet away from our position. He appeared to be hit in several places as he fell to the ground tightly clutching onto the satchel charge–looking explosive device that he was carrying.

Both the sergeant and I were unsure if the firing mechanism to his explosive device pin had been activated.

We didn't know exactly what type of explosive device he was holding on to, and for that matter, we didn't know for sure if the little guy was dead or not.

The sergeant told me to keep my rifle pointed at the shot-up VC who had fallen only ten feet from our bunker. By this time, the sergeant and the three marines had ceased firing at the near-naked VC who had been running past our two bunkers.

As the firing in our immediate area subsided, I managed to take a quick survey of the bunker the three marines were occupying and saw several dead loinclothed VC lying at the front end of their bunker. I counted at least seven dead bodies.

The three marines were not firing any longer, but they remained in the on ready position in their bunker. They were loading their M14s with fresh magazines and readying themselves for another wave of assault. *Later, these three marines were awarded medals for bravery; one of them turned out to be a close friend.*

Directly after several M14 shots were fired off, from either the three marines in the adjacent bunker or from other marines now crawling around our area, I heard four or five extremely loud explosions go off on the other side of our engineering tent where many of our aircraft were parked. The noise was so deafening my head and ears began to hurt very badly. I was motionless for a good while and, apparently, had suffered a slight concussion.

As a result of the explosions, small pieces of metal were hurling past my bunker and hitting the sandbags around me. I kept one eye fixated on the two apparently dead VC lying just ten feet from my bunker as the rest of me tried to bury itself in the sand.

It's impossible to pen on paper how frightened this young marine was during the many explosions, the near-naked VC running by his bunker, and the pieces of metal hitting the sandbags surrounding him.

Then, suddenly, I felt a warm and wet sensation on my right backside. I didn't feel pain at first, so I figured I had only pissed on myself from fright during the many explosions and intense small arms fire.

After ten minutes or so, I began to feel a slight amount of pain back there, so I managed to roll over and reach my hand back there for a more thorough examination. I touched the area that was warm and wet and brought my hand up to my face and noticed bright red blood covering my hand. I damn near fainted.

Even as a child, the sight of blood freaked me out. While viewing blood on my hand, I was very confused because there was very little pain associated with the vast amount of blood I was viewing on my hand.

The wound was located on my lower right butt cheek area, and it was impossible for me to look directly at it, so I had to lay there and assume things why I was bleeding. For a short time after my discovery, all sorts of weird thoughts came to my head, and I began to panic.

I came to the realization that I had been hit. By what, I didn't have the slightest idea, but I knew one thing for damn sure, and that was my black ass was bleeding. Since I had never been shot before, I began to think all kinds of crazy things. Like, was I about to visit my maker? I mean, clearly, what is one to think when one is bleeding from his ass, and the wound is in a location where one can't see it?

Quietly, the sergeant crawled over to me and asked me if there was movement on the part of the two apparently dead VC who were sprawled out in front of our bunker. I told him they hadn't moved, but there was more on my mind at the time and, without hesitation, rolled over on my side and pulled my trousers down and motioned to the sergeant to observe my ass wound.

He quickly shined his flashlight on my wounded area and, with a grin on his face, informed me that I would live and that I had most likely been hit with a piece of flying shrapnel and suffered what appeared to be a tear in my skin about an inch and a half long on the upper right cheek of my ass.

Suddenly, four to five loud explosions occurred, apparently on the metal planking where our choppers were parked, and the sergeant again told me, "Corporal, you'll live." Then he quickly left our bunker to join other infantry marines that were swiftly moving through our area.

Lord knows I was extremely relieved to know I had not been shot and that my wound wasn't serious. I then managed to roll over on my left side and remove my white handkerchief from my left rear pocket. I folded it up the best I could and applied it to the wound.

The hanky managed to stop the bleeding, and again I said a quiet prayer. I must have prayed a hundred times that dreadful night . . . but with all the hell going off all around me, I needed every one of them.

As I lay in my bunker reflecting on the events that had just taken place . . . I seriously can't see how one can survive a setting like this without embracing the faith of a religion. It's very difficult to explain the fear one endures during an episode such as this . . . Only combat veterans know this feeling . . . I experienced a small piece of this thing they call "combat." And I can't even think to imagine how our brave and courageous World War II veterans managed to keep their heads during all the hell they experienced.

While curled up in my bunker and administering first aid with my hanky to my right cheek buttocks wound. My mind began to wander again. I began envisioning how proud I would appear at the upcoming ceremony where my squadron commanding officer honored me by pinning medals of courage and bravery on my chest.

I envisioned him first pinning the Purple Heart Medal on my uniform for the bloody wound I had recently sustained. Then I reasoned maybe I would receive another medal or two for engaging in the firefight that resulted in the two apparently dead VC sprawled out in front of me.

While my mind was wandering, a few more loud explosions occurred, and I heard a marine shouting, "They're blowing up the choppers." This activity caused me to cease daydreaming and return back to reality.

Explosions and small arms fire ceased to erupt for a quite a long spell, providing the opportunity for my mind to wander again. I came to the realization that I couldn't report my butt cheek wound or anything that had taken place tonight. I also came to the realization that I wouldn't be receiving any medals and that I couldn't even report I was in this bunker with the sergeant.

I also came to the realization that if I were to report any of the activity that went on in this bunker tonight . . . I could end up getting court-martialed. What a bummer, but I could actually find my black ass locked up if the word was out that I was down here blasting away at the VC in this bunker.

The more I thought about disobeying their orders and possibly during time behind bars, the more adrenaline ran through my veins. I got so tensed up thinking they may throw the book at me that I accidently fired off a round in the vicinity of the two dead VC.

As soon as I fired the shot, the sergeant jumped back into my bunker and began aiming his M14 at the two dead VC lying in front of our bunker. I stopped him from firing and stated they did not move and that I accidently pulled my trigger. The sergeant was not happy with my answer and directed me to put my rifle on "safety" and to leave it there until it was necessary that I switch it back.

During the pause in the action, I thought that I had to figure out a story to get my ass from a possible court-martial. I even got mad at the thought that they would even consider placing me in the brig for sleeping in my work tent.

I reasoned I was a fighting marine, and fighting marines should be where the action is and not hidden in some bunker next to his sleeping tent while the fight is going on down by where the helicopters are parked.

I laid there in that bunker while daylight was soon to break and thought of all sorts of ways to get around the fact that I disobeyed a direct order from Master Sergeant Snyder.

I reasoned that I was involved with the sergeant in a firefight and that we bravely possibly saved the blowing up of one or two of our parked aircraft by being in the bunker directly behind my work tent. I also included in my reasoning that I even suffered a wound on my ass while protecting our aircraft.

I thought very hard on how I could adequately explain my situation in order to receive a possible Purple Heart, but sadly I kept arriving at the conclusion of being court-martialed for disobeying an order. My thought process was concluded as an extremely loud explosion sounded off, then another and another.

During these explosions, the sergeant E-5 crawled over to me, gave me a hand salute, and said thanks for helping him bring down the bad guys. Then he swiftly crawled out of our bunker. He soon disappeared from view, and I never saw the sergeant again.

After the attack was over, I personally searched our entire base for that sergeant. I remember his eyes were ocean blue, that he smoked small cigars and his hair was sandy red in color. His looks, his speech, and his personality resembled the actor who starred in the television western series *Wanted Dead or Alive.*

I finally ran into a marine corporal who knew him and was told he was, in fact, a member of the Third Marine Division and that he had requested a second tour of duty in Vietnam. His request was granted, and the corporal was informed the sergeant was shipped to a base close to Saigon.

Sergeant, if by chance you're still out there, please contact me, because I'm not sure I would be standing here today if it were not for your "slap" to my face, and all I want to do is formally say thank you!

The attack on MAG-16 based at Marble Mountain was officially reported as follows:

> A VC raiding party of 90 to 100 men quietly assembled in a village just to the northwest of the Marble Mountain Air facility. Under cover of 60mm mortar fire, four demolition teams struck at the Marble Mountain airstrip and a hospital being constructed by the Seabees. At least six VC armed with Bangalore torpedoes, satchel charges, and hand grenades, reached the MAG-16 helicopter parking ramp.

The VC's well-planned operation destroyed nineteen helicopters and damaged thirty-five others. Eleven of the thirty-five were damaged severely. VC was seen throwing satchel charges into open chopper doors.

Across the road from the helicopter matting was the newly constructed naval hospital which was nearly complete, and it was severely damaged. The raid by the VC took only about thirty to thirty-five minutes, and the Viet Cong withdrew, leaving behind seven-teen dead. Three Americans were killed during the attack.

"Ask, and it will be given you; seek, and you will find; knock, and it will be opened to you. For every one who asks receives, and he who seeks finds, and to him who knocks it will be opened."

—*Matthew 7:7–8*

"BIG DON THE WARRIOR."

Post-Attack Assessment

THE SUN BEGAN SLOWLY RISING up and over the rugged Marble Mountains, and it became clearly visible the two VC the sergeant had me guarded died instantly; both suffered head wounds. I could also clearly see the dark -colored object one of them had been clutching in his right hand was not an explosive device but was simply a piece of dark jagged metal.

Why he was holding onto this piece of dark-colored metal was a bit of a mystery to me; however, I was highly relieved the dark object wasn't an explosive device that could detonate when the poor little guy was moved.

The heavy explosive blasts caused by incoming mortars, had ceased for well over an hour, and the satchel charge and grenade explosions that caused heavy damage to our parked helicopters had also stopped. Sporadic rifle fire remained prevalent, but, for the most part, the attack was over.

Marines were walking about like there was not a threat of being harmed. There was a feeling of a weird calm that had come over our air base. As I observed our post-attack environment, all I could see was lots of gray-colored smoke bellowing up into the sky and hear a loud crackling noise resulting from the many helicopters burning.

The news had quickly spread about the severe firefight that occurred in my immediate area. Several officers and senior NCOs gathered to get a bird's-eye view of the many dead and wounded

VC bodies that were spread out in all directions around the sandbag bunker the three marines occupied.

Apparently, the news was rapidly spreading, because more and more marines began to gather around the adjacent bunker where the bodies lay; I thought it was a little strange that not a single marine approached me and inquired about the two dead VC bodies lying directly in front of my bunker.

I assumed the crowd of marines viewing the dead had automatically thought the three marines who were soon to be heralded as heroes had shot and killed the two in front of my bunker as well.

Not that it meant that much to me, because I wasn't sure who shot the two VC I was watching; it could have been the sergeant, or it could have actually been the three marines in the adjacent bunker. All I know is, I shot off several rounds from my M14 rifle at the running two targets and wasn't certain if I had hit one of them or not.

The one thing I am certain of is I have prayed each night prior to retiring to bed—that the shots I fired failed to hit anyone.

Also, I noticed that only one of the dead VC sprawled out around the adjacent bunker was carrying a firearm. The others were simply carrying satchel charges or hand grenades.

I also noticed that not all of them had a loincloth covering their private parts. A couple of the dead VC was as naked as a jaybird. I thought how clever, because they really blended in with the sand by attacking the base in their birthday suit.

Now there must be over thirty-five marines surrounding the adjacent bunker, and as stated earlier, not one of them questioned yours truly. They were all talking to the three marines. Occasionally, they would point in my direction, but not one asked me a word.

For a moment, the thought even crossed my mind that it was a racial thing. Maybe due to the fact that I was a brother, no one paid any attention to me. I thought how silly that could be, but was it?

You would have thought at least one marine would have ask me how two dead VC that lay in front of my bunker got shot up. Hell, they sure didn't shoot themselves. I figured it had to be racial. Then I quickly erased that thought from my mind. But, frankly speaking, at the time, it was difficult to arrive at any other conclusion.

During the next twenty minutes or so, the observing crowd of marines had swelled to a pretty good size; it must have been over fifty marines mulling around the adjacent bunker and talking to the three marines that had pulled a Audie Murphy on the enemy.

Frankly, I was getting pretty sick and tired of the three marines in the adjacent bunker getting all the attention. Then I suddenly came back to my senses and the realization that my ass was not even supposed to be within three hundred yards of this bunker. Since I wasn't getting any questions or attention, I felt this was a good time to slip out of my bunker and walk swiftly over to my work tent, the Engineering Office, which was a mere thirty feet away.

I quietly crawled out of my bunker, and as I walked past the dead VC that had the dark-colored metal in his hand, out of frustration, I decided to kick the object from his grip. I was a little pissed and kicked the object pretty hard. I was upset because all that time last night, I lay in my bunker, sweating it out, thinking all along, that this shot-up guy clutched an explosive that was ready to go off at any moment.

While I was kicking the object that was in the VC's hand, a couple of marine NCOs saw my actions and called out to me. I acted as if I didn't hear them, but they were persistent and ran over to catch up with me. They were a couple of staff sergeants and had observed me kicking at the dead VC and questioned me as to my purpose. I told them the true reason that I was pissed off due to the night long guarding and all, and they agreed with me and stated they would have been upset as well.

I felt relieved the two staff sergeants didn't ask me any further questions, because, after all, I was "not" supposed to have been in that bunker, and figuring I had performed an Academy award-winning performance on the two staff sergeants, I put a smile on my face and scampered on toward my work tent.

But what I hadn't realized is two more inquisitive marines had managed to listen in on my conversation with the two staff sergeants, a lance corporal, and PFC. They heard my reasoning for kicking the dark metal from the dead VC's hand and stated they didn't blame me for my actions. They asked me a few more additional questions about the dead VC, and during our conversation, the lance corporal pulled out a 35 mm camera and requested to take a snapshot of me standing over the dead VC that I had been ordered to guard by the disappearing sergeant. I agreed, and we walked back to where my bunker was located, and the picture was snapped.

We spent several minutes discussing my role during last night's attack and come to find out the two marines were members of my helicopter squadron. The longer we talked, the more we realized we had worked on some assignments together. I had to gather some information in order to perform proper aircraft logging of flight data, and these two marines spent several hours assisting me with that particular work assignment.

Since I had worked with these two marines, I felt I could confide in them. I briefly told them my situation about disobeying a direct order and that I would highly appreciate it if they would not disclose my identity as being seen in the bunker. They agreed, and we shook on it. Then I briefly walked away from the bunker and toward my work tent. (Later on, the picture taking marine provided me a copy of that photo as shown above).

After entering the Engineering Office tent, there were a couple of my fellow workers present, so I immediately began to blend in and appear busy by shuffling papers around and doing all sorts of things simply to appear fully occupied.

It was fully daylight by this time, and as my fellow marines were talking about the details of last night's attack, it became very difficult for me to simply set there and listen. In fact, some marines were fabricating stories that I knew were not true but reasoned that I best keep my mouth shut and not speak up and disclose the truth, and that I was where I was not supposed to be.

I found it extremely difficult to remain silent during the many bullshit stories I began to hear concerning the attack but the thought about the evil consequences I could possibly face. Just thinking about getting into trouble was overwhelming, and the thought of a court-martial and brig time was most frightening.

I was sitting on the left side of my buttocks due to the shrapnel wound I sustained during the firefight, and I reasoned I might give

myself away if I continue to do this, so I merely stood up and performed my work.

If someone had come up to me that early morning and asked
me my whereabouts during the attack, I didn't have a clue as to how I
would answer. So I kept busy and sort of out of the way to avoid vocal
contact with fellow marines entering and exiting our Engineering
Office.

We noticed several holes in our work tent and assumed they
were a direct result of the many rounds fired during the attack last
night. A couple of holes were directly in line to where my work station was, and a couple of my fellow workers were joking with me
about this fact, and finally one of them asked me where I was during
last night's attack. I began to provide some bullshit answer and was
interrupted by my supervising NCO Staff Sergeant Manny, calling
us all outside to muster in front of our work tent.

While we were lining up out in front of our Engineering Office
tent and undergoing roll call, I heard someone shout, "There he is,"
and I looked around, and a couple of marines were pointing in my
direction. I tried to turn my head so they wouldn't get a good look at
me, but that maneuver failed to work. They spotted me and swiftly
began to walk over to where I was standing.

As they came closer to my position, I panicked and cried out to
Staff Sergeant Manny that I had to use the head and that I had to go
right now. Sergeant Manny excused me from formation, and I broke
out into a run toward the same head I was trying to take a dump in
last night when I apparently spotted a few of the VC raiders. I ran to
the head and quickly squatted as if I had to perform number 2.

The marines who had spotted me followed me to the head and
shouted from outside the screen messing, "Are you the marine that
was in the bunker?"

I began to grunt heavily and played like I didn't hear them.
Then, boldly, one of the marines, a PFC came right up to where I
was trying to take a dump and shouted through the screen messing,
"Marine, are you the one that was in the bunker directly behind the
Engineering Office?" I answered no as sincerely as I could and began
grunting louder.

The marine PFC said he was sorry to disturb me during my business but said he could swear I was the marine in that bunker. He stated he was a journalist and attempting to piece together all the events that took place last night during the attack. I think I convinced him I was "not" the guy. So, finally, he walked away, and I felt extremely relieved. As that marine walked away, the thought intensified of a possible court-martial for disobeying a direct order, and it kept ringing in my ear, and it seemed to not go away.

Finally, I left the head and felt relieved that I had escaped further questioning from the inquisitive PFC. While walking back to the Engineering Office, the PFC walked up beside me and said in a whisper, "I don't know what your situation is, but I know you were the marine in that bunker, and from my vantage point of view, you did a fine job, Corporal."

I finally opened up to him and asked him why he thought I was the one, and he said he was in the bunker on the opposite side of the bunker the three marines were occupying and that he saw my every move. I told the PFC it was an extremely serious reason I was avoiding the disclosure. I told him the reason was personal, and he said he would not tell anyone and that he would also inform his buddy to not disclose my identity. I thanked him, then turned and walked away.

The good Lord answered my prayers that awful night of October 28, 1965, because I managed to successfully exit the Engineering Office without any other marines noticing me and melt back into my sleeping tent. The sixteen members of my sleeping tent were all discussing the attack when I quietly arrived.

My best friend, Tee, was the only marine who noticed me slip back into our sleeping tent. He quietly walked over to me and asked me, "Where in the world had I been?" I quietly told him I would explain why I wasn't in my sleeping tent and proper bunker position adjacent to my sleeping tent at a later time and that the story was entirely too lengthy to provide him an abbreviated version. He nodded his approval, and we quickly changed the subject.

Later that morning, I explained my entire episode to Tee, and he agreed with me that I shouldn't disclose what I had witnessed because my action was, in fact, disobeying a direct order during a combat situation, and I could get into a ton of trouble.

After Tee fully heard and absorbed my story, he came over to my bunk where I was sitting and sincerely said that he felt bad that I wasn't able to report the injury to my right cheek buttocks, and ultimately receive a Purple Heart. After thinking about it for a while, we both reached the same conclusion: is receiving a Purple Heart worth the risk of receiving a court-martial?

As the facts of the attack began to unfold, I soon found out I knew the three marines who occupied the bunker next to the one the sergeant and I were occupying. The three marines were assigned to my helicopter squadron. And they were even in my helicopter squadron while we were undergoing training in Futenma, Okinawa. They were good men, and there is no way I would have guessed that they were capable of the heroic things they did in that bunker last night.

The three marines were Corporal Mortimer, Lance Corporal O'Shannon, and Corporal Brule. They were credited with killing nine VC attackers and wounding two. There were dead VC bodies lying all around their bunker, and I thought the head count was far more than what was officially reported.

The three marines possibly could have even shot the two VC who fell in front of my bunker, because the bunkers were only about twenty feet apart, and I know for a fact, along with the sergeant and me, they were firing in the direction where the two had fallen. Mortimer, O'Shannon, and Brule was highly decorated, and each one deserving so.

During the post-attack assessment inquiries, it was officially determined by intelligence that approximately ninety VC quietly assembled in a village just to the northwest of the Marble Mountain Air Facility. And undercover of 60 mm mortar fire, four demolition teams, armed with Bangalore torpedoes and grenades reached the MAG-16 helicopter parking ramp, and totally destroyed nineteen helicopters.

They also severely damaged eleven other helicopters and slightly damaged twenty-four others. Across the road, much of the newly constructed field hospital was heavily damaged. According to military intelligence, this evasion was a well-coordinated hit-and-run attack.

The enemy was well equipped for this mission at Marble Mountain. Marines and intelligence team members recovered a considerable stock of fragmentation, concussion, and thermite grenades. They also recovered three Bangalore torpedoes, several Chinese Communist B-40 antitank rockets, and miscellaneous ammunition. They also captured several weapons, a 7.62 mm AK assault rifle, two .43 cal. automatic weapons, an automatic pistol, and several satchel charges.

When the forty-five minutes of intense fighting had ceased, and the Viet Cong had swiftly withdrew into the night, they left leaving seventeen dead and four wounded behind. American casualties were three killed, and several were wounded.

One of the American casualties was a person I knew pretty well and liked very much. He was a navy petty officer corpsman. I came into his acquaintance one rainy evening when he was looking for some information in one of our helicopter flight logs. I helped him locate this information, and it took us four hours or more. He was a former football player and avid fan. We hit it off from the very beginning. He had a great personality, and it was evident he didn't mind talking sports with a brother. We would talk about football and sports in general for long periods of time.

Medevac helicopters were deployed so regularly that it became customary for naval corpsmen to actually sleep in the assigned medevac helicopter that was parked on the ramp and scheduled to be utilized that particular night. It was reported my football talking buddy, the naval petty officer corpsman, volunteered to stand in for a corpsman that evening who came down with a bad cold. As normal, the naval petty officer corpsman snuggled up in the medevac chopper and fell asleep.

He didn't know what hit him, because he was asleep when his medevac helicopter was hit by several grenades last night, and he became one of the three Americans listed as KIA. I found later he was a famous US actor's older brother. All I know is he knew his sports and he was one hell of a nice guy.

Our South Vietnamese advisors reported about half of the attackers of our base last night was from North Vietnam and that four enemy prisoners captured last night were from a small hamlet in Quang Nam and Quang Tin Provinces.

Corporal Chris Fabris and Corporal William Tellis (Tee) told me some of the captured were from Quang Nam, and the reason Tee and Chris rushed this information to me immediately was they knew Quang Nam was the place where Tuyen and her brother, Trang, told us they would take the children if the war intensified in the city of Da Nang.

They further explained how they would take the children there primarily for safety reasons and that they had some elder family members living in Quang Nam. The elder family members were Quang Nam village dignitaries and that they also helped monetarily support Tuyen's care home.

Corporal Chris Fabris further informed me that he heard the hamlet of Quang Nam was where the VC assembled prior to attacking Marble Mountain. While Chris was telling me this, the only thing I could think of was the safety of Little Kim, Lanh, the other children, Thien, Tuyen, and Tuyen's three assistants.

As a result of the info Chris provided, I felt it was more than imperative that I make contact with Tuyen, Trang, or anyone associated with the care home. I'd already tried several times earlier this morning, but with the news Chris brought to me, I knew I had to somehow make contact. Tee and I worked in the Engineering Office; thus, we had access to telephones. The both of us were frantically calling and attempting to make contact.

Each phone number that Tuyen and Trang provided . . . we dialed, and we received no answer. I began to feel so helpless while failing to make contact but frantically kept dialing and dialing.

Out of pure exhaustion, Tee and I stopped attempting to call Tuyen and Trang's phone numbers. We stood up, left our desk area, walked over to our break area, and drank a soda. Then we held hands and dropped to our knees and began to pray.

Both our parents had taught us that when all else fails, pray, and our prayers would be answered. My prayer was simple and to the point. I asked the Lord to protect the children and to watch over them until this attack offensive by the VC was, in fact, over. I felt relieved each time I said that small prayer and sincerely felt the Lord was listening.

Tee said a similar prayer, and when done, we both remained in our praying position, and as if on cue, we both began to cry and cry and cry.

> *"Ask, and it will be given you; seek, and you will find; knock, and it will be opened to you. For each one who asks receives, and he who seeks finds, and to him who knocks it will be opened."*
>
> *—Matthew 7:7–8*

"MY BUNKER, THE VC THAT I WAS INSTRUCTED TO GUARD BY THE SGT."

Search for the Children

ORPORAL TEE AND CORPORAL CHRIS slept directly beside me in our sleeping tent, but for the past two nights, neither of us clocked any time sleeping due our sincere concern over the children's safety. I was the last one to talk to Tuyen, and that was well over a week ago. Each of us loved those kids and needed badly to obtain their status.

We spent hours calling on the phone attempting to locate them. We only had two phone numbers to dial in our search: the number to Tuyen's care home and the number Trang provided that dials directly to his police office desk.

Between Tee, Chris, and me, we had called these numbers no less than twenty-five times this morning, and each time we called, there was no answer. Prior to the attack on our base, I called these numbers, and someone would always promptly answer the phone. So one can imagine how aggravating it felt to not receive an answer during a time like this.

Chris had flown as a volunteer crew member on several flight missions in and around Quang Nam this past few weeks. He told Tee and me each time he flew over Quang Nam or close to the hamlet, his helicopter would sustain hits from incoming small arms fire. And Chris further stated the village of Quang Nam was normally classified by military intelligence as "hostile."

Chris began telling Tee and me some detailed accounts of one of the frightening incidents while flying over Quang Nam, and I immediately stopped him and shouted that I couldn't take it anymore. I explained to Chris that I simply couldn't stand to hear any accounts of how hostile Quang Nam was toward our American forces when, in fact, there was a possibility Tuyen had traveled there with her children and staff seeking refuse from the intensifying war activity around her home in Da Nang.

The four captured VC during the attack were from Quang Nam according to military intelligence. We were aware that Quang Nam was the place where Tuyen and her brother Trang several times told us they would take the children if the war intensified in the city of Da Nang. They told us they would transport the children there primarily for safety reasons and that they had important family members living in Quang Nam. They explained how the elder folks in Tuyen and Trang's family were Quang Nam village dignitaries and that they even helped monetarily support the care home.

Chris understood clearly where I was coming from and ceased talking about Quang Nam, and we three came to the solid conclusion that if Tuyen had taken the children to Quang Nam, they were "no doubt" in some sort of danger, and there was not one single thing that Tee, Chris, or I could do about it but to hope and pray.

At least a dozen times, that hot afternoon, we three knelt down and prayed. The power of prayer helped considerably, and it felt very soothing. But I can't put into words the hopelessness we three felt in regards to our concern over the safety of the children.

The knowledge that Little Kim (a.k.a. My Friend You) was possibly in danger was too much for me to bear. I would get sick in the gut each time I heard the name Quang Nam mentioned among marines at our base. I would say to myself, "Quang Nam . . . of all the places in Vietnam for Trang and Tuyen to have family members living."

Chris, Tee, and I found out after the third day of the attack that we were not supposed to make contact with any source outside of Marble Mountain. We understood the "no call out order," but it failed to stop the three of us from continuing our attempt to make contact with the children. We were obviously more discreet about our call out efforts, but we continued attempting to call and make contact.

As a matter of fact, we even stepped up our calling-out effort by asking the other members of the care home donating team to assist in this effort. Now there were six of us calling Tuyen and Trang's phone number in search of some information pertaining to Little Kim, Lanh, and the children. We six were all totally committed, and most likely not a minute would pass by where one of us were not dialing their phone numbers.

During our fourth day of calling, Tee thought he'd made a connection, because when he called the care home's phone number, a girl answered the phone. She wasn't Thien, Tuyen, or any of her lady staff. She spoke in Vietnamese, and after five minutes of Tee and her not understanding one another, the girl hung up, most likely out of frustration, and never answered the phone again.

We six hit the rack that night with a flicker of hope in our hearts. At least we knew someone was, in fact, at the care home, and we all hoped tomorrow we would hit the jackpot and make contact with either Tuyen or someone who spoke our language. It was extremely difficult for me to sleep that night, thinking about Little Kim—praying that she, Lanh, and the children were safe and sound.

The fifth day after the attack was an extremely heavy workload day. Many of our helicopters had been destroyed or damaged the night of the attack which equated to a ton of work by those working in the Aircraft Engineering Office, who were namely Tee and I. Both of my hands were cramping, resulting from the large volume of logging I was performing on our damaged aircraft.

I was working twelve- and fourteen-hour days logging data against our many damaged aircraft. My logging mate, Tee, had avoided working the long hours logging aircraft data. He was fortunate in that he was a popular crew member substitute, and due to Tee's popularity, he was being requested by our helicopter flight crew to fly as one of their flight crew members.

In essence, Corporal Tee managed to avoid some of the laborious tasks of aircraft logging, and to be truthful, I grew a little envi-

ous of Tee in that regard but that never "once" damaged our friendship. The two years Tee and I were together at three different Marine
Corps Air Bases (Quantico, Marble Mountain, and Chu Lai), we
never experienced one heated moment between us, and if you knew
him, you would quickly realize why.

He was simply one of the nicest guys on this entire planet. How
can one get upset at a guy like Tee? His giant grin would immediately
melt anyone's anger toward him. Tee was a special human being and,
simply stated, the nicest person I had met on earth. Hell, it wasn't his
fault he was called often to fly.

On the sixth day after the attack, Chris had been requested to fly
as a crew member on a rescue mission. One of our UH34D helicopters had experienced engine trouble and force landed near the hostile
hamlet of Quang Nam. Chris held a MOS of Jet Turbine Helicopter
Mechanic and flew nearly as many combat and/or medevac missions
as Tee.

The care home donation team reasoned that with Chris flying
into Quang Nam, he just may stumble across some valuable information pertaining to the whereabouts of Tuyen and the children.

The team waved Chris goodbye as his helicopter lifted and
headed inland toward the hamlet of Quang Nam. What a true
friend and supporter of the care home. Chris was born and raised in
south Chicago and wasn't afraid of anything. He was truly a blue-
eyed soul brother and hung with the brothers more than his own
kind. His speech and mannerism were more black than white. I
would fight in a foxhole with Chris at the drop of a dime. He was a
marines, marine. He was simply a cool guy who knew how to take
care of himself.

As his UH1E helicopter disappeared from view, I said to the
team members, "At last, we will receive a firsthand report about the
condition of the hamlet called Quang Nam when Chris returns."
There had been reports this little hamlet experienced some serious
fighting and unrest the night of the attack on Marble Mountain.

It was further reported that Quang Nam was the gathering place
for the ninety or so Viet Cong attackers who took part in the attack.
The team reasoned that if this were the case and if Tuyen had, in

fact, left Da Nang to seek refuge with her family members in Quang
Nam . . . she, the children, and her staff were, in fact, in danger.

Please, God . . .

Grant the children courage when times are bleak.

Grant them strength when they feel weak.

Grant them comfort when they feel all alone.

But, most of all, God, please bring the children home.

"TUYEN, THIEN, LITTLE KIM AND FRIENDS."

Finding the Children

UR TEAM OF DONATING MARINES who had been sponsoring Tuyen's care home this past year had assembled in our squadron's Aircraft Engineering Office tent once again today to make a countless number of phone calls in attempt to locate the missing care home children. A few of us were calling the phone number's Tuyen and Trang provided, and a few of us were random calling.

Tee hit the jackpot and managed to make contact with Trang. Tee placed him on speaker where he told us his sister and her three lady assistants had hastily taken the children and Thien to her uncle's estate located on the outskirts of a small hamlet in Quang Nam.

We asked Trang why Tuyen took the children to their uncle's estate. He told us his sister had been receiving reports from reliable sources in Da Nang that serious Viet Cong recruiting had been occurring in close proximity to the care home. And that she simply took the children to their uncle Tho's estate in hopes of seeking safety. He then said he had wished she would have consulted with him first prior to leaving.

He further told us a couple of the care home's older boys were recently approached by Viet Cong recruiters, and they warned the boys that they would be faced with serious consequences if they failed to join the VC and help them fight for their cause.

He said, as soon as Tuyen became aware of this particular incident, that she ordered her staff to quickly pack up the children's belongings and headed them off in the direction of her uncle's estate in Quang Nam.

Prior to hanging up, I asked Trang what he meant when he said he wished Tuyen would have called him first prior to leaving. After a lengthy pause, Trang spoke and quietly said most all of the hamlets surrounding Quang Nam were crawling with various factions of VC and that his sister was unaware of this activity. If she would have simply called him prior to going there, he could have informed her of this development. Then Trang suddenly broke down and began crying.

Not exactly knowing what to say, I said nothing and waited. Finally, he raised his phone receive, and said he would have Tuyen call me as soon as he made contact with her. In addition, he said that he'd been constantly calling his uncle's house and that he was getting no answer, and that he's currently preparing to drive up there, and that he would be leaving for his uncle's destination as soon as we finished our phone conversation.

I asked Trang if I could ride along with him, and he said certainly and that he would pick me up at the main entrance gate to our base in about forty-five minutes. Then he asked me, "How could you leave and avoid military disciplinary charges from being absence from duty?" I told him, "All of that business is my worry. I'll figure something out, but right now it's imperative that I help locate Kim, Lanh, and the remaining care home children."

Trang got my point and never brought that concern up again.

As soon as I hung up the phone, I began thinking up a scheme as to how I could travel with Trang to Quang Nam which was located about twenty miles north of our base, and avoid being charged with going over the hill.

Military intelligence recently classified Quang Nam as "off-limits" which could result in me leaving with Trang that more difficult. But despite the many obstacles and consequences laid out against me, I was determined to obtain the status of Little Kim, Lanh, and the other children.

As soon as I hung up on Trang, I immediately contacted a close friend and strong supporter of the care home. I knew if someone on base could help me with a plan to pull this off, it would be Corporal Chris Fabris.

Tee ran Chris down for me, and as soon as Chris stepped inside my work tent, he informed me that he had been selected as a volunteer crewman aboard a UH1E gunship and that their mission was to fly to Quang Nam and assist in protecting medevac helicopters that were attempting to airlift the dead and wounded, and transport them to our bases nearby naval hospital.

I interrupted Chris and told him of my plan to drive there with Trang and asked if he have any suggestions as to how I could make this happen. Chris provided me an action plan, and it was time for its execution.

When Chris left my workstation, I ran over to Marble Mountain's main security guard station and informed the head NCO security officer that I was going to soon be picked up by a Da Nang policeman and that he was going to drive me into Da Nang so that I could testify on behalf of four marine participants in a brawl with nine town locals.

The head security NCO told me that a Corporal Chris Fabris had just come over and provided him the heads-up and said that I was "cleared to leave." At that very same time, Trang drove up in his police car. I jumped in, and off we went.

As we left the base, I silently thanked my dear friend Chris Fabris for providing the scheme and clearing the path for me to join Trang on our much-anticipated trip. After roughly ten miles into our journey, Trang pulled his car over to the side of the road, placed his head in his hands, and began crying. I didn't have a clue as to what brought this on, so I simply would offer a kind word here and there.

After several minutes of crying, Trang slowly raised his head and informed me that he had been contacted by a trusted family member living in Quang Nam—that she was one of his favorite cousins and her name was Loan.

She was his uncle Tho's only daughter, and she directed him to immediately come to Quang Nam to officially identify Tuyen's body and two of her lady assistants, as well as several of the older children's bodies of those who had accompanied his sister to Quang Nam.

Trang further said that Loan would meet up with him upon his arrival in Quang Nam and that she had also been called "to officially identify the bodies of her father (Uncle Tho) and her younger brother (nephew Thu).

I then leaned down and hugged Trang and offered him my most sincere condolences for his beloved sister and quietly said, "Trang, things will be all right with Tuyen . . . She's in heaven right now . . . smiling down on the both of us." Then I told him what a great and courageous woman she had been to all of us at Marble Mountain, and those of us who were blessed with the grand opportunity to have known her loved her very much.

My kind words appeared to have helped a little because Trang soon pulled himself together and continued the short drive to his uncle's estate.

Upon our arrival in Quang Nam, Trang swiftly drove to where his uncle had lived nearly fifty years. After a quick survey of his uncle's estate, Trang drove a block down the street to Huy's home, a childhood friend whom his uncle had known many years.

Apparently, Loan had informed many of Trang's family members that he was arriving in town this evening, because when we drove up, they came running out from Huy's house, and we both were warmly greeted by no less than fifty people.

After making sure Trang and I were comfortably seated, Huy began the evening by toasting his two arriving guests. Then he began formerly introducing yours truly to each one of his house guests. I had never felt so important in my entire life.

After completing the formal introductions, Huy began slowly telling us how Tuyen, her childhood friend lady assistants, Uncle Tho, his youngest son Thu, and several of her care home adopted children were killed.

He began by saying Uncle Tho had strongly professed to be anti-VC for the past several years and that the VC had long attempted to infiltrate their township but was having very little success. The VC reasoned they were having very little success due to some prominent townsfolk speaking out adversely against them. The VC targeted Uncle Tho as being one of the prominent townsfolk who was speaking out against them. And they made the decision to raid his home.

Trang asked Huy if that was the only reason the VC attacked his home. Huy said he heard from one of the VC soldiers that their leaders simply decided to attack Tho's home in order to teach him and other prominent townsfolk living in his hamlet a strong lesson . . . which was to never go about professing to be anti-VC.

Huy then explained how Tuyen and her children arrived at Tho's estate about two hours prior to the VC raid—and that he and his wife had arrived at Tho's home to formerly greet Tuyen and her children only about twenty minutes prior to the VC raid.

He told how the chief VC leader ordered everyone in Tho's home to come outside and line up by a roadway leading up to his home. Tuyen was first to walk outside, closely followed by her three lady assistants. Thien defiantly came out next, tightly holding onto Little Kim and Lanh.

Once all of Tuyen's children had come outside and lined up by the roadway, one of the VC soldiers began asking if they wanted to join them and fight for their cause. Not a single one of Tuyen's children chose to join them, and at that point, Huy said it got ugly.

He told how the VC leaders began instructing his soldiers to start roughing up the children in an attempt to persuade them to join their cause. He watched as their persuading activity turned from a few slaps to the kids' faces to hitting them very hard in the back of the head with their rifle butts.

At this time point, he said Tuyen stepped in to offer protection and stop her children from further being hurt. As a result of her effort, she was immediately shot dead by one of the soldiers. Fighting back tears, Huy said one of Tuyen's lady assistants ran over to provide aid to her, and she was shot dead, as well. A second lady assistant also came to their aid, and she was struck in the back of the head with a rifle butt and died shortly afterward.

Huy told how Tho broke free of his captives and attempted to comfort both Tuyen and her lady assistants, and that he was shot by the chief leader and died minutes later. Huy further said Tho was shot dead while in an attempt to assist his fatally wounded father.

Huy began having a difficult time controlling his emotions and began to cry uncontrollably but did manage to say also killed during their courageous attempt to aid their beloved Tuyen and provide her comfort as she lay fatally wounded were five boys and two of her girls.

While firmly embracing each other, Trang and Huy were seriously crying by this time. I also had several tears hanging from my cheeks. As a matter of fact, I was crying hard as well . . . just like a newborn baby. My tears came more from anger than from grief.

Huy finally stopped crying and attempted to lighten the situation a little by changing the subject. He told us he had on several different occasions overheard some of the townsfolk talking about a very brave and courageous teenage boy who fought heroically during the attack.

Suddenly, Huy's wife came into the living room with exciting information, and they began speaking in their native tongue. I saw a telephone sitting there on a nearby end table and asked Huy's wife if I could use it. Upon receiving her approval, I immediately dialed Tee back at the base where he told me Chris Fabris had called in and reported it had been officially confirmed that the VC fighters who attacked Marble Mountain did, in fact, forcefully recruit many of fighters from this small hamlet in Quang Nam.

Tee told me that Chris further stated he had, in fact, personally verified six boys found among the deceased as belonging to the care home. And Chris had said the six boys had been forced to participate on the side of the VC in the Marble Mountain attack.

Not wanting to talk too long on their phone line, I said goodbye to Tee and told him I would check back soon and hung up. I then sat back down and politely asked Huy if he would tell me more about this brave young boy.

Huy thought for a minute, then said some close friends and family members told him they had witnessed bravery on the part of this young boy like they had never seen before.

They told Huy the boy vigorously fought the VC attackers in an attempt to protect his ten- or eleven-year-old sister. They told Huy the boy's younger sister kept shouting three words that irritated the chief VC leader and that finally the VC leader instructed his men to rough her up a little if she failed to cease shouting the three irritating words *My Friend You.*

They explained to Huy how the chief VC leader's men were getting extremely rough with the little ten-year-old girl, so rough with her that her harsh treatment became unbearable for her older brother to watch. They told Huy the chief VC leaders men began sexually mistreating the little girl which caused her brother to be outraged that he broke loose from his captives and came to her rescue.

Huy's friends said the little girl's brother put up a tremendous fight. They told how he courageously killed eight VC with their own weapons and severely wounded nine before being shot in the head at point-blank range.

Soon after Huy finished, I asked, "Why didn't some of the hamlet people assist in helping the little girl's brother fight off the VC?" Huy provided me with a sound explanation of how they were being held at gunpoint and feared for their lives.

He further told me there was, in fact, a few men who came to the boy's assistance but were quickly apprehended by VC soldiers and eventually tortured or put to death.

Trang reminded Huy the reason he was there was to identify his sister's body and assist in arranging for us to view the dead bodies of all the people who were killed in the raid two days ago.

Huy explained how he was tight with some of the hamlet's officials and that he was positive Trang's request could be arranged. He then stated it would be very easy to view one of the fallen. He said the hamlet folks were treating a brave teenage boy like a hero and that his body had been preserved and placed in an open casket to allow as many of the townsfolk who so desired to view this heroic boy's body.

As Trang and I made our way toward the heroic boy's casket, there had been a sign placed above the casket. I asked Trang to interpret, and he said the sign read, "Here lies the body of a teenage boy forever called the Brave One who courageously fought off soldiers that were hurting his baby sister."

The closer I got to the Brave One's open casket, the harder it became for me to take steps. Trang was practically dragging me. Obviously, I was afraid I would find Lanh's body lying there. As I drew close enough to see inside the casket and view the boy's face, I saw the cute little face of my close friend Lanh.

There were people walking behind me and beckoning me to move forward in order to provide them their opportunity to view the Brave One. I simply couldn't move, and no matter how hard I tried to step forward, I couldn't and was literally frozen there.

After several minutes of standing there, staring into the casket at the face of Lanh, I was finally able to move out of the path of the local townsfolk wanting to also view the Brave One. The mortuary people had Lanh dressed in a navy blue suit and a bright red tie. The wounds to his head were easily recognizable.

There is positively no way that I'm capable of expressing in words the hurt I felt while standing there viewing Lanh's body. I simply felt sick in my stomach and began to throw up. I spent a good twenty minutes throwing up while Trang attempted to administer minor first aid.

Eventually, I ceased throwing up and emphatically expressed to Trang that I must somehow put this behind me and focus my total attention on finding my darling Little Kim, a.k.a. My Friend You.

By the evening's end, we were able to view the deceased bodies of the majority of people involved in the recent hamlet raid. And Trang finally did, in fact, locate and identify the bodies of his younger sister Tuyen and her loyal childhood assistants. We also identified the bodies of several boys and girls whom Tuyen and Trang supported at their care home.

Later in the day, Huy informed Trang and me that Thien survived the ordeal, so Trang and I set out to locate her. We reasoned that when we located Thien, we would find the whereabouts of her favorite niece, Little Kim.

Trang began describing Thien to many of his childhood friends, and a clubfooted childhood friend by the name of Trong Tri came forth and told Trang where he had last seen Thien. Trong Tri stated he had seen Thien being cared for at a nearby medical clinic and provided Trang with directions.

After making several wrong turns, we finally located Little Kim's aunt Thien. We found her being cared for at a makeshift clinic. She was lying on a filthy cot in the hallway. And when she saw us walking up to her bedside, she began shaking with joy and began crying. They were happy tears, and it was obvious she was thrilled to see Trang and me.

Thien attempted to stand and formerly greet us, but due to thick bandages on her left arm, she was unable to, and a nurse and two aids approached us. The nurse informed Thien the doctors were about to perform surgery on her left arm.

While Trang conversed with Thien and her nurse, I managed to walk closer to her bedside and observed that Thien had suffered an apparent shotgun blasts to her left arm. The wound looked extremely bad, and I could clearly see where bone had been shattered.

While the two surgery aids were about to wheel her away, I quickly leaned down and kissed her on her cheek . . . as she whispered, "Corporal Don, please don't let them cut my arm off." Startled, I walked over and asked Trang if he was aware the doctors were about to amputate Thien's left arm. He softly said . . . he was aware.

With tears in our eyes, Trang and I leaned down and softly embraced Thien for seemingly a long while. Soon after, the two surgery aids lifted her cot up and wheeled her into an adjacent room where a team of doctors were waiting to perform amputation surgery.

I managed to say, "God will be with you," as they carried her past me into the operating room. Thien faintly said, "Thank you, Corporal Don."

In addition to her left arm, Thien's head was wrapped in heavy bandages. Trang managed to ask her nurse about the head bandages as we were being asked to leave the operating room. The nurse said the reason for her head bandages was she had suffered several blows to the head from an apparent rifle butt. The nurse said the doctors expected her to fully recover from the blows to her head.

Trang warmly thanked the surgery nurse as she was kindly escorting us out of the surgery operating area to a nearby waiting room. Prior to the nurse shutting the door, she told Trang that Thien's surgery procedure would take about an hour and that she would then be transported to the recovery room. She said Thien would remain in recovery for a minimum of two hours and that she would locate us when she is available to have visitors.

While we were inquiring with town locals concerning the whereabouts of Little Kim, a childhood friend of Tuyen and Trang's by the name of Van approached and told us he may know where the "shouting little girl" may be. We quickly followed him to a nearby coffin. When opened it, we found a shot-up little girl, but, thank God, it was not our darling Little Kim. Van apologized for the error, and Trang told him he didn't need to because all he was simply trying to do was to help.

A half dozen or more of the town locals came forth with information pertaining to the whereabouts of the "Shouting Little Girl," as Little Kim had become known, but none of their tips panned out.

One positive note is that each of the townsfolk claiming to possess knowledge of Little Kim's whereabouts did, in fact, proclaim that her aunt Thien knew the true whereabouts of the Shouting Little Girl due to the fact that she had been known to be very the last person to see her.

Trang and I reasoned . . . all we needed to do in order to locate the whereabouts of Little Kim was simply wait until Thien recovered from surgery. So we double-timed back over to the operating room section of the makeshift hospital and sought out the surgery nurse whom we had been speaking with . . . who was so helpful and informative.

We spent no time in locating the surgery nurse, and she informed us that Thien had been released from recovery and was then resting on her cot in the ward room. I strongly believe the surgery nurse had a crush on Trang, because she personally guided us to the exact location where Thien was resting.

When I saw Thien setting up in her cot, the first thing I did was to check her left arm, and it appeared to remain with her. So when we greeted Thien, she was obviously in a good mood. When we approached her cot, the first she did was to cheerfully display her left arm.

Then she began to explain that her doctors were able to save her arm and that it would remain sore a long time, but, for the most part, she could most likely expect a normal recovery in a few months. Then she began to softly cry, and again I cried a little with her . . . I'm pretty sure Trang cried a little, as well.

Noticing new bandages wrapped around her head area, I asked Thien about her head injury, and she merely laughed and said, "Corporal Don, my head is very hard." We three laughed; then we soon got back to the business of locating my soon-to-be adopted Little Kim, a.k.a. My Friend You.

When I asked Thien about Little Kim, all of a sudden, she got quiet, a strange look came across her face, and she turned her head just stared out into space, not saying a single word. Trang and I were a little confused by her actions but did nothing and granted Thien her space. Ten minutes went by, and I softly asked her again if she knew the whereabouts of Little Kim.

Thien looked directly in our eyes and began slowly telling us how the VC fighters began recruiting girls to join their forces, and Thien said the very first girl the VC approached at Uncle Tho's house for recruitment was Kim and that one of the VC leaders asked Kim for her name and that she loudly told him her name was My Friend You.

Thien began to softly cry and said the VC leader thought Little Kim was having fun and disrespecting him by telling him her name was My Friend You. So he slapped her across the face and again asked her for her name. After which, Little Kim began shouting, "My Friend You," even louder.

Thien explained how she was tied to a large tree but broke free and ran over to Little Kim in an attempt to convince her to tell the VC leader her name was Kim and to cease pissing him off by shouting, "My Friend You."

Fighting back tears, Thien explained how she was soon apprehended by her VC captives and tied even tighter to the large tree. She said that as her VC captives were dragging her back to where they had her tied, she was constantly pleading with her niece to tell the VC leader her real name . . . of Kim.

After a lengthy pause, Thien began again and told Trang and me that Kim totally disregarded her pleas and that each time the VC leader asked her name, she would shout back, "My Friend You." Holding back tears, Thien said this went on for several minutes until finally the VC leader consulted with a chief VC leader and came back mad and ordered one of his soldiers to strike Kim in the head with the butt of his rifle.

Thien explained that Lanh who had been tied up nearby over-heard the instructions handed down from the VC leader to strike Kim in the head with a rifle butt—and that Lanh broke loose and grabbed a rifle from one of the VC soldiers and began firing. With joy in her voice, she said by the time Lanh ran out of ammo, he had shot and killed five VC soldiers and seriously wounded three more.

Thien continued telling us with elation in her voice that when Lanh ran out of ammo, he took the rifle and skillfully used it as a club and began hitting several soldiers with it. She continued by joyfully saying Lanh inflicted much pain on the enemy soldiers as he kept swinging and hitting them with the rifle.

Nearly shouting with joy, Thien said it took eight VC soldiers to subdue Lanh and that even when they had him on the ground he was biting and scratching them. Then in a faint whisper, Thien told how the fighters shot Lanh in his head. She said the fighters contin-ued shooting Lanh because they were that afraid of him.

Crying uncontrollably, Thien explained how cowardly the fighters were to keep shooting her nephew like that and how regretful she was that she was tied up and unable to help him. She told us how a young village girl tried to help Lanh fight off the soldiers but that she too was shot to death. She then ended by saying she witnessed her brave young nephew take his last and final breath . . . Then she slumped down onto the flooring and began to weep.

Trang found a vacated hospital bed, and we quickly picked her up and laid Thien upon it hoping that she would discontinue her stressful conversation concerning Lanh's death and get some much-needed rest. After getting only twenty minutes of sleep, Thien set up and began talking again.

She said after being saddened by the death of her nephew, she immediately turned her focus back to Kim and began shouting at her to tell the VC leader her real name.

Thien explained that by this time Little Kim was shouting the three words, "My Friend You," at the top of her voice and that she was literally pissing off every VC leader who was within hearing range.

She said after Kim shockingly witnessed the shooting death of her brother . . . that she began shouting the words, "My Friend You," even louder. Then, suddenly, Thien's whole body began nervously shaking. Trang and I tried hard to calm her and to stop Thien from talking about her recent horrific experience, but she refused to adhere to our requests.

As I was gently massaging her neck, I leaned down and softly said, "Miss Thien, you must give this story some rest and get some yourself." With tears flowing down her cheeks, she looked up at me and said, "Corporal Don, someone has to know about this," and continued on by saying that by this time the chief VC leader had grown furious from Kim's constant shouting of the three words.

I asked her specifically why was the chief leader furious . . . She explained that because the chief leader didn't have a clue as to what Kim was shouting, and also he couldn't figure out why she wouldn't stop shouting the words *My Friend You.*

Thien said that she repeatedly pleaded for Kim to stop the shouting, that it was making the chief VC leader upset, but she said that Little Kim continued to ignore her and shouted even louder, "My Friend You, My Friend You!"

Thien paused for seemingly a long time, then softly said the chief leader had heard enough and that he had somehow determined the three words Kim was shouting were some type of secret military code or something of that nature. She said he quickly stood up and ordered his fighters to finally stop Kim from saying another word by placing a rag inside her mouth and taping it shut.

By this time, the suspense of not knowing whether or not Little Kim was harmed or not was getting too much for Trang and me to physically bear, so Trang interrupted Thien and sternly asked her what was the status of Little Kim and if she was harmed, and he ended up by asking Thien where we could find her.

When Trang asked his question of locating Little Kim, Thien broke down and suddenly fell to her knees and began painfully crying. Then she began coughing and vomiting like crazy. This went on for several minutes and even caused members of the medical staff to rush over and check on Thien. She ceased vomiting and promptly fell off to sleep . . . leaving Trang and me without a clue as to the whereabouts of my beloved Little Kim. All we simply wanted to know was if Little Kim was safe and sound. According to Trong Tri and other town locals, Thien was one of the last people to see Kim; thus Trang and I figured that we would receive instant information as to Kim's safety status and whereabouts.

Yet here Trang and I stand at Thien's bedside and, after several hours of being in her company, haven't learned one single thing about the safety status of Little Kim. And to be perfectly honest, this was beginning to piss both Trang and me off to no end.

About an hour had passed, and suddenly Thien awakened to specifically tell us that she hadn't personally witness Kim's final departure. Her reasoning was due to her constant struggle with her captives that she had been knocked unconscious by the two soldiers who were guarding her. She explained that she was told what had happened to Kim by reputable townspeople.

By this time, her surgery nurse had joined Trang and me at her bedside, and the nurse remained with Thien. The nurse explained she was ordered by her doctor to remain with her due to Thien's projected adverse reaction while telling us about Little Kim's disappearance. Trang and I were in total agreement because we didn't know what to do in case Thien began to experience these so-called adverse reactions or began bleeding again from her recent arm surgery.

The nurse checked Thien's arm bandages, propped her up in her bed, and provided her a cup of warm soup. Soon after which, Thien began telling us about what she had learned about Kim's disappearance.

Thien began by saying the last time she saw Kim . . . she was being led off into the jungle with both hands tied behind her back and a rolled-up sock jammed and taped to her mouth in their vain attempt to keep her from shouting, "My Friend You."

She quickly stated that she distributed flyers throughout the hamlet, requesting information concerning the whereabouts of her ten-year-old niece, and that yesterday a young pregnant girl named Mai came forward and told her that she had recently witnessed a young girl fitting the description in the flyer being led out into the jungle by soldiers.

Thien stated that Mai said when she heard the soldiers walking through the jungle that she hid from their view. And she witnessed a young girl with her hands tied behind her back being forcibly led through the jungle by about five soldiers.

And although the little girl had what appeared to be an old sock stuffed in her mouth, she kept attempting to shout out the words, "My Friend You." Mai had told Thien that when the little girl was successful in shouting out, "My Friend You'," the soldiers would knock her to the ground and torture her in disgusting ways.

Mai continued telling Thien the soldiers were radioed and requested by their leader; but prior to departing, they all gathered around the little girl, pulled out their things, and began urinating all over her. By this point, Mai emphatically stated the little girl was shouting out the words, "My Friend You," at the top of her lungs.

Mai said she saw one of the soldiers quickly turned and savagely hit the little girl in the head with his rifle butt. Believing he'd left her for dead . . . he quickly joined up with the other soldiers.

Thien explained how Mai ended by saying by the time she'd managed to crawl over to assist the little beat-up girl . . . that she had somehow vanished. Mai reasoned the little girl must have crawled away to safety or that she had crawled away somewhere to die.

Mai's recollection of events about Little Kim as told by Thien were extremely hard to listen to, but somehow we managed. Meanwhile, the nurse told us we had to leave for a few hours to allow Thien to get some much-needed rest.

As Trang and I waited on outside Thien's room, I can't tell you how many times I or Trang broke down and cried like newborn babies, but cried we did. And we both figured it was extremely difficult for Thien to inform us of Mai's encounter, but we reasoned she had to tell somebody . . . and tell it to somebody who really cared. And we certainly cared, and cared a lot.

I walked outside the makeshift clinic and sat down on a nearby bench and pulled from my shirt pocket a penciled picture Little Kim had drawn of me. I stared at that picture a very long time. She had, in fact, done a pretty good job on me.

After sitting there, spending nearly twenty minutes eyeballing Kim's drawing of yours truly, Tang walked outside to where I was and sat down beside me and handed me his field telephone . . . and to my surprise, on the other line was my close friend and dedicated Tuyen's care home supporter Corporal Chris Fabris. He quickly stated for the past week he had been up in this province flying as a volunteer crewman in a medevac chopper.

Chris further told me that Tee had provided him my MO and that he was sincerely worried about me back at base and for me to call him the first chance I get. I promised I would and asked him how long he was staying. Chris promptly stated his unit was about to return to Marble Mountain and that he only had about a minute. He also quickly told me that Trang had provided him a thorough briefing as to our purpose and had brought him up-to-date as to all the happenings at the makeshift clinic.

Chris then emphatically said he had been called to board his chopper, but prior to taking off, he had something important to tell me. I braced myself for bad news about one of our buddies . . . Chris said, "Corporal Clark, Trang told me about Little Kim's constant shouting of 'My Friend You.'"

I explained to Chris that I was aware Little Kim was fond of the sound of the three words but didn't know why she kept shouting them in the face all of that impending danger.

Chris very impatiently said, "Corporal Don, when Little Kim was shouting those three words . . . she was calling for you, Corporal Don. Don't you get it . . . ? She was reaching out for you."

It all was slowly becoming clear . . . because I had told her when she was ever faced with any danger to shout out those words, and a big bad marine would appear to rescue her. I simply couldn't take anymore and warmly thanked Chris before hanging up and collapsing into Trang's waiting arms. Then I totally lost it and broke down big time and began crying uncontrollably.

Trang left me so I could be alone, and while sitting there on that broken-down old stool outside the makeshift clinic . . . it all began to clearly come together. I realized why Kim kept saying our special three words. She was simply following our special code: Kim was calling out for the big bad marine who had proclaimed "he would always protect her."

This seventy-two-year-old marine will never forget this remarkable little angel, and I've had lived with her warm memory for fifty-two years. I'll never forget the wonderful talks at the café her brother and I had. What a remarkably brave and courageous young man.

I loved that little ten-year-old girl like a father loves a daughter. She was so special and fun loving. I loved her teenage brother like a father loves a son. He was streetwise and remarkably brave and possessed an inner glow of sincere sensitivity.

Little Kim and her older brother, Lanh, solidly touched my heart, and I'll never forget them for as long as I live.

"No matter how much we have failed, the love of God never ceases."

"YOURS TRULY – HOME BUILDER."

Thien's Concluded Statements

SOON AFTER LISTENING TO THIEN tell us about Mai and Mai's recollection of events surrounding our dear Little Kim, we had had enough for one day. And so had Thien who literally passed out after sharing Mai's story with us. We Trang and I helped Thien's nurse put her to bed, hoping she would enjoy a much-needed night's rest.

Trang and I talked with her nurse a short while and was assured by her nurse that she would recover from her arm wound. The nurses name was Be. Be was a great help to us, and as we began to gather up our belongings, we kindly said our goodbyes to her and to Thien's young American doctor. Then we exited the clinic and began our drive back to Da Nang.

The only subject we discussed during our trip back was if we should have stayed there another day to seek out Mai and attempt to validate her story, but like Trang said, "What good would that do? Why would Mai make up a story like that?" Then silence filled the car, and not another word was spoken during the remainder of our fifty-eight-mile ride.

Thank God, Corporal Chris Fabris was like a brother and on point, because when Trang dropped me off at Marble Mountain's main security gate at 4:00 a.m. that next morning, my reentry had been cleared by none other than one of my closest of friends Corporal Chris Fabris.

When I arrived in my sleep tent, I tiptoed past Tee's bunk and jumped in the sack and managed to get about three hours of shut-eye prior to our normal 6:00 a.m. wakeup call.

Shortly after six o'clock, Tee was shaking my bunk to fully awaken me and ask me about Thien's health condition and if Trang and I had any luck finding Little Kim.

Because of his fondness for Thien, Tee and I kept in close contact with each other all while I was up there, except for the very last day, so he was basically asking me if Trang and I had any luck locating Little Kim on our final day there.

We spent well over an hour discussing my findings up there. In addition all doing morning chow, we talked in detail about our many conversations with Thien. And I told Tee about what Mai had told Thien, so now Tee knew practically as much as I did.

For some reason, I kept dosing off and experiencing these weak moments, and expressed to Tee that I was simply bone-tired. At this time, we both came up with the idea of me reporting into sick bay with the hopes of getting some much-needed sleep.

For the first time in my three years of being a marine, I reported into early morning sick bay. I told the admitting nurse I was having a shortage of sleep problem and that I only got two hours of sleep last night.

My bullshit worked, because I was admitted into sick bay ward Ace Bravo and allowed to sleep that entire day. I needed the rest, and all was great, with the exception of being awakened by a corpsman every two hours to take my vitals.

I exited sick bay that evening feeling fresh as a daisy, and of course waiting for me was my dear friend Corporal Tee. I couldn't help but to notice that his constant grin was absent, and I had never seen him look like this before . . . He looked so down and distraught, so I promptly asked him what had happened.

Without hesitation, Tee began telling me that Trang recently called and told him Thien was dead, that she committed suicide by hanging herself with an electrical cord. And she was found by her surgical nurse near 1800 hours this evening.

Trang ended by telling Tee that he and his chaplain uncle would be leaving for her destination first thing in the morning. Trang also told Tee that she had scribbled a note and that he would provide info as to its content later that day.

Tee tried so very hard but was unable to completely finish discussing everything Trang had told him concerning Thien's departure. So he simply stopped talking, sat down on an old wooden bench, and stared out into space.

Tee was in love with Thien, and they had spent a lot of time discussing their planned lives together back in the States. Tee was even seeing authorities in Da Nang to arrange their marriage.

Obviously, Trang's news was hard for him to take, and he eventually stood up and collapsed into my arms. Tee began crying like a newborn baby. He was five feet six and weighed a little over 160 pounds, but he was muscularly built, and it took all the strength I could muster up to hold him up. Finally, an old gunny walked up to give me some much-needed assistance.

Tee cared an awful lot about Thien. She was a beautiful girl, and Tee fell for her the very first time he laid eyes on her, back at Marble Mountain's newly built field hospital. I tried hard to help my friend get through this. I explained to him she was currently in a much better place and that she was looking down on him, smiling and saying, "Everything is all right."

Tee didn't respond to anything I or the helping gunny was saying and didn't show any emotion . . . He just sat there on this worn-out wooden bench that was sitting outside our sick bay's door and continued to stare out over the heavens.

After thanking the departing gunny, I even tried to cheer Tee up by changing the subject and began talking about Lance Corporal Bernie's twenty-first birthday party that took place in Bernie's sleeping tent about a week back.

I reminded Tee of how we all kept celebrating Bernie's birthday, even after lights out and in the dark, and how we were telling jokes in a whisper, and all of us was sipping on stale warm beer.

I just knew I would get a smile on his face by reminding him of how hard we all partied that evening, and for the past several days, our base had been on high alert because there were reports of a possible VC attack.

None of us party hounds thought much about the base alert situation, because our base had been on alert so many times before without little or no resulting incident. We simply kept our party going and figured only a fool would mess with us half-drunk jarheads anyway.

My party discussion was simply a waste of time because Tee's thoughts were totally focused on Thien's death. I finally gave up on my attempts to change Tee's mood. So I walked a short distance away, giving him some space. I propped down on an old wooden crate to wait for my friend as he dealt with the tragic news of Thien's suicide.

Then, suddenly, one of our helicopter's squadron's crew chiefs came running out the sick bay door and saw Tee sitting there. Unknown to him that Tee was moaning the love of his life's death, he shouted out, "Corporal Tee, we are short a crew member on a medevac mission, and we would very much like you to join us."

Evidently this was exactly what Tee needed to snap him out of his moaning, because he quickly jumped up and asked the crew chief how much time he had, and the gunny sergeant shouted back, "You have just enough time to grab your rifle." We quickly embraced, and Tee scampered off toward the medevac chopper.

As stated earlier, Tee had worked his way to becoming a popular choice as a substitute helicopter crewman, and in addition, he was chalking up a ton of flight pay and making a good sum of money, I might add . . . by loaning some of it out and charging interest.

Thus far, in the Nam, I had been afforded the opportunity to fly over two dozen medevac missions, and every one of them was exciting. It was mind-blowing watching our pilots take hits to their aircraft, with .5-caliber rounds, but yet keep on flying calmly.

And I think I witnessed at least a dozen times where our marine pilots would land their helicopters in hostile environment with the enemy firing at them in order to save one soldier's life. And it was doubly amazing witnessing the marine copilot calmly take over the aircraft controls after his commanding pilot had been wounded.

In essence, I'm not sure of what the criteria is in order to receive a wartime medal. But what I know for sure . . . is these chopper pilots should be receiving some kind of recognition each time they take their aircraft up on a medevac. For those of you who were there, I know you totally understand what I'm saying.

"MY HOME AWAY FROM HOME"

"I SHOT A LOT OF THESE."

New Base Assignment

T HE FOLLOWING DAY, I LEARNED I had orders to catch a "hop" that day to a place a short distance north of Da Nang called Chu Lai. I thought this would be the first time Tee and I would separate while in the Nam, but it just so happened Tee had received orders to be stationed at Chu Lai, as well.

Later that day, I learned we were being assigned to the same helicopter squadron in Chu Lai. We flew on different helicopters to Chu Lai, but we got there at about the same time. About fifty marines from our old squadron at Marble Mountain were also airlifted up to Chu Lai to be assigned to one of the four helicopter squadrons in our new group—MAG-36.

For the first three weeks upon arriving in Chu Lai, Tee and I had to sleep on the ground in what is commonly referred to as a "Boy Scout pup tent." We didn't mind and, in fact, had fun. This reminded us of when we were kids and in the Boy Scouts, spending the night in a local community camping park.

But during the beginning of our fourth week at Chu Lai, things began to turn a bit ugly, at least for me. Sleeping in the elements in our little pup tents remained exciting for those of us who didn't mind waking up in the middle of night and witnessing our personal belongings floating out from our little pup tent. This was due to heavy rains, referred to in the Nam as "monsoons." During monsoon season, rains poured down from the sky for ten days and ten nights without relief. Daily accumulation would reach a staggering ten inches a day. Not only did you get drenching wet, but you literally stunk like hell. I'm sorry, you stunk like shit.

As a youngster growing up in the farm belt state of Kansas, I remember vividly how I loved it when it rained outdoors. My fondness of rain was prior to experiencing a monsoon season in the Nam. Today, I reside in Las Vegas, Nevada, and I'm not at all fond of rain and literally hate it when it rains, and everything about getting wet, that it stands for.

Our new home base in Chu Lai was practically new in origin and didn't even have an NCO "saloon" built yet. So Tee I and a dozen other jarheads simply gathered and celebrated our new home arrival by drinking warm beer out by a secluded old shack out near the seawater.

Chu Lai was quickly being inhabited by marines, Navy Seabees, and army personnel. Tent housing was hastily being constructed, and I was made a tent construction NCO commander. All this long-ass title meant was I carried the responsibility for constructing, within a prescribed time frame, my tent's flooring; erecting its wooden frame (according to spec); then placing and securing tarping over the tent's frame.

Our tent was constructed in near record-setting time, and it passed all of the applicable inspections. I might add it felt real good to sleep in our cots with wood decking as compared to our prior dirt/mud flooring.

It took only a week or so before practically all of the crew chiefs in MAG-36 learned of Tee's arrival.

That Tee enjoyed and was very good at flying as a voluntary flight crew member.

My good friend's reputation had preceded him, all the way from Marble Mountain; thus, he was quickly relieved of his duty of assisting in the constructing of our tent. Instead, Tee was off flying as a volunteer crew member and chalking up flight pay.

Somehow, my name had even been floating around our new squadron as a marine who enjoyed standing in on medevac flights. So the day my sleeping tent was completed, I was asked to fly on a medevac. I think my good buddy Tee was the person responsible in providing the helicopter crew chiefs my name.

During Thanksgiving Day of 1965, I was flying on my fifth medevac mission as a volunteer crewmember out of Chu Lai, and for the second time, I was ordered to take out some water buffalo with my weapon with hopes of exposing an enemy sniper. Our pilot was attempting to land our UH34D helicopter to rescue two wounded recon marines when suddenly our aircraft began getting hit by small arms fire from a sniper hiding in a herd of water buffalo.

The copilot ordered the three of us who were inside the belly of the chopper to return fire at two o'clock with hopes of killing the sniper. The sniper began rapid firing at our chopper, and our gunny crew chief was hit in both his legs. The remaining crew members in our aircraft, a baby face–looking sergeant E5, and yours truly lifted the injured gunny and attempted to set him in a rested position; but this seemingly simple task grew extremely difficult due to the large amount of blood spurting from the gunny's leg and causing the aircraft's aluminum flooring to become superslippery. After making our crew chief as comfortable as possible, we then commenced to frantically put our M14s in the auto position and began blasting away. The buck sergeant and I spent ten magazines each, eliminating our sniper. By the time we'd finished firing, our rifle barrels were glowing from all that intensity.

As our chopper began flying over our recent assault zone, in an attempt to locate the ideal place to land and complete our mission of rescuing the two wounded recon marines whom we had spotted below. Actually, the sergeant and I saw two young females dressed in civilian clothing sprawled out in the tall monkey grass about twenty yards east of the two recon marines we were sent to rescue.

When we landed, we were informed by the two wounded recon corporals that they were dispatched on a secret mission late last night and were cut down when they ran into these two female enemy fighters who were dressed as poor little farm girls. They stressed they were caught completely by surprise by these two pretty young girls. After they both were struck down, they told us how professional these two girls appeared to be.

They went on to tell us, after the two girls had taken them down, how they went about setting their trap. The lead recon corporal, who kept passing out while talking, managed to tell us how the two girls could have done them in hours ago, but due to their professionalism, they knew one of the recon NCOs would call in a crew of men or a chopper to rescue them. He went on to say that due to the severity of their wounds, they each had to lay there and watch these two girls hide inside the herd of about thirty water buffalo and began blasting away at our descending chopper.

Being an animal lover, it was extremely difficult to mow down these poor animals in search of the shooter(s). But it had to be done, and as we were landing, we were afforded the opportunity to count among the fallen eleven water buffalo and the two teenage girl snipers. We quickly body bagged the two girls and placed them inside our aircraft.

Speaking of body bags, they are what volunteer flight crew members normally carry, either from or onto awaiting aircraft. Another major task that volunteer crew members assist in is the lifting of wounded soldiers onto awaiting helicopters.

Personally, I liked assisting in the lifting of our fellow GIs. It made me feel like I was lending a helping hand to a fellow American who was in need. I didn't care if he was a marine or army soldier who was wounded or that he was white, black, brown, or yellow.

Seriously, I could give a shit less if the GI was from the blue states or the red states; it made me entirely no difference. I simply felt like I was helping a wounded or a fallen brother engaged in a war that many of us didn't want or actually believe in, but we gave it our all, anyway.

Meanwhile, back in Chu Lai and shortly after saying a silent prayer and asking the Lord for forgiveness for participating in the useless slaying of eleven water buffalo. It was getting late in the day and time to assist the lance corporal in carrying from our aircraft the two girl snipers.

When unloading dead bodies from our chopper, I never unzipped the body bag to take a peek inside at the body . . . be it one of the enemy or one of our boys, and it wasn't that I was afraid of what I would see inside . . . It was just simply a customary habit of mind.

The wind was heavily gusting this particular November afternoon, and my cover (hat) kept flying from my head. In an attempt to keep my cover (hat) on my head and from flying away, I accidently unzipped the body bag I was carrying, and to my amazement, it revealed a beautiful young girl. And she turned out to be a dead ringer of Little Kim, a.k.a. My Friend You.

This girl possessed Little Kim's identical facial features, her cute little nose, her complexion. This was absolutely amazing, and I must have stood there a solid ten minutes, staring down into this dead girl's body bag. Finally, I was able to take a step; Then I stopped and peered down into the body bag, and suddenly, I was standing there frozen again.

Then I suddenly dropped to my knees, tightly holding on to this girl's body bag as if I could never let go . . . Then I completely lost it . . . and began uncontrollably crying.

The lance corporal I was working with quickly ran over and tried his best to *relieve me of the body bag I was carrying, but I held on very tightly and wasn't* about to let go . . . at least any time soon.

Then another marine came over and began talking to the lance corporal, and their conversation was heading in the direction that I was heavily saddened by the fact that I had suddenly reached the conclusion that I had been the party responsible for taking the pretty girl's life which was inside the body bag I was hauling.

In listening to them attempting to figure out why I had lost it, the thought of me actually being the trigger guy never had crossed my mind . . . up until now. And the pain that I felt at that particular moment in my life can never be duplicated moving forward. The reasoning is simply my body or soul is not strong enough during this juncture of my life . . . to endure such pain.

Trying to live with these thought(s) as a marine is extremely difficult. The amount of sleep lost as a result of wondering whose round did, in fact, strike down one of these young and beautiful people, just like the girl I was trying to carry inside this body bag, is a story all into itself; and I can assure you that a many a marine has a story like this one to tell.

I finally managed to reach my destination, carrying her body bag, and figured by crying my heart out the entire distance actually helped in a special way for me to carry her body bag. The helpful lance corporal had attempted several times along the way to take her body bag from me and help me to carry her, but after I had witnessed her close resemblance to Little Kim, there was no way on earth I was going to let go of her body bag.

I spotted a priest walking and praying over some of the body bags that had recently been laid to rest, so I carried the little sniper's body bag over and kindly asked the priest to say some words over Kim's look alike. The young priest zipped the bag fully closed and provided a silent prayer.

Upon his completion, the priest gave me a slight head nod as if to acknowledge his prayer completion. I smiled down at the priest and silently said "thank you" with my eyes; then I placed her body bag down and silently said the Lord's Prayer and walked away.

After attending Easter mass in our newly constructed chapel at Chu Lai, Tee and I spent that entire Sunday afternoon reflecting upon our stay in Chu Lai. We were basically comparing our time spent at Marble Mountain versus our time based here at Chu Lai.

Our comparison was made rather quickly, and we concluded the off-base liberty life here at Chu Lai sucked as compared to the off-base liberty life in Da Nang. This conclusion was easily reached, and the reason is there was literally "zero" off-base liberty life here at Chu Lai.

One of us was traveling by taxicab into Da Nang for a full day of liberty most Saturdays. In Chu Lai, the both of us mostly did our laundry. And on Saturdays, if we were lucky, we would read mail from family or friends back in the world, because "mail call" normally sounded on Fridays in Chu Lai.

Tee and I flew on more flight missions as a volunteer crew member while stationed in Chu Lai as compared to Marble Mountain. Our services in flying on "sorties" as a volunteer crew member were so much in demand that selected pilots would actually ask for one of us to be part of the crew each time they flew on a flight mission.

Tee flew on four times as many missions as I did. He loved it more, and he could handle the sight of blood and guts a bit better than I, as well. I'm not sure just how many sorties Tee flew on, but it was a lot.

When I returned home, my buddies would ask me if there were times I had to fire my weapon while flying in those helicopters. I would reply by saying yes. And when my buddy would ask me to provide him a factual account of what I shot during my many volunteer flight missions, I would readily tell him that I don't honestly know.

Then I would attempt to explain to him that when you're flying in the air at several thousand feet and traveling at speeds of well over two hundred miles per hour, it's very difficult to pinpoint where the rounds fired from your weapon would land. And when you're flying on a night mission and engaged in firing your weapon, most times it's almost impossible to know what you're hitting.

During most of our flight missions in Chu Lai, Tee or I would assume that as many rounds as we fired, we must have hit something. We lay awake a many of nights wondering if we did, in fact, hit something.

Personally, I would wonder if I hit the enemy during my firing spree or if I hit an innocent person when I fire my M14. The truth may never be known, and it's one hell of a haunting feeling that stays with you for the remainder of your life.

The only way that I could go to sleep nights after firing my weapon was to say this prayer. "My Holy Father, who art in heaven, please ensure the rounds I fired did not hit an innocent person. Above all, please forgive me if I did, in fact, hit a person. Whether he or she was enemy or an innocent onlooker . . . Lord, please assist them, as I know you can . . . Thank you, Lord!"

As Tee and I continued comparing our tour of duty at Marble Mountain or Chu Lai, we finally came to the conclusion that the only merit in our complete tour in South Vietnam is that we witnessed a beautiful country and met some beautiful people and some orphaned children and that, as long as we live, *we can never forget them.*

Lanh and Little Kim, now known forever in my heart as My Friend You, you two taught the true meaning of caring, and I love you both so much.

While sitting here talking to my beautiful wife of fifty years (Marjorie Judy Hobley Clark) who blessed me with two beautiful daughters (Pamela and Carla). I told her back in May of 1966 that I had a story that I "just had to write," and here I sit in May of 2017 completing it. Kids, I sincerely hope I did your story justice, and, My Friend You, I will forever remain that big bad marine that will come to save you . . .

The End.

As time passed many Marines felt they were fighting a WINLESS WAR. Most are ashamed of the outcome, because every marine who fought and the fifty-five thousand who died . . . knew that if our American leaders wanted this war "won," we could have single-handedly won it in a matter of weeks . . . maybe days . . . maybe even hours.

Take that to the bank!

About the Author

D.
ONALD CLARK
- Born in Larned, Kansas, on May 14, 1944
- Raised up in the college town of Lawrence, Kansas, along with my younger brother, Kenneth, to the best parents on earth, Curtis and Gwendolyn
- Knee injury ended football at Kansas University during preseason practice

- Joined the marine corps in August 1962
- Life changed completely when Duane introduced me to the sweetest girl on earth: Marjorie Judy Hobley. We were happily married in November 1966, and still are.
- God blessed us with two beautiful daughters: Pam, May 1968, and Carla, August 1970.
- Rockhurst University, bachelor of science in business administration, December 1974
- Webster University, master's in business administration, 1979
- Hallmark Cards: fifteen years, retired in February 1979 as product scheduling director
- Avery International: ten years, retired in May 1990 as plant operations director
- Whitestone International: eleven years, retired in March 2001 as senior vice president
- Roosevelt Middle School: five years, retired in June 2006 as a math teacher, SDC

"ITS LONELY OUT HERE."

CARLA CLARK

- California State University Dominguez Hills 2001, MPA

- California State University Fresno 1998, BA

CPSIA information can be obtained
at www.ICGtesting.com
Printed in the USA
BVHW04s2341210918
528068BV00001B/6/P